Hilary's Trial

THE ELIZABETH MORGAN CASE

A Child's Ordeal in America's Legal System

Jonathan Groner

AMERICAN LAWYER BOOKS/SIMON & SCHUSTER
New York   London   Toronto   Sydney   Tokyo   Singapore

AMERICAN LAWYER BOOKS
SIMON & SCHUSTER

Copyright © 1991 by Jonathan Groner

Published by American Lawyer Books/Simon & Schuster
American Lawyer Books are published by
Am-Law Publishing Corporation
Simon & Schuster is a division of the
Simon & Schuster Trade Division
Rockefeller Center
1230 Avenue of the Americas
New York, New York, 10020

SIMON & SCHUSTER is a registered trademark
of Simon & Schuster Inc.
American Lawyer Books is a registered trademark
of the American Lawyer Newspaper Group, Inc.

Designed by Levavi & Levavi
Manufactured in the United States of America

10 9 8 7 6 5 4 3 2 1

Library of Congress Cataloging-in-Publication Data
Groner, Jonathan.
  Hilary's trial : the Elizabeth Morgan case : a child's ordeal in
America's legal system / Jonathan Groner.
     p.   cm.
  Includes bibliographical references (p.   ) and index.
  1. Foretich, Hilary Antonia, 1982–   —Trials, litigation, etc.
2. Morgan, Elizabeth, 1947–   —Trials, litigation, etc.
3. Foretich, Eric A.—Trials, litigation, etc.   4. Custody of
children—Washington (D.C.)   5. Child molesting—Washington (D.C.)
I. Title.
KF228.M65G76   1991
346.7301′7—dc20
[347.30617]   91-2283
                                                               CIP

ISBN 0-671-69176-7

Acknowledgments
and Author's Note

In the summer and fall of 1988, as Elizabeth Morgan's months in jail stretched on and as the mystery at the heart of her case deepened, the idea of writing a book about the subject began to form hazily in my mind. It was a chance conversation that October with Bruce Sanford, a Washington lawyer, that forced me to take my own idea seriously and pursue it. For that, I am permanently grateful to Sanford, a First Amendment litigator who has been a friend to any number of journalists.

If Sanford got me to the line of scrimmage, many others ran interference for me. My lawyer, Robert Barnett, helped me make my way in the publishing world and kept an eye out for my inevitable missteps. Steve Brill of American Lawyer Media, L.P., supported my idea from the beginning, put his personal prestige on the line for me, and provided invaluable editing assistance. The book could not have been completed the way it was, at the time it was, without him. Eric Effron and Ann Pelham, my editors at *Legal Times*, helped me work out a part-time arrangement that permitted me to research and write the book—and if they were frustrated by my sometimes irregular work week, they kept their frustrations to themselves. Jim Lyons, then the managing editor of the paper, helped me refine my ideas in the form of a coherent proposal. And other colleagues, including Kim Eisler, Eleanor Kerlow, Daniel Klaidman, Anne Kornhauser, and Judy Sarasohn, served as sounding boards for my thoughts.

Concerning the Morgan case itself, I had hoped when I began

this project to have complete access to everyone involved. As might be expected in as bitterly contested a case as *Morgan* v. *Foretich,* this did not occur. While Eric and his parents agreed to be interviewed, Sharon Foretich declined. My several approaches to Elizabeth Morgan for a detailed account of her life story were ultimately rejected. Despite Elizabeth's negative response, I have tried as best as possible, drawing on a large variety of sources, to include throughout the book her version of disputed events and her perspective on the passing scene. It cannot be overemphasized that this book is not anyone's authorized version of events and that no one involved in the case saw any portion of it before publication.

In addition to my interviews with more than 110 people and my review of dozens of technical and popular articles and books about psychiatry, psychology, pediatrics, child welfare, family law, and other subjects, this book draws on records, briefs, and decisions from all the major courts in Washington, D.C., and from many in Virginia. The most exhaustive publicly available source on the Morgan-Foretich dispute is found in the federal court in Alexandria, Virginia, and I made extensive use of that record. Materials in the National Archives, the National Library of Medicine, and the Library of Congress also proved useful to me. On Elizabeth Morgan's life, the best sources for me were her three published books.

Although this book encompasses much more than the legal issues of the case, legal issues form a part of it. A number of lawyers involved in *Morgan* v. *Foretich* spent considerable time explaining to me the case's convoluted history and the legal strategies they were pursuing, and I am grateful to them. Chief among them were Linda Holman, Elaine Mittleman, Stephen Sachs, and Valerie Szabo. Among the specialists, uninvolved in the case, who assisted me with insights into legal, psychological, or medical complexities were Judith Areen, Nicholas Beltrante, Pat Bennett, Donald Bersoff, Douglas Besharov, Frank Carter, George Cohen, Laurie Diamond, Annette Ficker, Rona Fields, Charles Fogelman, Milton Glatt, Bill Grimm, Abraham Karkowsky, Jill Krementz, Robert Liotta, David Lloyd, Joseph Poirier, Douglas Rendleman, Karol Ross, Richard Saunders, Diane Schetky, Howard Schulman, Gerald Solomon, Michael Valentine, Joseph Vander Walde, Elsa Walsh, Richard Wexell, Jim Wilt, and Jeffrey Zigun.

At Simon & Schuster, Alice Mayhew saw the possibilities inherent in my rough thoughts and brought them together to form a coherent whole. George Hodgman was as good a line editor as a first-time author could ever want. Rather than use his voice in my book, he did something for me that is more difficult and more effective: he challenged me to find my own voice and stay with it. Emily Remes and Felice Einhorn (along with David Kendall of Williams & Connolly) gave valuable guidance at the later stages.

Finally, Arlene, Sammy, Danny, and Sarah were the ones who gave me the understanding of family life that made it possible for me to write this book.

Jonathan Groner
December 1990

To Arlene, who helped me learn
what it is like to be a parent

Contents

Cast of Characters

The Morgans

Elizabeth Morgan
William Morgan, her father, a psychologist
Antonia Bell Morgan, her mother, also a psychologist
Jim Morgan, her older brother, a stockbroker
Robert Morgan, her younger brother, a lawyer

Sheryl Smith, housekeeper for Elizabeth
Leora Graham, housekeeper for Elizabeth
Fran Walton, housekeeper for Elizabeth
Narcisa Ramirez, housekeeper for Elizabeth

The Foretiches

Eric Foretich
Vincent Foretich, his father, a retired shipyard supervisor
Doris Foretich, his mother, a housewife and former art teacher

Evie Dimageba, housekeeper

The Lawyers

For Elizabeth:
Lane Gabeler
George Cronin
Robert Greenberg

For Eric:
Hugh Cregger
Betty Thompson
Robert Machen

Marna Tucker
Rita Bank
Hal Witt
Richard Ducote
James Sharp
G. Allen Dale
Stephen Sachs

John Lenahan
Thomas Albro
Elaine Mittleman
Melvin Guyer

The Experts

For Elizabeth:
Charles Shubin, M.D.
Dennis Harrison, Ph.D.
Mary Froning, Psy.D.
David Corwin, M.D.
Frank Putnam, M.D.
William Zuckerman, Ph.D.

For Eric:
Joseph Noshpitz, M.D.
Elissa Benedek, M.D.
Joel Ganz, M.D.
Catherine DeAngelis, M.D.
Arthur Green, M.D.
Edward Weiss, M.D.

Sharon's Case

Sharon Foretich
Cornelius and Mary Lou Sullivan, Sharon's parents

Mark Sandground, lawyer for Sharon
Valerie Szabo, lawyer for Sharon

Lewis Griffith, judge of the Fairfax County Circuit Court
Jane Delbridge, judge of the Fairfax County Juvenile and Domestic Relations Court
Bruce Bach, judge of the Fairfax County Circuit Court

Jean Albright, therapist for Heather Foretich
James McMurrer, psychiatrist for Heather Foretich
Elizabeth Finch, psychiatrist for Heather Foretich
Nancy Fretta, court-appointed psychologist
Joan Beach, court-appointed supervisor

Eric Foretich
P.F. Gero, *Sygma*

Elizabeth Morgan
P.F. Gero, *Sygma*

Hilary
Mark Baker, *Reuters*

Introduction

When I began researching this book, I had spent a decade as a practicing lawyer and a little more than two years as a full-time journalist. I assumed that my experience in both fields would be a great asset in sorting out the complicated truths, exaggerations, and fantasies of the Morgan-Foretich case. That turned out to be partly true. The lessons of both professions proved indispensable at every point. But I needed to draw on deeper resources as well. I found it impossible to plunge into the crosscurrents of the case without engaging my most human feelings as well as my most rational evaluative abilities.

The Morgan-Foretich case is, of course, the most publicized custody case of the decade, if not the century. The outline of the story—a woman sacrifices her money, her career, and her freedom to protect her child—touches a deep emotional chord. Here is a tale of irresistible drama and mystery. I want this book to convey some of that drama and to dispel some of that mystery.

But I can never let myself forget that at the center of the case is a small child—an infant at the beginning of the story, a schoolgirl at the point where my account leaves off. After all the lawyers, all the psychological experts, and all the media stars had their say, Hilary had to live with the results. She had had to grow up as the adults around her fought their private wars, spurred on by their own complicated motivations. Hilary's welfare was all that should have mattered. But too many people, pursuing personal and political agendas, lost track of her needs.

I have never met Hilary, and perhaps I never will. I am not a professional psychologist, psychiatrist, or social worker. But I have participated in rearing my own three children—always as an active parent, and for more than a year as their primary parent. This experience has influenced this book as much as anything else. My family helped me understand what it is like to be a child and a parent.

Hilary is not the only child in her situation. Her case is merely one of the best-known of the bitter custody disputes, many of which bring with them charges of sexual abuse, being played out every day in American courts. The details of the cases differ because human beings, their personalities, their backgrounds, and their financial resources differ. In each of them, though, parents are trying to use the courts to dictate intimate matters of love and trust. Anyone who knows anything about courts will not be surprised that they frequently fail at this complicated task.

Very early in my research for this book, I interviewed a well-known domestic-relations lawyer who is not involved in the Morgan-Foretich case. Much of what he told me about custody cases was predictable and depressing, but one statement came as a large surprise at the time. He had young children himself, he said, and if he were worried that one had been sexually abused, say at age three, he would not take the child to a mental-health professional for evaluation or therapy. "Kids get ruined by the system, destroyed," he said. These were the words of someone who knew the system, someone whose job it was to use that system for his clients as well as he could. This lawyer told me that if his own child were abused, he would talk to the child one-to-one, find out what had happened, and then try to "make the hurt disappear." He would not begin the endless process of psychological consultations and court hearings. He would bypass the system altogether.

I was stunned when I heard the lawyer say this, but now I understand what he meant. The courts are good at finding facts and issuing decisions but not very good at healing wounds or bringing families together. Their strength lies in the "adversarial system," pitting lawyer against lawyer, hired expert against hired expert. That is fine for an antitrust case or a contract dispute, but when a child's life is at stake, the adversary process hurts the person that everyone supposedly wants to help. We hear of one parent holding a microphone to the other's lips while transferring a child for visitation, in order to create a taped record; we hear of a parent furiously writing down everything a two-and-a-half-year-old says, again to use as evidence; we hear of parents suing each other for money damages, trying to ruin each other's careers and lives. Often, the "winner" is not the better person or the better parent, but the one whose lawyer is more crafty or whose expert witness is more convincing.

One of the wisest things ever said in the Morgan-Foretich case was uttered in court by Elissa Benedek, a distinguished psychiatrist testifying for Eric Foretich. When asked what future course of events was most likely to harm Hilary, she responded that "if this litigation continues and is protracted and Hilary is subjected to the kind of trauma that she has been subjected to, the multiple examinations, the multiple evaluations . . . she will become progressively more disturbed." When asked what would serve Hilary's best interest, she replied, "That the litigation stop, cease, and that Hilary be allowed visitation with all the important people in her life, her father, her grandparents."

Yet the courts, for all their imperfections, are all we have to govern the increasingly complicated world of domestic relations, where the battles grow more hostile every day. In today's world, it is not uncommon for children to be victims of kidnappings and counterkidnappings by parents and detectives. The use of these extralegal means brings society no closer to fulfilling the legal ideal of "the best interests of the child." The winner in these extralegal maneuvers is again the parent who is the most ruthless, resourceful, or stubborn.

In a civilized society, the courts, ill-equipped though they are, must make the decisions. Family courts are not inherently incapable of rendering at least some degree of justice in custody cases. But they must use wisely the devices available to them: mediation, supervised visitation, the appointment of special guardians for the child, and other techniques. In the Morgan-Foretich case, Judge Dixon of the D.C. Superior Court tried almost everything but still failed. At one point, he considered but rejected the course of interviewing Hilary in his judicial chambers to hear her story directly. Judge Dixon is not the villain of this book—most of his decisions made sense, and his colleagues and appeals judges almost unanimously lauded him. But he may have erred in not speaking directly to Hilary, whose words and thoughts were always filtered through someone else—a parent, therapist, or lawyer.

In 1984, long before the Morgan-Foretich case made national news, a Fairfax County, Virginia, judge got the message exactly right. Rendering a decision in a case involving Eric Foretich's previous marriage and his daughter Heather, then almost four, Judge

Lewis Griffith declared from the bench, "My concern is Heather. And I'm going to make her my concern until she is able to choose for herself. . . . I would hope that you [Heather's parents] would do everything to see that all reasonable requests . . . are met. And if you do, then each of you will have the satisfaction of knowing that what you have done is for the betterment and the benefit of someone that you love very dearly, your child. But she'll turn out to be what you want her to be. And if you don't, she's going to be a disappointment to all of us because it will reflect directly in her. We see it happen here every day."

What Judge Griffith said about Heather holds true for Hilary or for any child. If no one else will look out for a child, the judge must do so; but he cannot be there every day with the family, so he must do his best to make sure that the parents do so. There are no guarantees.

To say that I became emotionally involved in my story, to say that I care about Hilary, is not, I hope, to say that I approached my narrative with a bias. If I had any bias when I began this project, it was in Elizabeth Morgan's favor. But stubborn facts pulled me away from that conventional predisposition. If this book tells the Morgan-Foretich story differently than many other accounts do, it is because I made a judgment, months into my research, about the course that events probably took. And all we are dealing with is probability; no writer of nonfiction can ever "prove" this case either way beyond a shadow of a doubt. No investigator, no lawyer, and no judge was there to see what happened between Eric Foretich and his daughter. My account is one attempt to reconstruct reality in a convincing manner.

Ultimately, though, this is Hilary's story. And Hilary is ultimately the loser.

CHAPTER 1

The 1940s through
September 21, 1981

On March 11, 1983, Dr. Elizabeth Morgan filed a petition against her ex-husband, Dr. Eric Foretich, in the Superior Court of Washington, D.C. She sought custody of the couple's then seven-month-old daughter, Hilary, and requested child support. A casual reader of that day's document would have seen little to set *Morgan* v. *Foretich* apart from the deluge of custody cases that helps to fill the dockets of busy family courts across the nation. Every year, 2 million American children become involved in their parents' divorce, a number that has tripled since 1960; and each year, some 75,000 contested custody battles begin in the courts of the United States, after mothers and fathers turn to the legal system to solve the domestic problems they could not work out on their own. Many disputes drag on for years, and at any moment, hundreds of thousands of children are entrapped in the web of their parents' distressing accusations. *Morgan* v. *Foretich*, filed that March day, was one of these cases.

In some ways it was an extraordinary one. When the dispute began, Hilary wasn't even a year old; her parents' relationship had passed quickly from infatuation through divorce in little over a year. Father, mother, and daughter had never lived together as a family unit. And the length, expense, and intensity of the case became almost unparalleled in American history. But in its own crazy way, *Morgan* v. *Foretich* grew to embrace all the love, hate, obsession, suspicion, and anger that have characterized the custody wars of the late twentieth century. As an extreme example, it illuminates thousands of others.

According to one account, the ugliness started with the first session in court, which occurred just a couple of months after the petition was filed. Each of the principals came to court with a retinue of supporters. Eric Foretich walked in on the May morning of the hearing with his lawyer, with a child psychiatrist who was to be his expert witness, and with his parents, who had driven more than three hours from Gloucester, Virginia, to assist their son. Graying in her mid-sixties, Doris Foretich remained the sociable Southern clubwoman she had been for decades: cheery, devoted to home and family, something of a busybody. Her husband Vincent, a retired shipyard supervisor five years her senior, let Doris do much of the talking that day, as he did most days. He preferred to keep his feelings inside.

Elizabeth Morgan was also accompanied that morning by her lawyer, by a child psychiatrist of her choosing, by a social worker, and by her parents, who were taking her side as vigorously as Eric's were supporting him. Unlike Doris and Vincent, who had enjoyed four harmonious decades together, Antonia and William Morgan had been living apart for years. That afternoon, though, and for a good part of 1983, they were reunited. Friends always thought the Morgans an unusual couple—blustery William, a psychologist from Rochester, New York, and former CIA agent who loved nothing more than reminiscing about his World War II exploits, and quiet, reserved Antonia, also a psychologist, an Englishwoman who had met her husband while he was stationed in wartime London.

That morning in Superior Court, the first thing everyone did was to wait in an anteroom for a judge and a courtroom to open up. Doris remembers overhearing William tell his daughter, "Now, if the old man or the father had hurt her in some way, and we could tell about it, that would keep her from him." Doris was appalled: she had never realized how far Elizabeth and her family were prepared to go to win their case.

But before all the charges and countercharges was the romance. They were two doctors—he an oral surgeon, she a plastic surgeon. Eric, thirty-nine years old when they met, had already survived two failed marriages (he had a fifteen-month-old daughter from the second one) and dozens of relationships. His sandy hair, Virginia breeding, and worldly bearing had always seemed to attract women. Soft-spoken and charming in courtship, Eric sometimes showed a brooding, fatalistic side that had been nourished by family tragedy. Of three children, he was the only one who survived to adulthood, the only one left to satisfy his mother's emotional needs.

Despite his achievements, Eric never saw himself as successful; for him, failure was always lurking.

Elizabeth, with her dark brown hair and her deep brown eyes that signaled a remarkable intensity, displayed a self-assurance that Eric often lacked. Although she was not conventionally beautiful, men found her intriguing. An ambitious physician and a published author in her early thirties, Elizabeth could still project vulnerability to men and could turn on the feminine charm when she wanted to. Like Eric, she had found professional success; also like Eric, she had felt emotional emptiness. Closely attached to her mother well past the age when those bonds normally weaken, Elizabeth remained a bit naive in matters of romance. For her that fall of 1981 when she courted Eric, the time had come to get married and have children. Four, she thought, would be about the right number.

Those plans had quickly derailed. Just as the affair was beginning, Elizabeth found herself pregnant. After briefly considering abortion, she and Eric agreed to keep the baby and get married. From the beginning, however, the marriage was strained. Antonia lived with the couple, and Eric felt the burden of his wife's intense attachment to her. Both partners became disillusioned with each other and with the marriage, and neither worked to keep it alive. Eric became preoccupied with a grand home being built for him and his new bride; Elizabeth became preoccupied with her pregnancy, her surgical practice, and her writing. Tension built quickly. Elizabeth—accompanied by her mother—left Eric a few days before Hilary was born, after less than seven months of married life.

Hilary was the major concern of Judge Carlisle Pratt in the Superior Court that May morning. In custody cases, the court's major goal is to promote a child's best interests by maintaining as much family unity as remains possible after a divorce. But divorce, though it serves the needs of many adults, is a wrenching experience for children, especially for those too young to understand what is happening around them. Lawyers, judges, social workers, psychologists, and psychiatrists do their best to help, but most of them have long realized that their job is to control the damage, not to eliminate it. The task of the family court therefore is to find a combination of custody and visitation that will ease the pressure on the child and encourage relationships with both parents.

The judge's task of assuring that the children of broken families enjoy love and security is a difficult one. The judge, a stranger to the family, is asked to understand the parents' complex personalities and then to legislate harmony by court decree. What is at stake is not money, goods, or real estate, but the lives of children. Family courts, and the mediators, social workers, psychologists, and others they have enlisted to help them, can achieve at best a sort of rough justice. The first thing a judge looks at is how the family unit worked when it was intact: How did the parents show their concern for the child? Who spent time with the child? Who was the primary care-giver? Who was likely to provide the child with a healthy physical and emotional environment?

But in *Morgan* v. *Foretich,* there had never been a functioning family unit. The fact that Hilary had been under Elizabeth's care for seven months stemmed from the biological fact that it was Elizabeth who, after leaving her husband behind in her ninth month of pregnancy, gave birth to her. For most of the twentieth century, this would have been enough to earn Elizabeth custody of Hilary. For decades the courts indulged a powerful sex-based preference in favor of the mother, especially when such a young child was in-volved. But by the 1980s such biases had been abandoned. Under the law and policy of the District of Columbia, Eric and Elizabeth started out on an even footing in the custody battle. Eric could contest the issue, and he did: before the end of March, he also filed for custody of Hilary.

Eric had made it clear from the time of Hilary's birth that he wanted to participate in raising his daughter. He had taken hours from his practice in McLean, Virginia, to drive to her day-care home, where Elizabeth left Hilary about fifty hours weekly, to hold her in his arms and rock her. From the beginning, however, Elizabeth had refused to accommodate Eric's interest in the infant. "It never oc-curred to me that a struggle for custody would arise," she said in *Custody,* a book she wrote two years later. "I was her mother. Naturally I would raise her. I couldn't imagine it any other way. . . . No one, but no one, could make me leave her." "Nature," Elizabeth said, "didn't make men for rearing little children." Before the legal papers were filed, Elizabeth's best offer to Eric had been three hours' weekly visitation, in her living room, in her watchful presence. When Eric called his ex-wife in her medical office just before Thanksgiving 1982 to beg her to give him Hilary for four hours on the holiday, her secretary told him not to call the office. When he sent her a mailgram just before Christmas asking for some time with Hilary, Elizabeth told him to talk to her lawyer.

Eric's lawyer cautioned him in the spring of 1983 that from what he had heard about Elizabeth's behavior, a custody battle with her would be a titanic struggle. The prophecy was accurate. The case spun on out of control, tearing lives apart and tying the legal system in knots. *Morgan* v. *Foretich* became the biggest case in the history of the D.C. family court, with scores of witnesses and thousands of transcript pages. In 1989, the case's official docket sheet (summarizing the case's legal documents) filled more than twenty tightly packed pages. There were to be three separate custody trials in Superior Court, in addition to a full trial in a federal court and dozens of related proceedings in other legal forums. Magazine and newspaper writers and television producers were drawn to the story. Political coalitions formed and regrouped, and even the U.S. Congress had its say. The case simply would not die. That was largely because from the very start Elizabeth believed that she, and only she, knew what was right for Hilary. She would make the decisions for her daughter—not her ex-husband, not her lawyers, not Hilary's pediatricians or psychiatrists, and not the judges of the Superior Court.

Elizabeth learned her extraordinary tenacity from her father. Born Anthony Mitrano in 1910, one of nine children of poor Italian immigrants, he acquired his survival skills in the streets of Rochester, New York. His street smarts proved to be matched by a quick intelligence. Young Tony graduated from the University of Rochester in 1933 and went to Yale for a doctorate in psychology. He worked for a few years as a school psychologist in Rochester, where he developed a lively interest in the booming research field of psychological testing. Tony changed his name to William James Morgan in 1942, to avoid anti-Italian prejudice in the psychology profession, but he never changed his combative outlook on life. (The young psychologist's selection of "William James," the name of the distinguished nineteenth-century psychology pioneer, is noteworthy.)

William Morgan signed up as a psychologist for the Office of Strategic Services (OSS) in World War II and was sent to an old manor house in England to devise obstacle courses for Allied spies training to serve in Nazi-occupied Europe. But he wanted action, and although at thirty-four he was older and stockier than the ideal paratrooper, he convinced his bosses to let him drop as an undercover fighter behind Hitler's lines in France. "I had learned to think of myself as a hunted man. A spy who forgets that he is a hunted man is not likely to live very long," William wrote in his memoirs, *The OSS and I* (1957).

On a British train in September 1944, after returning to London from occupied France, William met Antonia Farquharson Bell, a beautiful Englishwoman on her way home from London to visit her parents in the country. Antonia, trained in educational psychology at Oxford and the University of London, had worked for the British Ministry of Information and had done research studies for the government on educational problems in India. The blunt American and the reserved British civil servant enjoyed a rapid wartime courtship and were married at a parish church in London on November 2, 1944. William was immediately sent away again by the OSS, this time to China, where he became chief of the U.S. intelligence mission in Taiwan. Antonia remained in England, where their first child, William James Morgan, Jr. (universally known as Jim), was born in July 1945. A few months later, William senior was asked to return to the United States to help staff the newly formed CIA, successor to the OSS; and in May 1946, the young family settled on Gallows Road, a major artery in Washington's Virginia suburbs. Jean Elizabeth (she rarely uses her given first name) was born there on July 9, 1947, and Robert followed two years later.

William's career blossomed in the postwar CIA. Although he never reached the highest level of management, he rose to deputy chief of the Agency's training staff and later became head of the assessment and evaluation division. There, he used his beloved psychological tests to predict which applicants had what it took to be undercover operatives. For a few years, Antonia stayed home with the children, putting her work as a psychologist temporarily on hold. Their Fairfax County neighborhood was rural then; Elizabeth described it as having "seventy-five people and a hundred and fifty cows." The Morgan children, lacking childhood chums, centered their lives around home, where the environment was described by family friends as intellectually competitive and intense.

The Morgans never coveted luxuries. Their plain wood-frame home was clean, well kept, and austere. The kitchen floor was cold cement, and for some years there were no blinds on the downstairs windows. William and Antonia emphasized achievement, not frills. Dinner-table conversations revolved around books and world affairs. Antonia's research had focused on how to identify and teach gifted children, whom she believed were not being challenged by the schools of the day. Both she and her husband felt that their own children were talented enough to benefit from special educational treatment.

In 1955, when Elizabeth was eight, Antonia wrote in *Scientific Monthly* magazine that gifted children are "a valuable national asset, possibly the most valuable one." She urged that all states administer the Stanford-Binet intelligence test to every elementary schoolchild.

Those identified as gifted should be placed in special classes or accelerated. In the majority of these cases, Antonia concluded, it was desirable for talented youngsters to skip a grade or two. In keeping with these theories (which have since passed out of favor), Elizabeth, who always scored very well in standardized tests, was pushed rapidly ahead. With her parents' encouragement, she skipped kindergarten and third grade, advancements that experts today might call emotionally risky.

Elizabeth was also given family responsibilities unusual for an elementary schoolchild. First on a part-time basis, then full time, William and Antonia opened a psychology practice together in their home under the name of "Aptitude Associates." A large part of their business was developing and selling psychological tests to schools and other institutions, and they also built up a busy consulting practice, specializing in troubled children who were having difficulty in school. William's advice to his patients tended to be blunt and direct. One former patient with a troubled past recalls him telling her, "I was a survivor in the war, and there was a reason for that. You tell yourself you are a survivor too."

Richard Thomsen, the retired headmaster of the Episcopal School in Alexandria, Virginia, who sent the Morgans dozens of problem children over the years, recalls that William and Antonia would often put troubled teenagers up in their house for several days of evaluation. From the age of seven, Elizabeth worked for her parents, letting patients in, announcing visitors, getting coffee, and fetching meals.

The demands of the practice taxed the capacity of the Morgan home, which was not especially large for a family of five. The living room became the clients' waiting room; the dining room was used by the Morgans' secretary; and the first-floor bedrooms were revamped for consulting and testing. The family lived in the basement. According to Elizabeth's recollections in *Custody* (her third published book), Antonia later regretted raising her daughter "in a dark house on a main road, isolated, with no friends." She urged Elizabeth not to repeat her mistake with her own daughter—and to find a life for her outside the family circle.

Elizabeth and her brothers became experimental subjects for the psychological tests William was busily devising. William testified in a deposition that he gave all three children a battery of tests of his own creation, including the "Morgan math test" and tests of logical reasoning, basic numerical skills, and verbal intelligence. He boasted that the three passed with extraordinarily high scores. The Morgan tests, about which William and Antonia wrote enthusiastically in the psychological journals through the 1950s, were based on William's work interviewing prospective intelligence officers for the CIA. A near-fanatical devotee of testing, William later saw the fashion of his profession pass him by, but he never wavered in the conviction that testing was the key that could unlock the door to human intelligence and personality.

By the mid-fifties, Aptitude Associates became a full-time occupation for both William and Antonia, who kept it open seven days a week, ten to fifteen hours a day. In 1955, when Robert, her youngest child, started school, Antonia went back to work full time, and two years later, William retired from the government to devote his time to his private practice. At that time William, like many of his OSS colleagues, published his wartime memoirs. *The OSS and I,* which deals exclusively with William's experiences in England and the European theater, received favorable though not spectacular reviews. Tautly written, it reveals little about the grand strategy of the war, emphasizing instead William's exploits in blowing up German bridges and leading a ragtag band of French Resistance fighters.

To their friends and business acquaintances, William and Antonia appeared perfectly respectable. William became the first president of the Virginia State Psychological Association and served for eleven years on the state's official licensing board for clinical psychologists. Antonia presented papers and lectured. But the frame house on Gallows Road seems to have been the scene of some rather extraordinary family dramas, often sparked by William's angry fits.

Antonia has testified that her husband would slap her "now and then," occasionally giving her a black eye; a psychiatrist who interviewed her years later says the couple apparently had a serious fight at least once or twice a week, usually after Antonia tried to "stand up" to her husband, who brooked little dissension. It was a turbulent home, Antonia said in a court deposition, and her husband was the source of the turbulence. "The children saw more than I thought," she said later. "I would shut the door but if I had had sense, I would have known. They said to me when we had awful fights, 'No one but you could live with him.' " Several times during these confrontations, William, who had owned guns since his days as a weapons instructor for the OSS, put a pistol to his head and threatened to kill himself.

At least once, according to an account from Antonia, William turned his anger at Elizabeth, threatening her with a golf club. "If you break that over me, will I have to pay for my funeral?" Elizabeth asked, according to her mother, who also said that the family then burst out laughing. William denies the incident, but reliable family history—Elizabeth's books and Antonia's deposition—suggests that it is consistent with William's personality.

William's blustering had an impact on his daughter. "It had taken me thirty years to untangle my feelings toward my father," Elizabeth said in *Custody* (1985). "When I was growing up, I always felt that no success of mine was enough to satisfy him." In her discussions with a psychiatrist years later in connection with the custody case, Antonia recalled Elizabeth as shy and afraid of meeting strangers and as having a serious fear of death; she attributed these fears to William and his demands.

The Morgan sons were also affected by their father's behavior; both were occasionally called in to calm William down. Elizabeth and her older brother Jim were often at odds, and Rob, the youngest child, was often thrust into the role of peacemaker. It was Antonia, though, who spent decades trying to patch up the differences. Elizabeth said later that her mother's "indestructible cheerfulness" was what allowed the family to survive upheaval and chaos. And Antonia began to blame herself for not being "patient enough" with William's moods.

William required a great deal of patience from others but exhibited little himself. He was extraordinarily demanding of his children, often taking it as a personal rejection if a child came home with a bad grade or was turned down by an exclusive prep school or an Ivy League college. Describing his family in a 1985 court pleading, William seemed to equate them with their educational achievements. He and Antonia, he said, "have in many ways contributed to the betterment of civilization including, but not limited to, the advancement of their children's education. James, the eldest, attended St. Andrews, The Episcopal High School, and Harvard; Elizabeth attended St. Agnes, Kent School, Harvard, and Yale; Robert, the youngest, attended St. Stephens, Groton, Yale, Harvard Business School, and Virginia Law School."

Despite her obvious intellectual ability, Elizabeth wasn't always an academic success. As she explained in her first book, *The Making of a Woman Surgeon* (1980), she did so poorly in a local junior high school that her parents sent her off to the Kent School, a prestigious prep school in Connecticut's Berkshire Mountains some ninety miles north of New York. Kent—termed "one of the nation's great schools" in a popular guide to private education—was in the midst of change in 1960, when Elizabeth arrived: that was the year that the school admitted girls for the first time. The thirteen-year-old Elizabeth, unwittingly a feminist groundbreaker, was a member of the first coed class.

As a tenth grader, Elizabeth was 5 feet 6 inches tall, weighed 125 pounds, and had reached full physical maturity. With a superior-range IQ of 129, she had the intellect to make it at Kent, but her emotions, it seems, couldn't keep up with her abilities. In *The Making of a Woman Surgeon,* Elizabeth said she went through rounds of bingeing, alternating with "terrifying stringent diets," during her first two years at Kent. "At the height of one pre-Christmas diet I was so desperate for food that I thought of the communion wafer at morning services as the first meal of the day," she wrote. In the early 1960s, anorexia and bulimia were hardly recognized, and Elizabeth's symptoms were not seen as indicative of emotional stress. (Researchers now believe that children from families where at least one parent is abusive appear to have an increased risk of anorexia and bulimia.)

Elizabeth was able to overcome her emotional problems well enough to succeed at Kent, an experience that she ultimately found fulfilling. (She later became a supporter and trustee of the school.) After graduation, driven by her parents' wishes and her own fierce desire to succeed, Elizabeth decided to pursue a career as a physician. It didn't hurt that she had scored high in the medicine category in a vocational test her parents gave her.

Elizabeth entered Radcliffe in the summer of 1963 at the age of sixteen. Like many people who enter a large university after a smaller, homier high school, she was not impressed. She found Harvard boring and impersonal, with famous faculty members who spent their time mostly on government grants. Elizabeth did well academically, majoring in biology, but still recalls "terrible bouts of depression" in college and self-conscious, awkward feelings around men. This is not surprising in an extraordinarily bright girl who was at least two years younger than most of her classmates.

As a junior, Elizabeth applied to Harvard medical school with the intention of skipping her senior year and starting medical school in the fall of 1966, at age nineteen. Much to her surprise, she was accepted. But her undergraduate dean and, surprisingly, her parents, said she was too young. "You need time to grow up," her mother said, "time for just meeting people, not feeling under pressure to work so hard all the time. You have to learn how to enjoy life." Elizabeth agreed, and after graduating a semester early, spent a term abroad at Oxford. She started medical school at Yale in the fall of 1967.

A first-year medical student at age twenty, Elizabeth still had a lot of growing up to do. She had never really been a teenager, postponing the romances and heartbreaks of most adolescents. To the extent that the demands of medical school permitted, she tried to catch up on those lost years. One of only nine women students in a class of about a hundred, Elizabeth recalls that she had "dozens of boyfriends" and "dated another person every week."

But she remained emotionally immature. "At twenty, I still developed a crush on almost every tall, handsome man who smiled at me. I knew I was not ready to marry and felt too vulnerable to get deeply involved with one man," she wrote in *The Making of a Woman Surgeon*. Her immaturity was exaggerated by her closeness to her mother. Ever since her early teenage years, when Antonia had been the force that kept the family together in the face of William's capricious anger, mother and daughter had learned to rely on each other for support. "While the rest of us were taking vacations with our boyfriends, Elizabeth was going to France with her mother," a friend later recalled. Elizabeth once wrote, "I never figured out how anyone grew up without my mother."

After graduating from Yale in 1971, Elizabeth began a surgical internship at the Yale New Haven Hospital. Medical school was still a male preserve in those days, and surgery was strictly men's turf. Elizabeth had to brush off her share of sexist remarks.

But Elizabeth, no conventional feminist, didn't want it forgotten that she was a woman. During her internship, she decided that she didn't like the white coats that surgical interns were required to wear on rounds. They didn't fit right, and they didn't project a feminine image. "These outfits made me look like a sack of Pillsbury flour," she griped. Elizabeth simply stopped wearing them, even after her supervisors warned that she looked unprofessional without them. Not every surgeon agreed with that assessment: one sympathetic doctor told Elizabeth, "Fantastic. You look like a woman again."

Many years later, Elissa Benedek, a University of Michigan psychiatrist who evaluated everyone involved in the case, concluded that Elizabeth "felt she was very special, different than anyone else." Elizabeth, Benedek said, was suffering from a personality disorder with some elements of narcissism. According to Benedek, Elizabeth saw herself as a special individual to whom the usual rules of society did not apply. The white-coat episode was one piece of evidence.

In 1973, during the second year of her surgical residency, Elizabeth attracted more attention when she was able to write a regular medical column for *Cosmopolitan* magazine, still controversial in those days for its sexual frankness. (Her entrée into the publishing world came by means of a contact of her brother Jim's.) *Cosmo* had been out front in the sexual revolution of the 1960s, and it continued the stance through the early 1970s. In May 1973, amidst the features about fun, fashion, and sex, "Your Body," by Elizabeth Morgan, made its appearance. Elizabeth worked hard to hit just the right breezy tone, and she did pretty well. Except for the annoying over-use of italics ("The *right* way to deal with a pimple is to leave it *alone*"), her writing is clear and concise, and the medical advice is unexceptionable: Use your diaphragm each time you make love; eat a balanced diet and don't overdose on vitamins; by all means try a sauna if you are healthy; see your gynecologist regularly.

Exhilarated by her first taste of fame, Elizabeth continued the column for seven years. She obviously had a flair for writing and began keeping notes on her medical education, notes eventually published years later as *The Making of a Woman Surgeon.*

While Elizabeth's writing took off, her medical career hit a snag. Yale's surgery department had hired too many interns and first-year residents for the year beginning in July 1973 and was forced to cut back. Only four of the thirteen residents would be asked to stay for the second year of residency. Elizabeth was not one of the four, but she quickly picked up a new position, back in the Boston area, as a resident at the Tufts New England Medical Center, a Harvard-affiliated hospital. In her last year, she served in the prestigious post of chief resident at two Harvard hospitals.

When Elizabeth turned twenty-nine in the summer of 1976, she had completed nine years of medical training. She could have taken the certifying examinations and opened a practice as a general sur-geon. Instead, she decided to go for an additional two years of specialty training to become a plastic surgeon. Unlike many plastic surgeons who prefer the more lucrative cosmetic surgery, Elizabeth was primarily interested in reconstructive surgery, in which damaged parts of the body are rebuilt.

In the summer of 1976, Elizabeth began her plastic-surgery res-idency at Yale. One of her supervisors, given the pseudonym Dr. Arnold Tewkesbury by Elizabeth in *Solo Practice,* her second book, was a well-known and influential surgeon with friends all over the country. The older doctor and the young, strong-willed resident clashed from the start. Tewkesbury was bored, cynical, arrogant, and disdainful, according to Elizabeth's account. Elizabeth was, in her own words, "insubordinate, rude, a typical outspoken, over-worked surgical resident."

It is easy to envision confrontations between the self-assured Elizabeth and Tewkesbury, equally obstinate and unaccustomed to dealing with women in a professional situation. Tewkesbury has never publicly discussed his side of the story, but one physician who was present that year and thinks highly of both Tewkesbury and Elizabeth explains that the program was "especially difficult. Male surgeons are notoriously macho, and you just don't cross them with impunity." Elizabeth soon left the Yale program, indicating that it was her decision to leave. She did her final year of plastic-surgery training back at Harvard, at the Cambridge Hospital and the Peter Bent Brigham Hospital. Francis Wolfort, the division chief who supervised her there, recalls Elizabeth as "bright and caring, with good judgment."

After Elizabeth and Tewkesbury stopped working together, they arrived at a "cordial animosity" (Elizabeth's description). Tewkesbury would not try to hurt Elizabeth's career, and Elizabeth would keep quiet about her complaints. This understanding ended, according to Elizabeth, after Tewkesbury made a sexual advance to Elizabeth at a medical convention. Elizabeth turned him down. Feeling rejected and hurt, the older physician decided to destroy the young resident—or that's how Elizabeth saw it. The situation may have been more complicated than that: Elizabeth admitted, after all, that she had been insubordinate and rude. Some years later, she told *People* magazine that during her training she had "become an absolutely difficult, quarrelsome, disagreeable battle-ax." She acknowledged assuming the stance intentionally, to fend off discrimination, adding that she turned off the pose when she realized she was alienating people.

In early 1978, Tewkesbury struck a blow at Elizabeth as she made plans to return to northern Virginia to open her practice. He wrote to the certifying board in plastic surgery that her work with him had been unsatisfactory and recommended that the time Elizabeth had spent training with him not be approved. The board's disapproval, besides hurting Elizabeth's reputation, would have forced her to retake a whole year of her residency. Elizabeth was depressed, worried that she had wasted a decade of her life and that she would never be able to practice surgery.

As they often did in times of crisis, the Morgans caucused to discuss the threat. Elizabeth described the scene in *Solo Practice*. "My brother Jim wanted to hire a hit man." William thought she should resign, and her younger brother Rob, by now a Harvard Law student, wanted to sue all two thousand board-certified plastic surgeons. Ultimately, the family decided on a more conventional path:

Elizabeth got several prominent plastic surgeons, including Wolfort, to write letters on her behalf, and in May 1978 the board declared her eligible to take the certifying examination.

Elizabeth's medical education was finally complete. She had survived the grinding experience "to prove myself, to me and to Daddy," she reflected. A couple of months later she returned to northern Virginia to open her practice. At first, she moved back to her parents' house (they let her use one of their consulting rooms as her medical office), and she saw her first patient in November 1978. Things were slow initially, and Elizabeth used the time between appointments to prepare a second draft of *The Making of a Woman Surgeon*. She had completed the first draft during her residency.

In January 1979, Elizabeth opened an office in McLean, Virginia, and that same spring, moved out of her parents' house. Twenty years before, her parents had bought a small house next door to theirs on Gallows Road. Elizabeth moved in there with her older brother Jim, who had abandoned a career as a writer and was training to become a stockbroker.

Elizabeth received privileges at nearly every hospital in the Virginia suburbs and slowly built up a very busy surgical practice. In 1979, she earned $100,000, an excellent income at the time for a doctor in her first year on her own. (Tewkesbury fired one final shot around this time, writing to several influential plastic surgeons in the Washington area to say Elizabeth couldn't be trusted to handle patients properly and suggesting that she be denied hospital privileges. The surgeons, impressed with Elizabeth's skill, paid little attention.)

Elizabeth's patients were struck by her calmness and sympathetic interest. "It helped that she was a woman, and an attractive, articulate, and gentle person," says Dr. Enrico Davoli, a McLean pediatrician who referred dozens of patients to Elizabeth. Elizabeth's name also started appearing on the all-important referral lists of some of the busiest doctors in northern Virginia. Her earnings quickly grew to more than $350,000 a year. "Elizabeth provided excellent care. She was very popular among hospital staff and nurses," says Csaba Magassy, a prominent Washington plastic surgeon who took a liking to the young doctor and helped her get started. "She did both reconstructive and cosmetic surgery, but she specialized in post-cancer and accident reconstruction. We're a small fraternity of plastic surgeons—only eighty-five or ninety in the entire D.C. area—and I for one welcomed having her around." One nurse who often worked with her says Elizabeth was a careful, methodical surgeon. In a 1980 *People* magazine feature, a nurse described Elizabeth as "one of the few doctors who gives nurses a fair break."

Elizabeth's success provided the money necessary to indulge her tastes for horseback riding, tennis, dinner parties, fine restaurants, and theater. Influenced by her mother's impeccable taste in clothes and finding Washington-area stores lacking, she made frequent shopping trips to Bergdorf Goodman's in New York. Elizabeth finally seemed ready to enjoy life, and Washington seemed willing to provide the opportunities. Slim and successful, she was considered one of the most eligible young women in the area. With her long dark hair and ready smile, she had no trouble finding men who wanted to date her.

But even well into her thirties, Elizabeth found it hard to escape her father's blustering intrusions into her life. William was approaching seventy, but he remained stubborn and difficult. In *Solo Practice,* Elizabeth recalled telling her father that he probably wouldn't think any man right for her. "He loves to direct people's lives," Elizabeth wrote. "It's his profession and he's a superb psychologist, but I was too old for him to be interfering with my life." According to Elizabeth, William wanted her to find a younger man, "perhaps twenty-five or -six years old so you can direct him."

Eighteen months after Elizabeth returned to Virginia, the Morgan family faced a crisis that would finally split it apart. Around the beginning of 1980, Antonia came down with an unexplained illness that started out like flu but refused to go away. Elizabeth immediately took charge of her mother. "With the bossiness of a doctor-daughter, I put her to bed and told her to stay there," she recalled in *Solo Practice.* Bedridden, Antonia fought off night sweats, painful joint swellings, and heart irregularities. Her doctors were perplexed, and she only got worse and worse. William, true to form, tried to cure the illness through sheer force of will. He urged his reluctant wife to eat ice cream and cookies to keep up her strength and apparently made other demands as well; Benedek, the psychiatrist, said that according to Antonia, William insisted that they have intercourse three times a week.

Elizabeth moved back home to help her mother cope with her illness and with her husband. William's eccentricities were becoming more pronounced. He began to burn firewood to save oil, dried his clothes on a clothesline, hung bedspreads in the windows instead of curtains, tooled around in his beat-up 1972 Blazer, and raised five goats to avoid the high cost of milk and meat. He salvaged old towels, notepads, and broken china, figuring they might come in handy someday. Finally, after thirty-six years of marriage, Antonia had apparently had enough.

One steamy June night in 1980, Antonia, accompanied by her daughter, left Gallows Road. According to a source close to the family, Elizabeth had suggested the move, telling Antonia in a peremptory tone, "Mother, you need to get away from Daddy." The two women took temporary shelter in Rob Morgan's apartment, then lived briefly in the Hampshire Towers in downtown Washington. Eventually, they settled down together in a small townhouse in the Dupont Circle area of Washington.

The family problems began to spill over into Elizabeth's life as well. The timing was bad. Early that July, her brother Jim introduced her to Raymond Shibley, a successful and well-established gas-pipeline lawyer in Washington. A gentlemanly, soft-spoken widower with no children, the fifty-five-year-old Shibley was a Yale grad—like both Elizabeth and William Morgan. Despite the age difference, Elizabeth and Shibley clicked almost immediately. Their first date, on July 9, 1980, was for dinner at the Jockey Club on Elizabeth's thirty-third birthday. They soon began a love affair that lasted until the end of the year.

"Elizabeth is a very interesting, articulate person, the brightest person I've ever met in terms of IQ," recalls Shibley, who has never remarried. "She had had an astonishing career, and I was interested in someone who had been able to achieve so much so quickly. When we first met, she autographed her book [*The Making of a Woman Surgeon,* which had just been published], and gave me a copy. But it became clear that her objective at that time in her life was to get married, and I did not wish to marry into that family. So I didn't continue the relationship."

Shibley had no problems with Antonia, whom he describes as "refined, quiet, well spoken." But William was a different story. Shibley still speaks, more perplexed than scared, of a time when William threatened to kill him.

"She [Elizabeth] had told me that in connection with one of her father's outbursts, he said he wanted her to stop seeing that man, and he intended to see to it that that result was achieved. I asked Elizabeth, 'By violence?' and she said, 'Yes.' " To this day, Shibley can think of nothing he could have done to offend William and can guess only that William was "being protective."

Shibley didn't actually fear for his life. He doubted that William would carry out the threat, but he had learned enough about the

Morgan family to develop a firm resolve not to marry into it. (William has denied ever threatening any of Elizabeth's boyfriends.)

Shibley recalls an evening toward year's end when Elizabeth returned from a trip to the West Coast. The couple had spoken briefly about marriage before the trip, and Elizabeth brought the subject up again. Shibley politely begged off, saying it was only a year since his wife's death and he wasn't ready. He drove her home, walked her to the door, and bent over to kiss her good night. "It's over," Elizabeth said, and walked away. He never saw her again.

Looking back on his six months with Elizabeth, Shibley says Elizabeth viewed her life as organized into neat chapters, like the chapters of her books. When she felt it was time to have a baby, she looked for the right man to marry, and if he wasn't interested, it was goodbye. And Elizabeth was used to getting her way. On the rare occasions when she was thwarted, she lashed out.

"She has a strong belief that her viewpoint is correct," Shibley says, "and that sooner or later, others will recognize that. She was not a feminist, but she was very perceptive about what it takes to motivate people to do the things she wants done."

Shibley also recalls Elizabeth as having an unusual interest in publicity and a remarkable ability to generate it. "She clearly indicated a strong desire not to lead a very private life," he says. "She had an active medical practice, but she was out of town a lot, promoting her book." *The Making of a Woman Surgeon* sold well, touching a chord among ambitious young women across America. Though just a few years older than the women who were then in college and medical school, Elizabeth spoke from a different vantage. She was among the last female American doctors who could count the women in their classes on their fingers. With her degrees from top schools and her success in a male-dominated field, Elizabeth was seen as a trailblazer for later generations.

But even as she was becoming a minor national icon, her career, her family, her romantic life (or lack of it), and her own demands on herself were overwhelming her. Elizabeth was working a lot of eighteen-hour days, and she still had to take the second phase of her plastic-surgery board examinations, an oral exam that surgeons must take after starting their practice. Antonia's continuing illness pushed her over the brink.

Although Antonia never demanded it, Elizabeth, a grown woman of thirty-three, felt her primary obligation was to her mother, not to her profession or herself. She chose to do for her mother what she would have expected her mother to do for her if she were ill.

She decided to take an indefinite leave from her practice, keeping her office open but performing only the surgeries she had already scheduled. "As women have known through the ages, the best person to nurse a mother back to health is her daughter," she reflected in *Solo Practice.* Her major regret was that she was a plastic surgeon, not a nurse.

Several years later Elissa Benedek, the psychiatrist, was to use Elizabeth's decision to cut back her medical practice, along with her decision six years after that to close her practice to study law, as evidence that Elizabeth was "occupationally dysfunctional." Benedek observed that Elizabeth seemed "somewhat overwhelmed" by her mother's illness. "Other female physicians are confronted with the same dilemma, caring for an aged mother, passing board examinations, many patients with many demands, and they find other ways of managing similar kinds of problems without closing down their practice," she said.

Elizabeth's decision may not have been so irrational. Antonia's illness, which was apparently diagnosed later as pericarditis, an inflammation of the tissue near the heart, was serious and prolonged. Antonia's doctors seemed powerless to treat it, and William was incapable of caring for his wife properly. Still, Elizabeth's choice to close her practice was an extreme, self-sacrificing reaction.

Eventually, however, Antonia's illness ended as mysteriously as it had begun, and in early 1981 Elizabeth was able to return to full-time practice after a break of several months. Antonia, sixty-six and on the way to a full recovery, retired as a psychologist. William stayed on Gallows Road and kept up the family business on a part-time basis.

Elizabeth was also able to resume her writing career, putting the finishing touches on *Solo Practice,* the sequel to *The Making of a Woman Surgeon.* The book, published in January 1982, covers the events in Elizabeth's life from her return to the Washington area through the period of her mother's illness and her decision to limit her practice. Like many sequels, the book lacks the power of the original, sometimes focusing needlessly on the details of Elizabeth's negotiations for office leases or some of the duller dinner parties she attended. Although well received by *The Washington Post* ("a fast-moving account of a concerned physician starting out in private practice. . . ."), *Solo Practice* is not nearly as compelling as *The Making of a Woman Surgeon.* The story line is simply not very dramatic.

Elizabeth left out names and identifying details of everyone—

presumably to preserve privacy. So the book is in most respects an unreliable source for the biographer. (Shibley, for example, is almost totally unrecognizable; it portrays him as a flashy Baltimore real estate broker rather than a staid Washington lawyer.) Still, the book reveals quite a bit about William's eccentricities.

Around this time, those eccentricities also found their way into the public records of the Fairfax County Circuit Court. On September 21, 1981, William filed three unusual lawsuits—two against Antonia, charging her with defrauding him of thousands of dollars of the family business's money, and one against Elizabeth, demanding that she pay him a total of $35,705 on a number of grievances. William claimed he had lent his daughter about $15,000, that she had taken silver and silver coins from him, and that she had failed to pay rent for living in the family home and for using some rooms for her medical practice. He even went so far as to ask for $1,070 for the rental value of his Blazer, which Elizabeth had used for a few months. For that, William fixed a rate of $5 a day. "He told me that she agreed to pay these things, and he sued her because he knew she was financially capable of paying," recalls Mary Cook Hackman, his lawyer from those days.

In the lawsuits against Antonia, William asked his wife to repay him large sums of money that he believed she had taken from the bank account of Aptitude Associates. He claimed that he discovered the money was missing during Antonia's prolonged illness, and that after doing some more investigating, he found that the purported fraud had been going on for almost a decade.

William's "discovery" coincided rather precisely with Antonia's decision to leave him, and Hackman sees a connection between the two events. "His real aim in all that mess was to get his wife back," she says. "I don't know exactly how he thought he'd accomplish it, but that was his aim. He simply couldn't understand how she'd want to live with Elizabeth in D.C. But Elizabeth's mother was very attached to Elizabeth. She would do whatever her daughter wanted her to do."

And, in his own strange way, William remained attached to Antonia. Despite all his lawsuits and his verbal and physical assaults, William apparently remained in love with her. Somehow he needed her around, if only to help him cope with his inner demons. As William put it a few years later in response to Antonia's petition for a divorce, "The complainant's perfidy is forgivable, provided that the complainant [Antonia] will agree to live with the defendant [William]."

In *Solo Practice,* Elizabeth noted revealingly in a slightly different context, "My mother had looked after him and shared the running of their practice for years. Without her, he was increasingly lost and increasingly angry." The couple's love-hate relationship may have worked the other way, too; as Elizabeth hinted years later, Antonia may have needed William around, simply because she had been with him for almost forty years and she didn't know how to face life without him. "For my mother, even separated, my father was the only man in her life," Elizabeth said.

On Christmas Eve, 1981, at the height of the couple's estrangement, William arrived at Elizabeth and Antonia's townhouse with a big plastic bag full of gifts. Elizabeth answered the door. When her father said he wanted "to hold my wife's hand and kiss her," Elizabeth blocked the doorway and told him that if he didn't leave, she would call the police. Elizabeth was "a pivotal player" in the breakup of her parents' marriage, William later declared. "She was very imperious then, and from what I understand, she still is," says Hackman, William's lawyer.

Confrontation, so routine with the volatile Morgan clan, was rare in the household in which Eric Foretich grew up. Eric was born and raised in Newport News, Virginia, just three hours' driving distance from Elizabeth. But the families could not have been more different.

Vincent, an engineer of Austrian descent, and Doris, a Daughters of the American Revolution member who traces her family through two hundred years of Virginia history, did not demand extraordinary achievement of their children—Eric, born in 1942, and Craig, born five years later. They cherished more modest hopes and dreams: a decent living, a lovely home, respect among friends and relatives. Their values were shared by many in Newport News, in those days a conservative, family-oriented city in Virginia's Tidewater area whose identity was heavily influenced by the large naval installations along the Atlantic shore.

As supervisor of marine architects at the Newport News Shipbuilding and Dry Dock Company, Vincent pursued a career similar to many of his neighbors but rose to a relatively high position. Eric's family had just a little more money, and a little more status, than most of their neighbors. Still, as hardworking churchgoers and solid citizens, Doris and Vincent fit in well in their community. "The whole family has lived in the Tidewater area for eons," says Linda Kelly, Doris and Vincent's niece. Linda's mother, Doris Foretich's sister Iris, lived near the Foretiches in Newport News, and Linda shared her childhood years with her slightly older cousins Eric and Craig. "Doris and Vincent always took a fine interest in people. Doris would dish out the ice cream and make you feel welcome," Linda recalls.

Doris Foretich, born in 1919, has lived nearly all her life in the Tidewater area. For twenty-two years she was an art teacher, with children of all ages coming to a studio in her home for lessons. But like many women of the generation that came of age during World War II, Doris centered her life around her family. Her nephews and nieces—three of her sisters raised their children in the Tidewater area—had the free run of her house. Christmas dinners and Fourth of July barbecues were always highlights of her life. Doris's other interests were equally conventional. With her gray hair and tailored wool suits, she looks the very model of the genteel clubwoman. Though not an intellectual, Doris has a lively curiosity about the larger world, and Linda Kelly recalls that Doris "was always studying for self-improvement." She took up bird watching after her children were grown, and had always painted, more for her own pleasure than for anything else. Her paintings of Eric's daughters hang in Eric's house.

Doris is a determinedly middle-class woman with many of the values of the Old South. Raised a Methodist, Doris remains a regular churchgoer. "As God is my witness," she is apt to say, or, "May the Lord strike me dead."

Doris carries a hint of resentment against what she sees as big-city sophistication and cynicism. In a letter to Elizabeth in 1985, alluding to Elizabeth's years as a columnist for *Cosmopolitan,* Doris wrote: "No Pollyanna am I, but I *know* there is more beauty to life than you are capable of seeing. Perhaps you hung out with the Cosmo group a bit too long."

Her husband Vincent, like many American men of his generation, remains controlled, stiff, still ramrod-straight in his mid-seventies. Born in 1914 and raised as a Catholic in Newport News, Vincent was able to fulfill at least part of every Catholic boy's dream by studying at Notre Dame. But the money ran out, and he left a year short of his bachelor's degree in engineering. Although Vincent never finished college, his talents were in demand as the nation mobilized for World War II. In the early 1940s, Vincent began his successful career of nearly forty years at the Newport News Shipbuilding and Dry Dock Company. When he retired in the fall of 1979 as manager of production engineering, he was supervising hundreds of engineers. He held one of the most responsible positions in the company, and because 90 percent of the company's work involved defense contracts, Vincent received a security clearance from the FBI.

Like his wife, Vincent continued his education over the years. Trained as a chemical engineer, he studied architecture and home construction in his spare time, and in the early 1980s, nearing seventy, designed an elaborate Georgian home for Eric in Great Falls, Virginia. Vincent also loves to build boats, and he and Eric still own a sailboat together and spend occasional weekends maintaining it. If Eric inherited his mother's fondness for the fine arts, he also absorbed his father's passion for order, logic, and neatness.

In Vincent's later years, a psychologist described him as "not by character self-revealing or very self-reflective. He tends to be conventional, subscribe to traditional ways of looking at things and does not want to get into emotional expression." This is a fair assessment. Vincent tries to keep his life and his emotions under control. The home he designed for Eric is a Georgian mansion modeled after the president's house at the College of William and Mary. Its symmetrical lines reflect a mind uncomfortable with disorder. When Eric became embroiled in child-custody problems, Vincent started writing summaries of key incidents, meticulously numbering events in his neat, all-capital-letter handwriting.

Vincent Foretich was not an easy man to have as a father. Until Eric was about ten, Vincent occasionally hit the boy with his belt. When Eric let sports come before his studies, Vincent stepped in. He wanted his sons to make something of themselves. But unlike the Morgan children, Eric and his brother do not seem to have suffered any particular stress. Looking back on those years, Eric and his friends describe scenes reminiscent of TV shows like "Leave It to Beaver."

"Boring middle class is the best way to describe us. You had families that were young, very family-oriented, everybody had children. The people all knew each other," recalls Jonathan Gibson III, a boyhood friend of Eric's who now practices law in the Tidewater area.

Unlike most of his friends, Eric was sent out of his neighborhood for elementary school. He attended an inner-city Catholic school fifteen miles away from home but switched to public school for junior high and high school. He wasn't an especially motivated student, spending more time thinking about girls and sports than about his studies. "He seemed to discover girls around age fifteen," his mother says. "He always seemed to have a girl around."

Friends and family consistently recall Eric as rather a ladies' man in high school and college. He is not conventionally handsome, but women seem to be attracted to him because of his intelligence and courtly manners. He projects a boyish vulnerability and softness that many have found difficult to resist. Once when Eric was about fifteen, a friend from the swim team invited him to watch an older acquaintance, whom Eric had never met, perform in a summerstock production in Williamsburg, Virginia. After the play, the actor invited the boys back to his apartment and plied them with mixed drinks; Eric recalls downing two or three scotches. Unaccustomed to alcohol, Eric collapsed, sick and heaving, on a bed. A couple of hours later he found the actor in bed with him, trying to fondle him. Eric got up, picked up his things, and left. That was the end of the matter. Some psychologists later attempted to use the incident to show that Eric had been scarred by sexual abuse, but it appears to lend but weak support to such theories.

In 1958, when Eric was sixteen, his mother gave birth to a girl, Doris Paula. Sick from birth with a congenital blood ailment, the baby died after only five weeks of life. According to family lore, she received "the wrong blood" during a transfusion. The family took it very hard, and it fell to the teenage Eric, the oldest child, to keep them together. His brother Craig was eleven then, too young to be of much help, and Eric, along with an uncle, made the funeral arrangements. Doris and Vincent, dazed by grief, were unable to do so. "I think it had a lasting effect on me. None of us has ever really gotten over the loss," Eric later recalled.

In 1960, Eric graduated from Warwick High School in the middle of his class. Since early childhood he had wanted to become a doctor, but his grades were mediocre and he was rejected by William and Mary, his first choice for college. Instead, he enrolled at a far lesser school, Lynchburg College in Lynchburg, Virginia, where he started as a business major. He soon switched to biology and found himself excited about his studies for the first time. Eric's grades suddenly improved: at the relatively undemanding college he discovered he could make As with minimal effort. In the middle of his sophomore year, he was able to transfer to William and Mary.

Eric had to work hard, but somewhat to his surprise did well academically and lettered in soccer, swimming, and track. He also enjoyed a fairly conventional college social life. He tried to pledge a fraternity but was unable to join; the school's administration closed the house because of the poor academic work of some of its members. Eric's own grades were excellent, however, and before graduation he visited the Medical College of Virginia in Richmond with an eye on either a medical or a dental career. When he got top scores on the pre-dental examination, he made up his mind and enrolled at the dental school. He hoped to have an opportunity to pursue some DNA research he had started.

Around this time, Eric met Katherine Sue Arrington, a petite, attractive elementary schoolteacher two years his senior. Vincent tried to convince Eric that at twenty-two, he was too young to marry, but to no avail. In 1965, Eric and Sue were married at a Presbyterian church in the bride's hometown of Hayside, Virginia. After the ceremony, the couple moved into campus housing near the dental school. But almost immediately Eric discovered that his father had been right: he could cope with the requirements of dental school but not with the requirements of a marriage. Eric, still emotionally immature in his early twenties, simply didn't try to make the marriage work. Most of the fellows in his crowd were single, and although Eric recalls he had "every good intention," he became more and more attracted to the carefree life he had left behind. Other women also caught Eric's eye, though he says he never had an affair at this point.

During the summer of 1968, the Foretich family suffered another blow when Craig Foretich was killed, at age twenty-one, in an accident on a Virginia highway. He was about to begin his senior year at the University of Virginia in Charlottesville. By all accounts, Craig, who had been previously treated for alcoholism, had been drinking when his car went off the road that night. Many years later, Eric told a psychologist that his brother was a drug user and had been taking lithium under the direction of a psychiatrist. Greg Williams, once a fraternity brother of Craig's and now a Washington lawyer, confirms this. "I was told that Craig had a pretty serious drug problem, marijuana and probably heavier things. He was kind of into the counterculture, a bit of a loner. But he always had great admiration for Eric," Williams says. Craig's death placed a heavy burden on Eric. As the only surviving child, he was suddenly the focus of all his parents' hopes and ambitions.

Vincent and Doris grew closer to Eric, who was then twenty-six years old, married, and long since out of his parents' house. Doris obviously leaned more on her son than before, and this dependency may have taken its toll. Eric and Sue's marriage was already shaky, and Eric's relationship with his mother in this difficult period apparently strained the marriage.

Eric graduated from dental school in 1969 and entered a prestigious oral-surgery internship program at New York's Harlem Hospital, associated with Columbia University. When he visited New York to find a place for him and Sue to live, he realized he didn't really want to stay with his wife. "I was very self-centered and had very little concern for the other person involved," Eric recalled. "The decision to become single again troubled me, but once I had made it, I couldn't go back on it." The couple was divorced about a year later, in December 1970.

To this day, Eric wistfully refers to Sue Arrington as a "very, very steadfast, loving, caring person," and says they left the marriage as friends. He blames himself for the failure of the marriage and for the impulsive behavior that would continue to complicate his romantic life. His professional life was in order, but he seemed unable to form a successful relationship with a woman. "Eric's selection of women has been bad. He has good insight into investments and real estate, but he just can't pick women," says Michael Fry, a D.C.-area plumbing contractor who has known Eric since 1972.

After his first marriage broke up, Eric enjoyed the single life he had coveted. He found his Southern charm as effective with New York women as it had been back in Virginia. As he describes it, he worked hard and played hard. At one point in the three-year period, Eric rented an apartment in a Manhattan building that, to his amusement and surprise, was also home to an extraordinarily large number of flight attendants. "It was stewardess heaven. I had more girlfriends than you can imagine," he says, looking back on the period as a hedonistic episode he has long since outgrown.

When his years of training were over, Eric returned to Virginia in 1973 to set up a practice. He continued to enjoy the good life there, moving into Marina Towers, a building in Alexandria, Virginia, with a lot of single young professionals. He was still dating a New York-based airline stewardess, who eventually moved to the Washington area hoping to encourage the relationship.

Eric's first job was with Norman Coleman, an older oral surgeon who hired him as a salaried dentist in his practice. After a few months, Eric bought the practice and also became chief of oral surgery at two hospitals in northern Virginia. His career was prospering. He opened offices in Virginia and in a fashionable neighborhood in Washington, and picked up a part-time teaching post at the Howard University dental school. Eric was elected president of the Greater Washington Society of Oral Surgeons.

"He had a terrific practice. He would get referrals from all over," says Peter Sauer, then the head athletic trainer at American University, who signed Eric on as the consulting oral surgeon for the athletic department. Eric was on call to treat athletes at the school who suffered injuries of the mouth or jaw. In his early thirties, with his training complete and his professional career established, Eric Foretich seemed to have the whole world in front of him.

Eric's relationships with women remained his one source of disappointment. As usual, he was looking for love and finding only unfulfilling relationships. His playboy life was rapidly losing its allure.

In August 1976, a dentist friend of Eric's introduced him to Sharon Sullivan, a nineteen-year-old part-time fashion model for Bloomingdale's and Saks Fifth Avenue. "You'll get your rocks off just looking at her," Eric recalls the other dentist saying. Not surprisingly, Eric's attraction to her was primarily physical.

Sharon, who had taken college courses through the years but never graduated, was thrilled to be dating a successful oral surgeon. Eric was immediately captivated by the tall, strikingly beautiful brunette. The couple embarked on a love affair that Eric's friend Michael Fry recalls as a classic whirlwind romance, with evenings at the ballet and the symphony and dinners at Washington's finer restaurants. Sharon was impressed with Eric's intelligence and sophistication. He was impressed that wherever he went with Sharon, "every man in the place would turn his head. When she was nineteen or twenty and she had her makeup on, no woman in the D.C. area could match her."

When the couple announced their marriage plans, Fry and some of Eric's other friends had their doubts, and Vincent was concerned about the disparity in age and education. But there was no swaying Eric, and on August 5, 1977, he and Sharon were married in a Catholic ceremony at a church in downtown Washington. The couple bought a condominium apartment in the Regency, a fashionable building in McLean. He was almost thirty-five years old; she had just turned twenty.

The speedy courtship deteriorated into a turbulent marriage. Sharon noticed a diametric change. Eric seemed indifferent, even hostile, since the wedding. The Southern gentleman who had courted her with flowers was replaced by a tense, unpleasant husband who could blow up without provocation. She particularly recalls one anniversary evening when he took her to an expensive French restaurant and angrily broke four champagne glasses. He told her he was frustrated with the marriage. (Eric recalls being angry that day but denies breaking the glasses.)

During the four-year marriage, Sharon, who had had a diseased kidney removed at age three, carried two pregnancies to term. She recalls that Eric was at his worst when she was pregnant. "He was so worried about me gaining weight that it was an obsession . . . ," she said later in sworn testimony. "He made a big issue out of me running with him and working out, and if I did not run and if I could not work in his office and entertain and work out and do everything, I was a bum and I would be lazy, there would be ridicule. . . . Eric had this idea of making me what he thought I could be . . . and it was beyond my own capacity."

Throughout her first pregnancy, Sharon recalls, Eric kept telling her that the baby would die. What was worse, he made the prediction flatly and without emotion; it was as if he didn't care. Sharon felt she was carrying a child her husband didn't really want. It didn't help that when the child, a boy, was stillborn, Eric hardly reacted at all. Eventually, Sharon reconciled herself to a loveless marriage. She no longer expected anything from Eric except a steady income. She had stopped trying to make the marriage succeed.

From Eric's point of view, Sharon was the problem. He had concluded that Sharon wanted him only as a ready source of income. Eric had enjoyed the cultural life of New York, and he wanted to enjoy the best of Washington: gallery openings, theater at the Kennedy Center, concerts by the National Symphony. He told a psychologist almost a decade later that being married to Sharon, whom he saw as a flighty, poorly educated, unsophisticated woman, was like being "married to wind."

From time to time, Sharon would talk about entering the Miss Virginia segment of the Miss Universe contest. A friend involved in the contest told her she was a sure shot to win. But Eric thought beauty contests weren't exactly a good idea for the wife of an ambitious oral surgeon. All those nights away from home in hotel rooms with middle-aged men, Eric said, couldn't do either of them any good. "Sharon had one valid complaint against me," says Eric today. "I didn't flatter her. I refused to feed her ego. I thought these contests were suspect. I wanted to put her through school, and her mother went so far as to complain that this was causing Sharon too much stress."

Sharon's life lacked direction and substance. She never settled on a career; in addition to modeling, she dabbled in computer sales and freelance fur retailing. She also ran up bills, once using Eric's American Express card to order some $20,000 worth of diamonds from a mail-order ad in *The Wall Street Journal*. When she told

Eric's friend Peter Sauer about the jewels, she swore him to secrecy like a teenager who didn't want her mother to find out what she had done. Eric eventually returned the diamonds and got the merchant to cancel the charge.

One of Sharon's complaints about Eric was that he was too close to his mother. He wanted his mother and his wife to be best friends, Sharon explained. According to her, Eric called Doris almost every night, and about every other week Doris and Vincent would make the 175-mile trip up from Tidewater, or Eric and Sharon would drive down. (Eric says he did call his parents but not nearly as frequently as Sharon believes.) Another nagging concern of Sharon's was that Eric had bought a beach house jointly with his parents rather than with her. A lawyer friend of Eric's, perhaps sensing that the marriage wouldn't last, had suggested that arrangement. Sharon saw it as a slight to her.

Eventually, Eric's relationship with his parents helped deal his marriage to Sharon its final blows. In the fall of 1979, Vincent retired from the shipyards at age sixty-five. He and Doris had always looked forward to a trip to Europe; Eric and Sharon, enjoying their new-found wealth, had gone the previous year. The four of them planned a nine-day European trip at Christmastime.

Around the time that Doris and Vincent were planning their trip of a lifetime, Sharon learned that she was pregnant again. But her kidney problems, exacerbated by the pregnancy, also flared up just as the vacation approached. Sharon begged off for health reasons; she wanted to have this baby. So Eric ended up going on the trip with his parents—and without his wife. While they were away, Sharon had to be hospitalized for about a week as a precautionary measure. She resented Eric's absence.

After her release, Sharon, largely recovered, picked up her husband and her in-laws at the airport. In what was surely one of the more uncomfortable half-hour rides any of the four has endured, Sharon sat in the front seat next to Eric and chatted with him but conspicuously refused to speak with Doris or Vincent. The four drove to Sharon's parents' home for a very tense dinner. The next day, Sharon decided she had had enough of what she saw as a one-sided marriage. Eric and his parents made all the decisions; her needs didn't matter. She felt she no longer had any reason to prove to Eric how strong or capable she was. All she wanted was a healthy baby, and staying with Eric wouldn't help bring that about. She left him that day and spent the remaining six months of her pregnancy living with her parents. The couple made some halfhearted efforts at reconciliation during that period and attended childbirth classes together, but the marriage remained in disarray.

On June 3, 1980, Sharon gave birth to a daughter, Heather Nicole Foretich. Eric had been at his beach house when his wife went into labor, but he was able to drive back to Fairfax Hospital in time to spend a full day of labor with Sharon and to be the first person to hold his baby daughter. After Heather was born, Eric slept the next night in Sharon's bed by her side. But almost immediately, Eric and Sharon's problems began to spill into Heather's life. The next day, there were angry quarrels and an obstetric resident had to ask Eric to leave his wife's room. The doctor was afraid that the stress would push Sharon's blood pressure to dangerous levels.

When Sharon was discharged after two weeks in the hospital, Eric asked her if she wanted to give their marriage one more try. Somewhat to his surprise, she agreed, and they went home together to their apartment in the Regency.

To Sharon, the next fifteen months were like playing house. She "poured herself into her child and her apartment," she recalls, and Eric poured himself into his work. Sharon says Eric was a good father when he was around, taking his part in feeding and diapering the baby. But he was still consumed with building up his practice. Often, he would leave for the office before Heather was awake and would come home after she fell asleep.

Sharon's health did not improve. She frequently had to take kidney medication intravenously through tubes attached to her arm. Often it was Eric, not his ailing wife, who would awaken when Heather cried at night. The marriage did not improve either. Several times Sharon packed her clothes and the baby's and left to spend the night with her mother. Then she would have second thoughts and ruefully return to her husband.

According to Sharon, Eric came home one September evening in 1981 in a dark mood, frustrated about something that happened in the office that day. "I don't make enough money," she recalls him saying. "You just don't understand. You don't understand anything." Sharon was sitting in a wing chair in the den, hooked up to her intravenous tubing. Heather was playing on the floor. When Sharon seemed to ignore Eric's laments, according to her account, he tried to get her attention by jerking on the plastic tube. The needle stayed in her arm, but the medicine started "falling out all over the place." She thought Eric was trying to kill her. The next day, Sharon left Eric and went to see her lawyer about a divorce.

A few weeks later, she learned she was pregnant. That pregnancy ended with a miscarriage.

Eric insists that although he often yelled at Sharon, he never pulled the tubing out of her arm. He believes the story was invented to blame Eric for Sharon's decision to leave. In that way, rather than find Sharon guilty of wrongfully deserting her husband, a divorce court might find that Eric had "constructively deserted" Sharon by making it intolerable for her to live with him. Whatever really happened that evening, Eric's second marriage was over. The divorce lawyers would pick up the broken pieces.

This breakup, unlike that of Eric's previous marriage, involved a third human being, a little girl just over a year old. Through the months of strife, Eric and Sharon had loved and cared for Heather. Her needs had to be taken into account. But during much of that fall Eric was unable to devote much attention to his wife, to his daughter, to his busy oral-surgery practice, or to the lavish Georgian home for which ground had just been broken in Great Falls. A few weeks before, he had met a woman he thought would solve all his problems, a woman with intelligence, charm, and beauty who seemed to love him for who he was, not for his income or his lifestyle. That woman was Elizabeth Morgan.

CHAPTER 2

Late August 1981 through February 18, 1983

In late August 1981, Eric Foretich and Elizabeth Morgan met for the first time—in the recovery room of Fairfax Hospital in Fairfax, Virginia. Both were caring for patients just coming out of surgery. Eric, who had only the vaguest knowledge of Elizabeth and her books, introduced himself first. "I have a couple of cases to discuss with you. Let's have lunch sometime," the sandy-haired surgeon suggested. Later, he asked his secretary to call Elizabeth's secretary, and a business lunch was arranged for the first Friday in October, the earliest that the doctors' schedules permitted.

The lunch conversation quickly veered from medical matters to more personal topics. According to her later testimony, Elizabeth noticed Eric's fatalism as he told her about his problems: the deaths of his brother and baby sister, his two failed marriages, the difficulties with Sharon, who had walked out on him permanently two weeks before. That very day, a Fairfax County judge had granted the couple a legal separation, awarding Sharon temporary custody of Heather. Eric was granted temporary visitation rights. Eric remembers talking about Sharon and Heather during his first lunch with Elizabeth. They were very much on his mind. But he dismisses the idea that he spoke of the deaths of his siblings. It was, after all, their first time together.

Elizabeth and Eric do agree on one thing: both sensed a powerful mutual attraction that afternoon. Eric invited Elizabeth to dinner the next weekend at a fine Washington restaurant, and she accepted. The couple soon realized that they shared other interests. Eric, a ballet fan, was impressed with Elizabeth's knowledge of dance. Though she professed ignorance, she knew what she was talking about. Elizabeth was attracted to Eric's Southern charm, and she sympathized with his insecurities. She thought she could be good for him.

By mid-November they were seeing each other steadily, and Elizabeth had started to think about marriage. She was hoping for a wedding after Eric's divorce from Sharon became final the following September. Eric, although completely infatuated, says he wasn't thinking about marriage at that time: he was still sorting out his feelings about Sharon and hadn't even begun to focus on their property or custody arrangements. He didn't even know where he was going to end up living. When Sharon left him, he had stayed in the Regency, but he didn't know who would finally be awarded title to the condominium.

Still, Eric's first weeks with Elizabeth were among his happiest. He liked the idea of Elizabeth: he was thrilled to find a woman who had been educated at Harvard, Yale, and Oxford, a woman whose mother spoke with a proper British accent. Elizabeth was also a well-known surgeon, a published author, and even something of a media star. She was a great catch, not bad for a kid from the hinterlands whose parents never finished college. Eric saw Elizabeth's accomplishments reflecting on himself.

Eric seemed like a teenager with a crush. One autumn afternoon, almost breathless, he called his friend Peter Sauer and whispered, "I have a new honey. I want you to meet someone special." The three soon met for dinner, which Sauer describes as "one of the most strained evenings I've ever seen." According to him, Elizabeth stared "stone cold," made a few perfunctory remarks, then departed. She had driven herself to the restaurant after seeing a patient, and she left alone. "She's a lunatic," Sauer told Eric. "Drop her." Eric told his friend to butt out of his life.

Despite what Sauer says he saw, Elizabeth was apparently genuinely attracted to Eric, and she thought she could help him. "He had a lot of problems with the tragedies in his life . . . and I hoped to help him solve those problems," Elizabeth said years later. As love-struck as Eric, Elizabeth wrote her *Cosmopolitan* editor that she had just met "a wonderful man who looks like Lord Byron."

The romance soon took an unexpected turn. Late on Thanksgiving evening, Eric and Elizabeth sat up talking at Elizabeth's Washington townhouse. Antonia had said her good nights. Eric made a sexual advance; Elizabeth acquiesced and asked if she should run upstairs for her diaphragm. In the end, they decided that pregnancy was unlikely. Eric says it was the first time they ever made love.

A few days later, Elizabeth told her lover to sit down. "I'm pregnant," she said with an air of certainty. "I just know." Within ten days, she had medical confirmation: her child was due in August. After briefly considering abortion, Elizabeth decided that since she planned to marry Eric anyway, she would simply start a family a little bit earlier than expected. Eric, influenced by his Catholic background, saw no moral justification for abortion, though he would have agreed if Elizabeth had wanted one. He was traditional enough to believe that a man should stand by a woman he had gotten "in trouble." He wanted to give his child a name and assure its legitimacy. He couldn't just walk away.

Vincent, however, suspected that Elizabeth was out to manipulate his son. He counseled Eric to forget her and to start over with someone new. Eric's friends also begged him to drop Elizabeth. "If she wants to take care of that baby and has the money, let her," Bill Hale, a cousin of Eric's, advised. But Eric couldn't do something he thought was wrong; he couldn't abandon Elizabeth.

The couple hastily planned a marriage. At a Sunday-night caucus with Hugh Cregger (Eric's lawyer in his divorce from Sharon), Eric, Elizabeth, and the senior Foretiches mulled their options. Abortion had already been ruled out, and an immediate marriage in Virginia was also out of the question: Eric was still legally married to Sharon. That divorce couldn't be final until September, and by then, the baby would be born. Eric and Elizabeth had to act faster.

Cregger suggested that Eric solve the Sharon problem by going to Haiti to obtain an immediate divorce. Sharon would not be present, but that wasn't necessarily a difficulty. Some courts in the United States, Cregger said, would recognize what is known as a "unilateral divorce"—secured by one of the partners without the other's consent. After that, Eric could immediately marry Elizabeth in Haiti. Networks of lawyers up and down the East Coast could arrange quickie unions in these situations; for the right price, it was easy to tap into the network. For Eric, secrecy and speed were essential; if Sharon found out what had happened, she would surely use the threat of an adultery charge, or a bigamy complaint, to exact a high price from Eric in their property settlement. (Sharon had hired Mark Sandground, a hard-nosed divorce lawyer.) The whole plan smacked of deceit and the divorce might not hold up, but in his zeal to legitimize his unborn child, Eric went ahead.

Elizabeth later denied knowing that Sharon was being deceived, but she seems to have been fully aware of the scheme. She has testified that she told Eric that attorney Lane Gabeler had represented her in the litigation with her father. According to Elizabeth, Eric told her that Gabeler suggested that the couple might want to contact an Alabama lawyer she knew who could work out the logistics of a Haitian divorce.

Gabeler denies that she participated in the actual arrangements but does remember being consulted about whether the Haitian marriage would be legally valid if challenged by Sharon. She had said that the marriage would probably stand up; a Virginia judge would prefer to rule the child, a Virginia resident, legitimate.

The Alabama lawyer, who had arranged dozens of Haitian divorces, made things move rapidly. On January 22, 1982, Eric and Elizabeth flew to Port-au-Prince, where a divorce hearing was held the next day. The wedding ceremony took place on Monday, January 25. In his hotel room, feeling buffeted by forces beyond his control, Eric sat down to write a letter to his eighteen-month-old daughter Heather. He told her how guilty he felt that he had begun a new marriage and a new life with a new baby. He said he knew she'd probably never forgive him. Maybe later, when she was old enough to read the letter, she would understand.

Eric and Elizabeth were now married, but Elizabeth was committed to a February book tour for *Solo Practice,* so they delayed setting up a home together. Finally, in March, they moved into a rented house in Great Falls, a wooded suburb along the Potomac some forty minutes from downtown Washington. Settled in Revolutionary War times, Great Falls is a quiet retreat for the affluent and for young professionals seeking a distinctive address. The house was also a short drive from both Eric and Elizabeth's offices.

After the final breakup with Sharon, Eric had stopped the work on the Georgian home under construction on a huge lot in Great Falls. Now the work resumed. The house would do nicely for him and Elizabeth and their children. The rental would do until then.

Antonia Morgan moved in with the newlyweds from the beginning. Elizabeth explained that her mother had no other home. Antonia and William remained at war. Eric agreed to have Antonia move in, presumably on a permanent basis.

There was also a temporary boarder in the small ranch house. Bill Hale, the cousin who had advised Eric against the marriage, moved in while he supervised the electrical work on the new home. Hale, an electrical engineer from Newport News, had been temporarily assigned to a project in the Washington area and agreed to work on Eric's house in exchange for free rent and an hourly labor rate. Eric acted as his own general contractor, and Vincent, the old shipyard supervisor, dropped by often at the site to make sure everything was in order.

Eric wanted to build the home for his new bride, but Elizabeth never showed the slightest interest in the new house. She liked the buzz of city life. Eric didn't seem to sense her lack of excitement.

Neither Eric nor Elizabeth invested much time or effort in their relationship during their brief time together. Forged from a brief attraction and a fortuitous pregnancy, the marriage never really had a chance to develop and the sparks quickly burned out. It was a curiously cold relationship, a marriage of convenience rather than affection. Instead of pooling their resources and incomes, the couple kept everything separate, like roommates. Both Bill Hale and Eric recall Elizabeth and Antonia writing down their grocery expenses on a tablet on the wall. Each week they added up the expenses, dividing them into three equal parts.

Eric and Elizabeth had many competing demands on their time. Eric, a professional worrier to begin with, was fretting that his surgical practice wasn't growing fast enough. He had to spend time with dentists and doctors who could refer patients, and he had the house in Great Falls to attend to. There were also the nagging problems with Sharon, who he says had already vowed to "ruin him" in their divorce settlement. At this point, Eric had temporary visitation rights with Heather but didn't know whether Sharon would use their daughter to exact a better settlement.

Elizabeth was even more preoccupied, usually leaving the house before eight in the morning and not returning until after seven. Her mother drove her to work. Many days, she spent more time alone with Antonia than with her husband. If Eric and Elizabeth had dinner together during the week, it was often at a local Hot Shoppe—with Antonia.

Elizabeth, pregnant at the time, was not physically up to par. She was vomiting frequently and also developed a urinary-tract infection that forced her to be hospitalized for a few days in the fourth month of pregnancy. But she didn't cut back her hours. She signed a contract with Little, Brown & Co. for a third book about her life, tentatively entitled *Surgeon, Wife and Mother.* The book, eventually published under the title *Custody,* would begin where *Solo Practice* left off. The idea was to explain how the successful medical woman was able to combine marriage, motherhood, and a career. Elizabeth was always a disciplined writer, and she was already taking notes about everything she and Eric said and did. She would often stay late at her medical office working on the book.

According to Bill Hale, Elizabeth didn't seem to take the marriage seriously. Eric had his furniture, china, and other belongings moved to the house, while Elizabeth just brought the bare minimum. Eric rented out the Regency condominium to pay rent on the house he was sharing with Elizabeth, but Elizabeth never rented her townhouse in Washington. She says she kept the house vacant because it needed plumbing work and, in any case, she was too busy to find a tenant.

There were other problems, and Elizabeth's extraordinarily close relationship with her mother exacted a heavy toll. According to Hale, Elizabeth prepared attractive plates of food for her mother while ignoring Eric. And many evenings around half past ten, instead of sitting down with her husband to compare notes about the busy day, Elizabeth would lock herself in the bathroom with Antonia for hours. Antonia would soak in the bathtub while she and Elizabeth chatted.

Eric thought it odd that a grown woman and her mother would routinely walk around naked in front of each other, as Elizabeth and Antonia did. Elizabeth verifies that she and her mother often got ready for bed together and that this included Antonia taking a bath. Antonia has also confirmed the fact that the bathroom meetings took place every night. A friend of Elizabeth's who observed her with her mother recalls that the relationship was "very strong, almost as if *they* were the couple. There was none of the normal love-hate relationship between mother and daughter. Elizabeth was so polite and deferential to her mother, it was like playing a record at the wrong speed."

Elizabeth gives a different explanation for the sessions. She has testified that the bathroom was the only place the two could speak privately. Eric was becoming increasingly angry and frustrated with his life, she remembers, and he would take his frustrations out by launching into tirades at her. Elizabeth says that hour-long tête-à-têtes were necessary so she could maintain her composure. (Eric says he first noticed the bathroom sessions back at the D.C. townhouse when he and Elizabeth were dating, and a person who has known the Morgans for years recalls that Antonia and Elizabeth had the same kind of sessions back in the Gallows Road home, long before Eric entered the picture.)

One day in the spring of 1982, Hale noticed water dripping from the bathtub onto the ceiling of his basement apartment. Assuming that Eric and Elizabeth were together, he tiptoed gingerly upstairs to offer any help he could. Instead of finding the embarrassed new-lyweds, he saw only Eric, standing in the hall beside a locked bath-room door. Eric raised both hands and shrugged. "What have I gotten myself into?" he asked his cousin. Hale, equally perplexed, shrugged back.

A couple of days later, Eric thought he had a solution and sug-gested to Elizabeth that they try bathing together. "No, thank you," came the cold, distant response. "My mother and I have been doing this for years."

Eric felt that his new wife had closed him out. Elizabeth, he decided, didn't have much of herself left to give him. By his own account, Eric was "very needy" in those days. He had changed his life radically to marry Elizabeth. He had hoped she would recognize how much he had given up for her—and would provide the emo-tional support to cope with Sharon's demands. But Elizabeth was remote and unsympathetic, and Eric found himself calling his par-ents often to ask what he had done wrong. With their advice, he learned after a few weeks to adjust to a marriage that he found seriously lacking. He began to believe that marrying Elizabeth was an even more serious mistake than marrying Sharon.

Elizabeth thought Eric had made her just his latest problem, in-stead of letting her help him solve his problems. He would wake up late at night and lash out at her: he blamed her for getting preg-nant and for ruining his life. His money was slipping away, he would tell her, and she didn't love him. Elizabeth says she needed to escape and to get a chance to breathe. Eric never really cared for her, she decided later. He was cruel and unkind. He seemed to be angry with the world, angry with women, angry with her all the time.

Antonia says that Eric was angry or moody most of the time. Nothing ever seemed to make him happy. She says that she wanted her daughter to make the marriage work, despite her own "physical revulsion" toward Eric and his "perfectly obvious" personality prob-lems. Even though she quickly concluded that there was little hope for the marriage, Antonia encouraged Elizabeth to keep it going.

In May 1982, Eric and Elizabeth decided to try to salvage their relationship. They hoped a change of scenery would make a differ-ence in their foundering marriage. The couple—with Antonia in tow—went to England to sightsee and visit family. During a ten-hour automobile drive while Antonia was staying with one of her relatives, Elizabeth and Eric finally had a chance to have a real husband-wife chat. Eric recalls that Elizabeth spent most of the time trying to convince him to give up his visitation rights to Heather. She didn't enjoy having the little girl around, and besides, she argued, little children belong with their mothers. Eric was appalled. He loved Heather and wanted her to be a permanent part of his life. He was not at all sure that Elizabeth wanted to remain in his life, and there was no way she would make him give up his daughter.

After the trip, Eric began to have further doubts about Elizabeth's intentions when he noticed what appeared to be a draft of the first chapter of her latest book lying on the living-room coffee table. Elizabeth, it appeared, was ready to reveal the intimate details of their marriage for public viewing. Eric was offended, with good reason, he thought. He confronted Elizabeth, who said he had no business prying into her private affairs. Elizabeth later said that what Eric saw was not an actual chapter but merely a chronology of events from their marriage.

The Washington rumor mill began to hum with stories about the unusual circumstances of Elizabeth Morgan's pregnancy and marriage. They surfaced in print on July 11, 1982, in Rudy Maxa's "Front Page," a gossip column in *The Washington Post*'s well-read Sunday magazine. "Rumor has it that Dr. Elizabeth Morgan, the Washington plastic surgeon and author, is pregnant," read an anonymous question in the column. "I thought she was single." (Maxa confirms that he invented the questions as a way to present gossip he had heard around town. The questions were never attributed to actual readers.) Maxa "responded" that Elizabeth had married Eric Foretich and that a child was due the next month. He also noted, correctly, that the marriage was Elizabeth's first, and incorrectly, that it was Eric's second. The marriage to Sue Arrington had escaped his notice.

Elizabeth had not contacted Maxa on her own but had confirmed the story. She wasn't happy in her marriage, but she didn't want anyone to think of her as an unwed mother.

The person who was shocked by the story was Sharon, who learned for the first time that Eric had married someone else. Furious and humiliated, she called him that morning. "What on God's earth is going on there?" she demanded. She recalls his reply as cool and dismissive: "I knew you were going to call me one of these days. I knew it. You wouldn't understand. I can't explain it to you because you certainly wouldn't understand." But she had the trump card. He was an adulterer and a bigamist, and she could prove it. He wasn't morally fit to see Heather, and she'd make sure he never saw his daughter again.

Eric blamed Elizabeth. During a Sunday-afternoon stroll in a park along the Potomac, he told her about Sharon's call. The whole complicated plan had unraveled in the worst possible way, he said.

Sharon had read about it in the *newspaper,* of all things. Eric, feeling betrayed, decided that Elizabeth had spoken with Maxa to embarrass him. Eric believed he had given up so much for Elizabeth, and now she had turned on him.

According to Elizabeth's deposition, *The Washington Post* had called Eric just before the column appeared to ask him which of his wives he was married to. That same day, according to Elizabeth, Eric pushed her down on the floor and violently kicked her in the stomach in a fit of anger. (Eric says he and Maxa have never spoken, and Maxa confirms that he never contacted Eric at any time. Elizabeth testified that she did not seek any medical attention, surprising for a physician who had allegedly received such a serious blow in the last months of her pregnancy. Neither Bill Hale nor Antonia saw or heard any physical violence during the Morgan-Foretich marriage. Antonia, certainly no friend of Eric's, testified that Elizabeth never spoke of any such episode. Eric vaguely recalls that Elizabeth went to the hospital emergency room late in her pregnancy but says it was because she had slightly injured a ligament near her uterus during intercourse with him.)

Elizabeth continued to see patients up to the end of her pregnancy. She felt tired, embittered, and unattractive. She decided that her marriage was a failure: Eric was intelligent and charming, but was also moody and depressed.

Eric, for his part, still felt angry and suspected that Elizabeth was using him. He thought she wanted the baby but not the husband or the daily routine of married life.

As Eric expected, Sharon and Mark Sandground, her lawyer, made the most of Maxa's column. Sandground threatened to reveal all the details of the Haitian divorce and remarriage at a public divorce trial. Eric hired Betty Thompson, a tough-as-nails divorce lawyer who knew Sandground well, to try to restrain Sandground's demands. But Eric was dealing from weakness. On August 13, he signed a tentative settlement with Sharon requiring him to pay $1,600 a month in combined alimony and child support. Sharon got the Regency condominium, and Eric had to make the mortgage payments. In return, Sharon was to pay the condo fee and to give Eric reasonably liberal visitation with Heather. Eric was allowed to see her two weekends a month and five hours every Wednesday afternoon.

Late that afternoon, as Eric recalls it, he swung into traffic in his old Mercedes, silently assessing the settlement. He realized that Sharon and Sandground were celebrating a big win. He knew that he could have gotten a better financial settlement if it weren't for Elizabeth and the Maxa column, but he wanted to put that behind him. Elizabeth's baby was due any day. Besides, he had tried to pull a fast one on Sharon and wasn't proud of what he had done. He probably deserved to get caught. With the baby and the new house, scheduled to be finished in the spring, his income would drain off very quickly. Sharon's $1,600 a month wouldn't help.

Eric stared at a double scotch in a McLean bar on his way home from the lawyer's office. Somehow, someone would have to help him meet these crushing obligations. When Eric got home that evening, he flopped down on the bed, still trying to figure it all out.

Elizabeth walked in, catching Eric in mid-thought. He told her that he had a new financial burden to face and that he needed help. It isn't clear exactly what load he asked her to shoulder. Eric says he wanted to make sure she shared in the upkeep of the new house. Elizabeth contends that Eric asked her point blank to help pay his alimony. "I didn't really listen to his proposed financial details," Elizabeth said in later testimony. "I think his suggestion was so wrong that there was no hope for our relationship. I was terribly, terribly upset. It simply brought to a head the fact that he had no feeling for me, he didn't care for me, he thought nothing of me except as a source of revenue."

Elizabeth stood up and walked the few steps from the bedroom to the bathroom. Antonia, concerned about what she had overheard, peeked in from the hallway, and the two women huddled for a few minutes in rapt conversation. Elizabeth made her decision: she had reached the end of the line with Eric. She would be out of the house in minutes. It was just after 9:00 P.M.

Elizabeth threw a few of her things into a large plastic bag, and both women trudged out into the warm August night to begin the forty-minute trip back to Elizabeth's Washington townhouse. Eric watched the blue and white Buick disappear down the dark country road. First Sharon, now this, he thought. What would happen to him next? Eric later realized he should have seen it coming. He remembered that for a couple of weeks before her departure, Elizabeth had begun to leave her car on the front lawn. She must have figured it would be easier to make a clean getaway like that. The next day, Elizabeth returned with her brother Jim to get the rest of her things. Eric wasn't home at the time.

The following Friday, Elizabeth went into labor, and on Saturday, August 21, 1982, Hilary Antonia Foretich was born at Sibley Hospital in Washington. She weighed 8 pounds 8 ounces. The baby's first name was Eric's choice; not surprisingly, Elizabeth selected her mother's name as her daughter's middle name. At birth, Hilary turned blue and briefly had trouble breathing. The obstetrician used a suction tube to remove an obstruction from the baby's vocal cords. Otherwise, Hilary's passage into the world was uneventful.

Eric attempted to visit Elizabeth in the hospital during labor, but she had ordered him barred from both the labor and delivery rooms. She told him his presence would upset her.

Eric showed up in the recovery room just as Elizabeth was being wheeled out of delivery. He carried two dozen red roses. Elizabeth's love for her husband reawakened. In *Custody,* Elizabeth said she had never been so happy to see him than at that moment. He was a difficult person, she knew, but maybe they could work things out for Hilary's sake. Eric pleaded with her to come home with him and the baby, but Elizabeth firmly said no. She was still in love with Eric, but her doubts remained.

Whatever accommodation Elizabeth was willing to make for Eric did not include her daughter. Elizabeth wrote in *Custody* that from the moment she left the hospital with Hilary, she was determined to be the only force in her daughter's life. It never occurred to her that Eric would show any interest in the child. Nor did she want him to: "I am utterly convinced that when a little child is taken from its loving mother, even for visitation, it may lose its natural protector and its security. Men are all very well, but nature didn't make men for rearing little children."

Elizabeth's brother Rob drove her home to the Newport Place townhouse early the next week. Hilary was a difficult infant from birth, constantly crying and never settling down to a sound sleep. From the beginning, Elizabeth hired night nurses to help with the baby so she could conserve her strength to go back to work—feeling financially strapped, she had allowed herself only four weeks off— and Antonia did whatever she could. For just a short time, Hilary's birth seemed to bring the Morgan and Foretich families to a rapprochement. Eric and his parents visited a couple of times a week, and William dropped by once with a bottle of Chivas Regal for Eric. William was in an expansive mood; a few weeks before Hilary was born, Antonia had convinced him to drop the lawsuits he had filed against her and Elizabeth. "Fathers deserve a bit of acknowledgment too," he told his son-in-law. Elizabeth hoped the joy of the new baby would somehow help her father to deal with his anger. Maybe he could learn to enjoy a placid retirement.

During the weekend of September 18, William and Antonia, although they were still living apart, went to Bermuda for a brief vacation. That Friday evening, Elizabeth dropped the four-week-old Hilary off with Beverly Smith, her medical secretary, and went shopping at Bloomingdale's with Eric, looking for a baby gift for a mutual friend. Things were turning around for them. Or so both of them thought that night.

Elizabeth had decided to give the marriage another chance. She didn't really believe Eric was stable enough for her; she feared his anger and was saddened by his depression. But she wanted more children and was willing to have more with him.

Eric, stung by too many rejections, dared to hope that his bad luck with women might finally be over. Eric and Elizabeth spent the night together that evening at Newport Place, beginning a period of reconciliation in which Eric visited his wife a couple of times a week. But when Eric tried to pick up Hilary, Elizabeth told him severely, "Put her down. She's not yours to pick up."

Antonia was still not ready to let William come back fully into her life, so she continued to live with Elizabeth. And Elizabeth, who had resumed her surgical practice after her maternity leave, did not wish to subject the frail woman of sixty-eight to the demands of an infant. The small house couldn't accommodate a live-in housekeeper. So Elizabeth started dropping Hilary off, from 8:00 A.M. until 6:00 P.M. five days a week, at the home of Linda Mason, a day-care provider in McLean.

Hilary's hours with Mason were soon extended even further. When Elizabeth had surgery scheduled for early mornings, she sometimes dropped Hilary off as early as 7:00 A.M. For the first few months of her life, Hilary spent a great deal more of her waking time at the sitter's than at home. Elizabeth felt a twinge of sadness that Hilary was a commuter by the age of one month. She seemed to be doing well in day care, but Elizabeth noticed that the infant was very tired at the end of the long day and did little but cry.

The reconciliation between Eric and Elizabeth did not last long, and Elizabeth says money sparked the couple's final break-up. In early October, Eric and Elizabeth had signed a contract to lease space for a joint medical office in McLean. Each agreed to pay half the cost but, according to Elizabeth, Eric kept reducing his share until she was stuck with most of the burden. This confirmed Elizabeth's suspicion that Eric was merely using her as a source of funds.

Eric never believed finances were the real reason for Elizabeth's departure. He says there never was much of a dispute over the office lease. He says he made it clear that he was merely temporarily short of cash and that he would eventually pay his full share of the rent.

Eric says the final breakup began after a dinner invitation from a dentist friend who wanted to meet his new wife. Eric accepted with pleasure for Tuesday evening, October 12. At six-thirty that evening, half an hour before they were supposed to be there, Elizabeth called Eric and said she wasn't coming. He was able to persuade her to go later in her own car. But when she finally showed up, in an unhappy, preoccupied, agitated mood, Eric knew his life had changed forever. He decided that Elizabeth had never really wanted the marriage. Just a few days later, she said goodbye.

That farewell appears to have occurred on the weekend of October 16. On Friday morning, Elizabeth called Eric at his dental office and told him she wanted to terminate their joint lease arrangement. The following Sunday, she sat him down on the couch at her Newport Place house. "It's over," she said icily, using words reminiscent of her statement to Ray Shibley two years before.

And from then on, it *was* over. Elizabeth cut Eric out of her life, declaring him a non-person who had to be separated from their daughter to the full extent that legal processes permitted. "My reaction was instinct, not reason," Elizabeth wrote later in *Custody*. From the very beginning, long before any charges of sexual abuse arose, Elizabeth vowed that no one could make her give Hilary up, even temporarily. Hilary occupied the center of Elizabeth's emotional life in a manner that a psychiatrist would later consider abnormal. "It is a serious problem in social relationships for an adult woman to find her four-year-old child is her best friend," Elissa Benedek concluded years later.

Eric believes that he had been important to Elizabeth only as Hilary's biological father. According to *Custody,* Elizabeth's brother Jim told her, "Whatever else your ex is good for, he's got good genes." Eric recalls Elizabeth saying in their last conversation that she was still willing to have more children with him, just as long as they didn't live together. Eric says he rejected the proposal as absurd and demeaning. Elizabeth denies making the proposal, but Eric certainly understood her to be saying just that. In a November 11, 1982, letter to Elizabeth, he asked rhetorically, "Did I ever leave *you,* or did I ever suggest that we have more children and not live together?" And Doris, in an anguished letter to Elizabeth two days later, argued: "You terminated the relationship and proposed that you and he continue to have children but remain apart. I refuse to believe that you, a doctor, would ever consider having offspring with one whom you really thought was unstable."

Four days after the breakup, Eric tried again to salvage a marriage that was probably unsalvageable. He wrote to Elizabeth on October 22:

Although I too have had occasional doubts about the sincerity of our marriage, I strongly feel it is inappropriate to terminate so important a relationship before it has had a chance to flourish. The positive aspects of our personalities and interests have oftentimes been subjugated to the untoward circumstances of the day or the emotional behavior of others.

This is not to say that everything can be perfect, because we are human and we each have our idiosyncrasies. Yet I know I can bring you happiness.

As your life is important to you, so is mine, and so there is no frivolity in what I am trying to say. These words come from someone who is willing to make a commitment predicated upon mutual respect, admiration, and love.

I have made no mention of our daughter because she is the product of our relationship but not its foundation.

It is unnecessary to mention my love for her, but she gives me such a special joy when I hold her, a feeling that only a parent can have.

Her future is extraordinarily important to me. I hope I can be with her as a parent with whom she lives.

Please let us not close the book on our lives before at least I can officially extricate myself from my former tether. Please give me the chance to display to you the consideration I would like to offer you.

Elizabeth, I love you very much. In my life, I have never met another woman who offered me as much intellectual and emotional stimulation as you. There is no other woman with whom I want to share my affections. I am not perfect, but I have special sensitivities that I think can enrich your life.

If after a reasonable time, after I am free of the other bond, it is necessary to go separate paths, then we at least will have given it our best.

These words are from my heart and my prayers. I mean them with all sincerity. Please, although you may have reservations, open your mind to my request.

Elizabeth replied four days later: Eric was a wonderful man and a wonderful father to both his daughters, she said. But the marriage had to end. Elizabeth added that she wished she could have made Eric happy but was sorry she had not succeeded. She told Eric that he had had a difficult year and that he should spend some time recuperating from his emotional traumas.

Eric was not quite so ready to give up. He and Elizabeth had never really had a marriage, he said. Why not at least try now to have one? The accidental pregnancy, the hasty wedding ceremony, and the nagging problems with his "former tether" to Sharon had preoccupied both of them. It was true, he conceded, he had been testy and difficult to live with. But was that a reason to end a marriage so abruptly?

"Elizabeth, you are a marvelous woman. You are both beautiful, and intelligent and gifted," Eric wrote to her. "I know I can never replace you. Yet I know I cannot change your mind. I will no longer try. I know you have loved me. . . . Like a fairy or gazelle, the shadow of you is always with me, but when I reach out, I cannot touch your soul."

Although Eric had finally given up on his marriage, he made it clear to Elizabeth that he was not giving up his right to be part of Hilary's life. Elizabeth's first offer to Eric in that regard had the virtue of simplicity. George Cronin, an associate of Lane Gabeler and Elizabeth's lawyer at the time, told Eric that in exchange for his agreeing to relinquish his parental rights in their entirety, Elizabeth was willing to let him see Hilary in her home from nine o'clock to noon every Saturday morning. Eric turned that offer down as insulting. A little child needs a father as well as a mother, he believed.

After this, Elizabeth refused to let Eric visit Hilary at her house. He tried to come by once, just after their final breakup, and they ended up yelling at each other. She told him he had "terribly upset" her, so all future visits would have to take place at Linda Mason's day-care home, a few minutes' drive from his office.

Eric rearranged his scheduled surgery to permit him to see Hilary three or four times a week, a couple of hours at a time. Mason did not object, but Eric soon found the arrangement less than ideal. It was difficult for him to have any quiet time with his daughter in the hurly-burly of the day-care home. He wrote to Elizabeth, "Although I am fond of Mrs. Mason and believe her to provide excellent care and emotional support for our daughter, I believe more suitable arrangements should be made at least temporarily. Her paternal grandparents will be visiting this weekend and I am sure they would prefer to visit with Hilary in a somewhat more private setting."

Elizabeth, however, made no concessions. All the visits occurred in Mason's presence; Elizabeth didn't even let Eric leave the day-care home to take the infant for a walk.

The conflict escalated throughout the fall and into the winter. Eric made repeated efforts to see Hilary, only to find out that Elizabeth would not make her available. Just before Thanksgiving, Eric had his secretary call Elizabeth's secretary to ask whether Vincent and Doris could bring Hilary to Eric's apartment for four hours the next day. Elizabeth was with a patient and did not return the call. The next day, Elizabeth's secretary responded that Elizabeth refused to accept personal phone calls at the office.

On December 22, Eric sent a mailgram to Elizabeth at her office.

It read in its entirety: "My parents and I request that Hilary Foretich, my daughter, spend a portion of the upcoming holiday with us in my home. Please contact me regarding this arrangement." Within fifteen minutes Elizabeth had dashed off a curt letter telling Eric not to contact her at the office on personal matters. The visitation was impossible until a formal custody arrangement had been completed, Elizabeth said, and if Eric wanted to talk further about visits, he should contact Cronin, who had been advising Elizabeth about a divorce. Impatient, she flew to Haiti and ended the marriage in January 1983.

Fortunately for Eric, his settlement with Sharon (the tentative one he had signed the day Elizabeth first left him) had not yet been reduced to a final document, so Eric was still negotiating with Sharon. He believed that Elizabeth had agreed not to divorce him until he freed himself of that obligation. Instead, she had gone off and gotten her Haitian divorce. "How was Haiti?" he could not help writing. "I guess your promise to keep us intact, at least on paper, until my affairs cleared up, just couldn't hold up to the attraction of the Caribbean, what with the weather being so nice there this time of the year."

The divorce was not the only abrupt separation that winter. In mid-February, Elizabeth stopped sending Hilary to Linda Mason. She believed that the six-month-old baby was failing to grow as she should and wondered why the food she left every day for Hilary never seemed to be used up. Hilary's pediatrician, Dr. Voja Russo (who rapidly became Elizabeth's friend), told Elizabeth that the babysitter probably wasn't feeding Hilary enough. Although Hilary's food could have been left over for any number of reasons, that was enough for Elizabeth. She found Hilary another day-care provider, Diane Cotter.

On the afternoon she fired Mason, Elizabeth called Eric to inform him. But she failed to tell him the location of the new day-care home. Eric wrote two snappish letters to her. The situation, he said, was "untenable." He could not locate his daughter, whom he hadn't seen for three weeks.

In a February 18, 1983, letter, Eric tried for a moment to bypass the squabbling. "I believe we would both be served by preventing a Machiavellian struggle over our infant daughter," he wrote. "As this would not be in her best interest, neither would it be consistent with my feelings toward you. I still harbor an abiding respect and tenderness for you." But Eric ended the letter with a warning: "Be advised, that what I seek is fairness!"

CHAPTER 3

March 11, 1983, through May 26, 1983

The Machiavellian struggle began three weeks later—in the D.C. Superior Court with Elizabeth's March 11 petition for custody and child support. Eric, frustrated that he and his parents had been relegated to visiting Hilary at day-care homes, struck back with a counterclaim seeking temporary custody, or at least the right to overnight visitation. The new case was assigned to the court's family division, which handles all disputes over child custody. The docket number, D 684-83, would remain permanently attached to the case for as long as it lasted.

At the time of filing, the case was not assigned to a particular judge. At that point, the Superior Court (the District of Columbia's general trial court) did not ordinarily permit a single judge to remain involved in a continuing matter. The judge could shift on a day-to-day basis, depending on availability. Nine judges rendered decisions on *Morgan* v. *Foretich* before court administrators finally decided to assign a permanent one.

Along with his counterclaim, Eric asked the court to order a psychiatric evaluation of Elizabeth, a reasonably common procedure in contested custody cases. Eric thought Elizabeth had behaved irrationally toward him for almost a year, and he hoped to convince the court that she was an unfit mother. Such an evaluation might convince a judge to name Eric as Hilary's primary custodian and to limit Elizabeth to visitation rights.

In child-custody disputes, U.S. courts are governed primarily by the standard of "the best interests of the child." The rights of the parents (such as the right to have access to the child, the right to be involved in the child's upbringing, and the right to make decisions about the child's life) are important. Legally, however, the child's needs come first; the courts are supposed to serve the child.

The "best interests" standard is deliberately couched in vague terms, in order to permit judges to tailor decisions to the unique strengths and weaknesses of the parties involved. Because of this, domestic relations cases are, as lawyers put it, extremely "fact-bound." Attorneys rarely put much stock in legal precedent. Rather, custody lawyers attempt to paint their clients as stable, loving, and healthy, while trying to establish the opposing parent's less attractive attributes.

Juries are not used in custody cases; judges hear witnesses from both sides and craft solutions designed to create a nurturing environment for the child. No one wins or loses in family court—at least in theory. Judges sometimes complain about having to assume the role of psychologists or social workers, mediating disputes between parents rather than handing down judgments for one side or the other. But this is the way the system is supposed to work.

Eric and Elizabeth, like most parents caught up in custody cases, didn't see things that way. They wanted to win, not to conciliate. They bypassed the lawyers who had advised them on their marriage (Lane Gabeler and George Cronin for Elizabeth, and Hugh Cregger for Eric), and brought in attorneys who had more experience at presenting a case in court.

Eric was represented by John Lenahan, a former Washington prosecutor with a small litigation firm in Fairfax. After serving as a medical consultant in a malpractice case Lenahan was trying, Eric asked Lenahan to represent him in the custody case. Lenahan is more of an all-purpose litigator than a family-law specialist. A lawyer's lawyer, he does his talking in court, not in press conferences. In *Custody,* Elizabeth compared Lenahan's appearance to a shark's, and the analogy is apt. With his fixed, intense stare, clipped questions, and often sarcastic dismissal of witnesses, Lenahan is a formidable cross-examiner.

Elizabeth hired her own trial specialist—Robert Greenberg, a Washington lawyer with a heavy domestic relations practice. Unlike Lenahan (better known as a bulldog litigator than as a conciliator), Greenberg is equally comfortable when settling a case or trying it to the bitter end.

Settlement without trial, however, soon proved elusive in *Morgan* v. *Foretich.* Elizabeth and Eric, each with a personal agenda, each supported wholeheartedly by parents and other family members, were pursuing irreconcilable goals. Elizabeth told Greenberg that she wanted Hilary all to herself. Eric, although he made it clear that he would settle for something short of full custody, told Lenahan that he and his parents were entitled to a major role in the infant's life. In practical terms, that meant the right to overnight visitation.

Elizabeth and Eric both had their arguments. In *Custody* and in court testimony, Elizabeth expounded her "primeval urge to protect and love and fight and die for my child," and her firm belief (an odd sexual stereotype for a pioneering feminist) that men are unfit to perform the "traditional woman's role" of child rearing.

Elizabeth has also explained that she had seen Eric act negligently in caring for Heather (she thought she had seen the two-year-old wander too close to the construction site at Great Falls). Eric, Elizabeth said, was too absent-minded to be entrusted with custody.

Finally, Elizabeth testified that since Hilary was only a baby, she was too psychologically fragile to easily tolerate visitation. "I felt from everything I had been told that the separation anxiety of a little nine-month-old . . . would risk terrible harm to her," Elizabeth said.

Separation anxiety, which can occur when a very young child is taken away from a parent, is real, but not inevitable, permanent, or life-threatening. Many couples who care about the welfare of their children work out arrangements that prevent either parent from becoming a stranger to the child. Instead, Elizabeth seemed overwrought, determined to keep Hilary away from her father rather than to support that relationship.

Eric, angered, began to pursue his own agenda, one that was also not necessarily in Hilary's interest. Beyond his concern about Elizabeth's emotional stability, he worried that Elizabeth and Antonia would raise Hilary in an environment he considered sterile and overly intellectualized. He failed, however, to take into account the fact that Hilary had already bonded with her mother in her first seven months of life. He didn't seem to appreciate the fact that for a tiny infant like Hilary, overnight visitation was bound to be an ordeal, at least at the beginning. (Eric explains that if Elizabeth had permitted reasonable daytime visits, he would not have insisted on overnights. Stung by Elizabeth's obstinacy, he pushed stubbornly forward with his own plans.)

Greenberg and Lenahan scheduled a *pendente lite* hearing on custody and visitation for May 16, 1983. At such a hearing, a judge decides the issues on a temporary basis, pending a full and final resolution of custody and visitation. In a busy urban court, a year or more might pass before the rendering of a final decision, so the result of the *pendente lite* hearing mattered a great deal to both Eric and Elizabeth. Hilary would be nine months old at the May trial; she might be two or even three by the time final custody was determined. During these crucial years, Hilary could easily form ties with one parent at the cost of the other.

Because family situations, and a child's best interests, can change, custody decisions are never considered final until the child reaches adulthood. They can always be altered if one party proves a need. But Eric and Elizabeth both knew that the judge's first decision could set the tone for the entire case.

Eric's concern grew when he heard that Elizabeth was moving into a new home. This would make it even harder for him to see Hilary, he realized. She would no longer be sent to outside day care, where Eric could at least count on seeing her on a reasonably regular basis. Instead, Elizabeth would hire babysitters to take care of Hilary at home. Eric feared that Elizabeth would enlist her employees and her mother in her plans to keep him away from Hilary.

The first nanny Elizabeth hired that spring was nineteen-year-old Sheryl Smith, the daughter of Beverly Smith, Elizabeth's office assistant. She was a former secretary in Eric's dental office, but that didn't seem to matter to Elizabeth, who needed to hire someone quickly. Sheryl, who had been an occasional evening babysitter for Hilary, had asked Elizabeth for the job. Elizabeth, though she knew it would be temporary—Sheryl was taking a break from junior college—was enthusiastic. "She was the answer to my prayers—someone to come to the house, someone whom [Hilary] knew and liked."

In a March 30 letter to Elizabeth, written two days before her move, Eric expressed serious concerns about visitation. "I suppose this means I will have no access to Hilary except through the courts. For Hilary's sake, it is certainly my wish that we could have better communication. My prayers beseech Christ to open our hearts so that compassion and understanding can enter our lives." In response, Elizabeth offered Eric three hours' visitation a week with Hilary, from 11:00 A.M. to 2:00 P.M.—with forty-eight hours' notice.

Elizabeth's new home was on Westover Place, a quiet street in northwest Washington, in a newly developed community of luxury townhouses. Newspaper advertisements pitched Westover to people who sought the feeling of exclusiveness: "When it's important to have the proper address," the ads read.

Elizabeth's home was the largest and the most expensive of Westover Place's five models. There were French doors on the main level and a master bedroom suite two levels up from the street. The model was advertised at $250,000, pricey for a Washington townhouse in 1983, but Elizabeth's surgical practice was doing well. Her gross income, before office expenses, was $127,000; after expenses she was making about $6,000 a month. Elizabeth decided Westover would be a good place to raise a little girl. "I could imagine [Hilary] kicking in the sandbox with friends in the summer," Elizabeth said.

The security of the neighborhood was another advantage, as was its closeness to the Washington National Cathedral. Elizabeth, a practicing Episcopalian like her mother, quickly became active at St. Alban's Church on the cathedral's premises and became friendly with Rector Francis Wade and his assistant minister, Caroline Pyle. She began teaching at the parish Sunday School.

Eric had also moved into a new home that spring: the Georgian mansion was finally ready. Eric was able to enjoy a comfortable but not necessarily lavish lifestyle. He was netting almost $4,000 a month from his oral-surgery practice, but his home was his major asset. Built for about $400,000 in construction and land costs, it would probably sell in the early 1990s for about $1.3 million.

Eric wanted Hilary to think of Great Falls as her home in the same way as Westover Place was. To help him get overnight visitation, he turned to Joel Ganz, a Washington child psychiatrist whose specialty was in evaluating children and their families in custody hearings. Ganz was becoming disillusioned with his career choice. He had seen too many parents put their own needs before their children's—and destroy their children's stability. (He later left psychiatry and became a manager of a fast-food restaurant.)

On May 12, Lenahan asked Ganz for full evaluations of Eric, Elizabeth, and Hilary, and a recommendation to the court. "Dr. Morgan has developed an attitude of dislike and distrust of Dr. Foretich," Lenahan told the psychiatrist. Because of this problem, the lawyer explained, Eric had not seen his daughter in two months, and Elizabeth's latest settlement offer was laughable. Ganz agreed to take the case—and met immediately with Eric and his parents. He also saw Hilary. But Elizabeth refused to see him, except in court.

She had also brought in a specialist. At Greenberg's suggestion, she had asked Lora Daniels, a Washington social worker in private practice, to perform a home study leading to a custody recommendation. Daniels visited the Westover Place home of the Morgans, where William, in another attempt at reconciliation with Antonia, had recently moved in. She played with Hilary and met her mother and grandparents. Lenahan advised Eric not to meet with Daniels, fearing that her mind was irrevocably made up in Elizabeth's favor.

He was partly wrong. Daniels recommended that Eric be granted visitation rights, though she was against overnight visitation because of Hilary's tender age. To allay Elizabeth's anxieties, Daniels proposed that she be allowed to be present at the visits.

Ganz's recommendation was quite different. He agreed that, ideally, a child Hilary's age should not be asked to undergo overnight separation from her primary parent. But Elizabeth, he noted, had handed Hilary over to other caretakers almost from birth. Despite her protestations that only she could raise her child, Elizabeth had not really been doing so, the psychiatrist thought. Eric, Vincent, and Doris seemed to love Hilary. If the judge could foster that relationship, Ganz thought, it would give Hilary a sense of permanence that could not be achieved by Elizabeth's ever-changing array of babysitters. Although Ganz knew that overnight visitation would present problems at the beginning, things would settle down and the Foretiches would bond closely with Hilary.

As the date of the *pendente lite* hearing approached, relations between the Morgans and the Foretiches began to deteriorate seriously. Eric had made an emergency motion in the Superior Court, asking a judge to permit a brief visit before the hearing. Judge Eugene Hamilton had obliged with a temporary restraining order requiring that Elizabeth hand Hilary over to Eric at 9:00 A.M. on Saturday, May 14, for a nine-hour daytime visit that would last until six o'clock that evening. As Saturday night approached at Westover Place, William Morgan grew angrier and angrier. He was fuming when Eric—one minute late—arrived at the door with Hilary. "I'd better straighten this man out," he told Elizabeth. "Let me handle this, honey. I'm a man. You shouldn't have to speak to him."

According to Elizabeth's account in *Custody,* William invited Eric in for a man-to-man chat. Doris and Vincent stayed outside in the car. William commanded Eric to take a seat at the dining-room table while Elizabeth stayed in the room and Antonia whisked Hilary upstairs. "Where did you take her? What did you feed her?" William barked at Eric. "When did you change her diapers? When did you bathe her?" Stung by William's belligerent tone and his questions, Eric refused to answer. "This is beginning to sound like an interrogation. Don't shout at me!" Eric recalls replying.

Vincent remembers that the noise was loud enough for him to hear twenty feet away in the car. Vincent knew something about William's past and had heard that he kept guns in his house. He got out of the car to check on his son's safety. As Vincent approached the townhouse doorway, Eric was retreating in the face of William's verbal barrage. Vincent retreated too, casting a backward glance at the portly psychologist.

"He doesn't know what I'm like when I shout. I wasn't shouting,"

William told his daughter as Eric left. William knew well how furious he was capable of becoming. So did Elizabeth. In *Custody,* she explained that she had never heard her father "shout" at Eric, and in a deposition, she described his tone that evening as "average." She knew what William was like when he really shouted.

It is unclear why William developed his intense aversion for Eric, though it was not the first time he had conceived a violent dislike for one of his daughter's lovers. Apparently he had decided, soon after he met his prospective son-in-law, that Eric was homosexual. William later said that Elizabeth hadn't asked him for permission to marry Eric, but that if she had he would have told her not to marry that "pervert."

"I have no indication that he is a man's man," William said in a 1986 court deposition. "Would I go hunting with this man? The answer is no. Would I go fishing with this man? The answer is no. Would I play poker with this man? The answer is no. . . . Homosexuals tend to be paranoid. Perverts tend to be paranoid and suspicious. They don't talk. They are slow to react. They protect themselves as much as possible." William said he knew this because he had encountered "a lot of deviants" in his decades as a practicing psychologist.

On May 16, the Monday after the confrontation between William and his former son-in-law, Elizabeth and Eric appeared in the D.C. Superior Court to begin the *pendente lite* hearing before Judge Carlisle Pratt. Each was accompanied by a retinue of supporters: Elizabeth had Robert Greenberg, the lawyer; Lora Daniels, the social worker; both her parents; and Dr. Edward Beal, a child psychiatrist who was prepared to testify that overnight visitation would be harmful to Hilary. Eric had John Lenahan, his courtroom advocate; Joel Ganz, the psychiatrist; and his parents. The air in the small Superior Court anteroom was tense with anticipation.

Doris Foretich's recollection is clear. She was sitting two rows behind Eric, Vincent, and the lawyer, and four rows behind her sat Elizabeth and her parents. As she recalls it, William Morgan turned to Elizabeth and said, in a clearly audible stage whisper, "Now, if the old man or the father had hurt her in some way, and we could tell about it, that would keep her from him." Doris wheeled around and stared at William, and Elizabeth also glared at her father and placed her finger on her mouth in a gesture Doris recognized as requesting silence. Later that day, when she got the chance, Doris told Vincent and Eric what had happened.

When the hearing began, John Lenahan made a reasonably strong case, bringing out Eric's interest in being a good father and his determination to be part of his daughter's life. He also mentioned Vincent and Doris's willingness to move up from Newport News to help care for Hilary; Elizabeth's instability (her sudden turn against Eric and her attempt to keep him away from Hilary); and her long work hours. Finally, he pointed out that Hilary had a half sister whom Eric saw on a regular basis. It was important to encourage her relationship with Heather. "To argue that sisters . . . should not be allowed to be together and to know one another at this early stage in their life because of some suspicion on the part of a parent who has never seen them together that the natural father can't care for them is ludicrous," Lenahan declared.

Elizabeth took the stand to explain why overnight visits would be bad for Hilary. "I didn't mind her seeing her father," she wrote in *Custody,* recalling her testimony. "But she was high-strung. She needed stability. If she went away overnight, she'd be terrified. It would be bad for her, very bad. I knew it. I didn't know why I knew. I was her mother. I just knew. I wanted to scream at the judge. Please don't destroy my child, please! . . . I burst into tears. The judge's face froze in anger at my tears. I wasn't supposed to cry."

Robert Greenberg, making Elizabeth's case more calmly, argued against any overnight visits until Hilary turned two. He said that Hilary had bonded emotionally with Elizabeth; that Eric was unstable; and that Hilary's care was more than adequate. Privately, Elizabeth knew that Dr. Ganz had found her weakest point—her decision to put Hilary in day care fifty hours a week from the age of one month. Eric knew his weakness was the simple fact that Hilary had already gotten to know Elizabeth better than she knew him.

Daniels and Ganz had a long talk in the courtroom corridor, away from the principals and the attorneys. They agreed that the courtroom was an inappropriate place to work out the dispute and, as Daniels described the discussion in a letter, they "recommended that [Eric and Elizabeth] sit down together to work this out with help from the mental health professionals they had consulted." However, according to Daniels's account, "Dr. Morgan, upon the strong recommendation of her lawyer, refused to go along with this plan. There seemed to be no way in which good mental health principles were going to be attended to, and I withdrew from the situation."

Daniels says it was Greenberg's intransigence that torpedoed the possible settlement—and forced her out of the case. Greenberg, the lawyer, appears to have rather a different view. Although he declines to be very specific about his representation of Elizabeth, he hints strongly that the intransigence came from his client. "In general, if the client's goals are attainable, I'll do the case," Greenberg says. "What her goals were, and whether they were attainable, I would rather not say." Ganz agrees with Greenberg that it was Elizabeth, not the lawyer, who prevented settlement talks from getting under way.

The *pendente lite* hearing continued on May 26, and this time Judge Pratt handed down his ruling. "I'm the judge here, and I'm the one who's got to make the decision, not the damned psychiatrists," the heavy-set judge declared. As often occurs in family courts, both sides won a little and lost a little. Elizabeth retained custody of Hilary, but Eric was granted overnight visitation. Hilary would visit with her father every other weekend from 4:30 P.M. on Friday until 5:00 P.M. on Sunday, as long as Vincent and Doris were living with him. The first visit would take place on the first weekend in June. In the near future, said the judge, there would be a hearing and a decision on permanent custody and visitation. Dr. Beal, the psychiatrist Elizabeth had picked, had apparently succeeded in convincing the judge that overnight visits would be difficult for Hilary at her age, but not that they would destroy her.

Eric agreed to continue paying Elizabeth $350 a month in child support. Partly at Lenahan's suggestion, Vincent and Doris immediately left their home on the waterfront in Gloucester, Virginia, and moved in with Eric in Great Falls, more than three hours away. Eric was still a busy surgeon with weekend and evening hours, and he needed help in caring for a daughter who was not quite ten months old. Judge Pratt had also thought it might defuse the obvious tension in the case if Hilary were exposed to extended family members in addition to her parents.

By most people's standards, Elizabeth had won the first round. She had gained the right to raise Hilary pretty much as she pleased, and she had 85 percent of Hilary's time. But she recalled in *Custody* that she left the courtroom that day in despair. "It stinks," was all she could say to her lawyer. "It stinks."

As Elizabeth probably saw it, Daniels, the social worker she had hired, had tried to compromise her case, and Greenberg, her own lawyer, had found her goals unrealistic and hadn't even tried to achieve them. Beal, the psychiatrist, had tried to help her but must not have been convincing enough. It was clear that she needed others to take her side.

CHAPTER 4

June 1983 through December 1984

Not long after Judge Pratt's decision, Elizabeth Morgan got a call from Sharon Foretich. Sharon thought she had heard three-year-old Heather say she sometimes bathed with Eric during their visits and that she had "touched his hot dog" in the tub. Sharon had solved the problem, she told Elizabeth. She had warned Eric to stop bathing with Heather, who was too old for it. In any case, Eric had denied ever bathing with his older daughter.

Elizabeth, hanging up the phone, saw no reason to suspect Eric of doing anything inappropriate with either of his daughters. But she took Sharon seriously enough to tell her parents about the call.

Hilary's third overnight visit with the Foretiches fell over the weekend of July 2 and 3. Doris, Eric, and Vincent had taken her to Gloucester to show her off to the relatives, but Hilary had gotten sick on the way home. She had fever and diarrhea and her thighs were reddened. On Sunday evening, Elizabeth noticed the redness while changing Hilary's diaper. She called it to her father's attention. "This child has been molested," he said without hesitation. "Somebody, Eric or Vincent, has put his penis in between her thighs and rubbed it."

This was an extraordinary diagnosis for a grandfather to make on a child who was, after all, less than a year old. Plenty of children that age occasionally have red thighs, for various reasons.

Elizabeth took Hilary to Georgetown University Hospital, where the emergency-room doctors diagnosed the little girl as suffering from diaper rash. They said it could have been aggravated by Hilary's being cooped up in a hot car for hours. (Eric says the air conditioning in his parents' Mercedes was not working that day. Elizabeth told the hospital nurse that Hilary had been in a non-air-conditioned car for five hours.)

William blamed the diagnosis on the absence of semen. "A smart guy like Eric is not going to let the semen remain," he said. By 1983, however, most medical experts were well aware that sexual abuse is not always contingent on the presence of semen; it is, in fact, rather unusual to find semen even in undisputed cases of abuse. And in this case the doctors were actually looking for evidence of abuse; Elizabeth admits to having told them that it was a possibility.

William, not surprisingly, insisted on believing that the Georgetown doctors had misdiagnosed Hilary's problem. "People don't like to fool around with molestations," he said. "They don't like to hear about it."

Elizabeth later testified that she thought sexual abuse was "impossible" at this time. But she, like her father, seems to have had abuse on her mind in 1983. In *Custody,* in her account of the hearing before Judge Pratt, Elizabeth described another case called before the court that same day. In this case, a father was granted unsupervised visitation with his four-year-old twins even after acknowledging that he was a homosexual and an alcoholic who had experienced sexual relationships with his brother and parents. His children, according to Elizabeth's description, had been admitted to the hospital with anal tears, fissures, and genital swelling. "Did he rub the baby's face over his penis?" Elizabeth quotes an attorney as asking the man's ex-wife. In a deposition, William Morgan gave a similarly graphic description of abuse, describing a case in his clinical practice in which a man "carried his stepdaughter around in his arms and would, with his penis, violate her." Like her father, Elizabeth seems to have had abuse on her mind.

Elizabeth has since admitted that the case she described in *Custody* never actually occurred, at least not that day in the D.C. Superior Court. She says it did take place before a Fairfax County judge months before. But in a 1988 *Washington Post* interview, the judge she thought had heard the case, Barnard Jennings, recalled no such hearing. Elizabeth explained in later testimony that even in a non-fiction book like *Custody,* "it's standard to take episodes and telescope them in time, so that the time sequence is not necessarily true." Many non-fiction writers would disagree. (*Custody,* although subtitled *A True Story,* appears to have some incongruities of time and inaccuracies of various sorts. It never mentions Eric and

Elizabeth's brief reconciliation, portrays Eric rather than Elizabeth as having filed first for custody, and places Elizabeth's trip to Haiti for the divorce after the custody filing.)

The Georgetown diagnosis accelerated the bitterness between the Morgans and the Foretiches. A few weeks later, William said that Vincent "took that child, like a bundle," and hurled Hilary a distance of six feet toward Elizabeth when he was bringing the baby back after a visit. If Elizabeth hadn't been there to catch Hilary, William said, the baby would have hit the sidewalk and possibly suffered brain damage. William said he saw the whole thing from the patio.

Eric disputes this account. "Elizabeth was walking down the sidewalk very rapidly, and my father got out of the car with Hilary. They had a collision, and he gave her Hilary. Then she acted like he had tried to push her or bump her. She recoiled because of how fast she had been going. Bill Morgan yelled out, 'Don't you hit my daughter,' or something like that, and my father and Bill exchanged harsh words."

Vincent tells a similar story: "I extended Hilary to Elizabeth, and she yelled at me, 'Don't you hit me with my baby.' But she had walked right into Hilary." Eric points out that the Morgans would inevitably have filed police charges had anyone actually thrown the baby girl. But no charges were ever filed.

During the summer of 1983, the Foretiches hoped that the Morgans would reconcile themselves to the visits as time passed. But as the every-other-weekend visitations continued, the Foretiches were more and more disheartened by what they saw as obstinate and disagreeable behavior by Elizabeth. Frequently, after handing Hilary to Eric, Elizabeth would put a microphone to his lips and follow him to the car. The microphone was attached to a tape recorder, and Eric assumed that Elizabeth was hoping to capture any angry words or curses for the judge. Eric says he never went for the bait. (Elizabeth has acknowledged using the recording device but says she wanted to deter Eric and Vincent from yelling at her in front of Hilary. She also says she wanted to record the special instructions she gave Eric when Hilary was sick.)

As the visits continued, the two families broke into disputes about the way in which Hilary was being transferred from parent to parent. Eric recalled that as the weather turned cooler, Elizabeth would leave Hilary on the top step of her house in a sundress and diaper, without socks or shoes. Doris recalls that later, even when ice covered the steps, Elizabeth left the little girl on the stoop to avoid having to actually hand her to Eric. (Elizabeth agrees that she put Hilary on the steps but says she did it for Hilary's good, to minimize the trauma involved in handing her over. In any case, she says, she always stayed next to her daughter, and never put her out on the ice.)

According to the Foretiches, Elizabeth was always extremely reluctant to allow Hilary to leave her. She clutched the baby tightly to her chest and sometimes refused to hand her over to Doris and Vincent. Only Eric, she said, could legally take the child, so Eric was forced to interrupt his dental appointments and drive over.

Despite these incidents, the eighteen months after the *pendente lite* hearing were a happy time for the Foretich family. Just before Pratt's order in Hilary's case, a Fairfax County judge had given Eric the right to weekend visitations with Heather and had scheduled them for the same weekends as Hilary's. (The other terms of Eric and Sharon's divorce remained unsettled, even after a year of hearings before a "commissioner"—a lawyer appointed by the court to take testimony and make a recommendation to the judge.) The Foretiches hoped that the two little girls, just about two years apart in age, could get to know each other during these weekends and start thinking of each other as sisters.

"These were the best times," Eric recalls. "We had a routine. We'd pick up Hilary first in Washington. Then we'd go pick up Heather, then drive out to the Tysons Corner Hot Shoppe, and all five of us would have dinner. Everybody would laugh. These were the most precious moments I've ever had in my life." Doris took the lead in the day-to-day care of the girls, bathing and dressing them; Eric was often occupied with surgical emergencies and with friends.

During these weekends, the Foretiches noticed that Hilary had trouble sleeping. "She had sleep disturbances," Eric acknowledges. "She would wake up and scream once or twice a night. But they were manageable. Either my mom, my dad, or I would wake up and attend to her."

Three-year-old Heather, the Foretiches say, never had any problem sleeping and never woke up at night. Sheryl Smith, Elizabeth's daytime housekeeper for the first several months of visits, said she didn't notice that Hilary had any sleeping problems. She never had any trouble putting Hilary to sleep for her nap, didn't find her unusually fussy, and never noticed any unusual crying spells.

Elizabeth saw some problems at night but did not view them as serious. On September 8, 1983, in a hand-delivered note entitled

"Instructions for Eric," Elizabeth said that Hilary would occasionally wake up at night crying, apparently afraid of the dark. At that point, she said, Hilary would need a lot of comforting before she fell asleep again. Later in this period, Elizabeth got into the habit of sleeping in the same bed with Hilary, building a wall of pillows between them.

Sleep disturbances are not uncommon in one-year-old children, and the problem could have been the tension surrounding her visits with her father or even just an unfamiliar bed. Normal sleeping difficulties, which often result from separation anxiety, are generally outgrown as the child grows up.

Hilary wasn't the only victim of separation anxiety. For Elizabeth, Hilary's weekends away were a source of constant worry. And her time with Hilary at Westover was marred by her continuing clashes with her father. William insisted that Hilary have a bath every time her diapers were changed. He took her out for hours on outings against Elizabeth's wishes. "[Hilary] has plenty to contend with," Elizabeth told Antonia. "I don't want her confused by what happens at home. . . . Sometimes after Daddy and my ex, I wonder if I'm the problem. Maybe I'm just a bitchy, bossy surgeon—but [Hilary] has to have stability, doesn't she?" Antonia nodded a silent assent.

Elizabeth finally decided that Hilary was being emotionally scarred by her father's mercurial behavior. "I would rather you didn't take [Hilary] out alone," she told him. "I know when I'm not wanted," he replied before returning to the old house on Gallows Road in August 1983. Still, William stayed in Elizabeth's life, continuing his campaign to root out all traces of Eric and his family from the life of his daughter and granddaughter. "I would let Elizabeth know I didn't trust these people," he has said. ". . . I think that a pervert is a pervert is a pervert and I've tested a lot of them."

Hilary's problems soon took what Elizabeth saw as an ominous turn. For a week after her visit with the Foretiches on September 10 and 11, Hilary seemed to wake up in the night more than usual. Then on Saturday evening, September 17, almost a week after she returned from the visit, Hilary, who had been playing happily, suddenly reared up and bumped her head on the floor. When Elizabeth picked her up, her eyes rolled upward and her body stiffened and turned white. She stopped breathing for a brief moment. But before Elizabeth, a trained physician, could start mouth-to-mouth resuscitation, Hilary's breath came back. After two hours, Hilary had returned to normal.

Elizabeth was concerned that Hilary might have had a *grand mal* seizure, the kind typical of epilepsy. (She got more worried after a second episode, lasting five or six seconds, took place a few days later.) Elizabeth called Dr. Voja Russo, the child's pediatrician, who recommended a Washington neurologist named Bennett Lavenstein.

"No one will ever believe me, but she's having seizures because the visitation is frightening her," Elizabeth told Antonia, who agreed and commiserated with her daughter. No one else would take their side—except another mother, she said.

Like many doctors who would examine Hilary, Lavenstein found nothing wrong with her. He performed an electroencephalogram, which came back completely normal, but was unable to repeat the test while the child was asleep: Hilary was too agitated to sleep in the doctor's office. In the absence of any positive findings, Lavenstein decided not to treat Hilary with medication; phenobarbital, the drug of choice then to control seizures, can harm the development of a child's brain. Lavenstein, a specialist in the field, told Elizabeth that Hilary's seizures had nothing to do with the visits to Eric. He said they might be caused by minimal brain damage suffered by Hilary during birth—at the moment when lack of oxygen made her turn blue. Elizabeth, however, said in her book that she "just knew" that the seizures were reactions to the visits. She knew because she was a mother.

Elizabeth admitted in a later deposition that no physician ever believed that the seizures were a reaction to the visits. And even though the weekends in Great Falls continued for another two years, Hilary never had another seizure.

Eric never saw Hilary experience anything like a seizure. He has always maintained that Elizabeth exaggerated what was a normal temper tantrum, either to prove a point or because of a honest mistake. In a phone conversation with Elizabeth the Monday after the seizure, he asked her whether she might not be blowing the event out of proportion. Elizabeth, who thought Eric wasn't taking the problem seriously enough, fired off a letter to him that evening. Recalling her medical background, she told him she viewed it as a potentially life-threatening episode of *grand mal* epilepsy. If Hilary had been left by herself briefly in a bathtub, she might have drowned, Elizabeth admonished Eric. "I am sure that you, as a concerned father, will not take this lightly," Elizabeth ended the letter.

In a letter the next day, Eric replied that he did not mean "to be accusatory or to question what you had done." He pledged to cooperate with Elizabeth to find out what was wrong with Hilary, but he couldn't resist some sarcasm: "I have certainly no reason to doubt your ability to differentiate seizure disorders, based upon empirical observation, when one considers your medical training."

Elizabeth said that it often took Hilary seven to ten days to "recover" from a visit with Eric. At this point it would be time for another of the weekend visits that she considered the source of all Hilary's difficulties. Elizabeth seems not to have considered the possibility that something in her household or her relationship with Hilary could have been the problem. After all, Hilary's "upsets" seemed to occur when she was with Elizabeth. Doris Foretich, Hilary's primary hands-on caretaker during her visits to Eric, says that the very thought of going home to Elizabeth could disturb Hilary. By the time Hilary was eighteen months old, she began to recognize the route the Foretiches used in driving her back to Westover Place, and she would cry on the way back. "If she cried when she went home, it was because she wanted to be there with us," Doris has testified.

At this stage, Eric and Elizabeth maintained a semblance of cooperation in dealing with Hilary's problems. But just a month after the seizures, Elizabeth received an extraordinary letter from her father, urging resistance rather than accord. In a deposition three years later, William read his entire letter of October 15, 1983, into the public record. In it, he first describes the "emotional deterioration" he noticed in Hilary following her visits with Eric. William then provides an incorrect summary of the Foretich family history, saying that Eric was under psychiatric care during his marriage to Sharon and that Craig Foretich committed suicide. Then William continues to build his case against Eric:

> . . . As a psychologist, I believe that the courts must be damned when the courts neglect a child's proper development. If I were her mother, if I were you, I would no longer permit Hilary to be taken away for so-called visitation rights. At the most, I would insist that Eric and Eric alone visit and play with Hilary under supervision in your home or in a mutually acceptable place where Hilary could be watched and be protected from yelling and screaming and violent behavior to which the Foretiches are prone. Supervision would be provided by you or mother or by me or by Jim or by Rob. If the court would not agree to such a relationship, then I would refuse to let Eric see or be with Hilary. I would rather serve time in jail for contempt of court, rather than to further permit the atrocious deterioration of a child who had so much promise.

There was no mention of sexual abuse, but the letter introduced a scenario that Elizabeth would later play out very effectively. William's "instructions"—to keep Hilary from the Foretiches even at the risk of contempt of court—couldn't have been much clearer.

Elizabeth was already aware of the danger of a contempt citation. Moreover, the thought of someday hiding Hilary away from Eric had almost certainly crossed her mind, although she was not yet emotionally ready to do so. Discussing the events of 1983 in *Custody,* which sets forth her thoughts at the time of the events described, Elizabeth said, "I couldn't steal away in the night with [Hilary] and disappear. I felt sorry for the mothers who felt they had to, in order to protect a child." At another point in *Custody,* Elizabeth says a lawyer advises, "You can take her away to England. You would have to plan on not ever coming back. And don't tell your ex. He can stop you at the borders." Again, Elizabeth rejected this course of action.

In his October 15 letter, William made it clear to his daughter that she should get rid of her lawyer, who he said was not working in her best interests. By the end of the summer, Elizabeth had parted company with Robert Greenberg, her lawyer in the May *pendente lite* hearing. In a 1989 interview, Greenberg made it clear that he withdrew because he thought Elizabeth's goal of eliminating Eric from Hilary's life unattainable. "She was a bright, engaging person, but we had a disagreement over strategy," Greenberg says.

In September 1983, Greenberg referred Elizabeth to Marna Tucker, one of Washington's best-known divorce lawyers. Tucker, who had just been elected the first woman president of the D.C. Bar, is a strong supporter of feminist causes: in 1990, she received the National Women's Law Center's annual award for leadership on behalf of women. She has a very solid reputation as a conciliator, a lawyer who gets things done at the settlement table, not in court.

The Morgans apparently took an almost immediate dislike to Tucker. According to Elizabeth's account in *Custody,* Jim Morgan told his sister that "Mrs. Jones" (a composite character in the book who has many of Tucker's traits) was too conciliatory and ladylike. "That lawyer of yours. She's got to go," her brother told her. "You don't have a warm, sympathetic negotiation on your hands. They're saying you're an unfit mother. . . . Change lawyers, Elizabeth." Elizabeth was soon to follow that advice.

Not long after William's letter to Elizabeth, Eric got a chilling premonition of what he could expect from his ex-wife. That October, at a meeting of the northern Virginia chapter of the William and

Mary Alumni Association, Eric ran into an old friend, Robert Machen, president of the alumni group that year. Machen, a domestic relations lawyer, spent years as an Army psychologist and went to law school late in life. Eric had known him from his own years as a board member of the chapter. Eric confided to Machen that he was having problems with his ex-wife over visitation.

Machen, who had never met Elizabeth, didn't hesitate with his reply. "Be careful," he told Eric. "Before this is over, you'll be accused of abusing your child. My advice to you is never be alone with your child. Always have someone in the room with you. Don't bathe the child, wipe the child, or change her clothes. The way it sounds to me, your ex-wife will be vindictive." Machen knew from his law practice that abuse allegations in custody cases were increasing, but Eric didn't believe it could happen to him. "That's so extreme," he replied. "Elizabeth would never do anything like that."

Eric, however, took Machen's advice. From then on, he says, he never spent a minute alone with Hilary (except on a couple of occasions when he drove her back to Westover Place alone because his parents were tired).

On his own, Machen tried to make sure Eric was following his advice. The lawyer, who soon took on Eric's representation in his property settlement with Sharon, began to drop by the Great Falls home unannounced to make sure that Hilary was properly chaperoned. Eventually, Machen's records reflected that he visited his client and friend during thirty-two of the next thirty-four visits. "I found that his parents were there all the time," Machen recalls. "I never had any basis whatever to conclude that Eric had done any of the things he was later accused of doing, and I learned a lot that convinces me he didn't do them." Doris Foretich confirms Machen's account: She says that during the visits, she would "watch over the children, like a watchdog, a friendly watchdog," to make sure no one had a pretext to charge that anything improper had occurred.

Back at Westover Place, there were more changes for Hilary. In September, Sheryl Smith left her job as Hilary's babysitter to go back to school. Her replacement was Leora Graham, a thirty-two-year-old black woman who had already raised a twelve-year-old son of her own. Elizabeth was elated, as she often was when she first found a new lawyer, a new doctor, or a new housekeeper. "Like Mary Poppins, she had come into our life, an answer to my prayers," Elizabeth wrote, with her usual exaggerated theatrics.

Leora Graham remembers a rather troubled child. "She did a lot of crying for a child. She'd have a nightmare. She'd wake up from her nap and she would cry a lot. Giving her a bath was very difficult for me, very hard," Graham said in a deposition. Often, she said, Hilary's crying fits came after visits with the Foretiches, when the child seemed to need extra reassurance. Graham, however, never saw any unusual diaper rash or any physical illness in the time (nearly a year) that she spent with Hilary. Graham, who was with the child almost full time, says Hilary was no sicker than the average child.

Elizabeth, however, remained perplexed about Hilary's crying. Once, Hilary started screaming when she woke up in the middle of the night and did not stop until ten in the morning. Elizabeth took her to Dr. Russo, who prescribed Benadryl, a sedative. "It's all you can do," Russo said; she agreed that the stress of visitation might be causing Hilary's problems.

Elizabeth asked her lawyer, Marna Tucker, what she could do to help Hilary. In early November, Tucker's partner Rita Bank and Eric's lawyer, John Lenahan, sat down with Dr. Edwin Kessler, a distinguished Washington child psychiatrist who had directed the division of child and adolescent psychiatry at Georgetown Hospital for twenty-seven years. Kessler has treated and evaluated thousands of troubled kids, but he still recalls the meeting with Bank and Lenahan as extraordinary. Usually, before getting involved in a custody battle, he held introductory meetings with the spouses and children. In this case, however, before Kessler met Eric, Elizabeth, or Hilary, he agreed to talk to the lawyers for both sides. They had cast themselves in the role of mediators in an attempt to control their clients' anger and reach an accommodation. With the consent of Eric and Elizabeth, Lenahan and Bank had picked Kessler to evaluate the whole situation and to make a recommendation to the Superior Court about custody and visitation. (The court case was continuing on the back burner. The parties were expecting a hearing on permanent arrangements for Hilary to begin sometime in January or February, 1984.)

Kessler met first with Lenahan alone. "We want to avoid the adversarial role of the court," the lawyer told the psychiatrist. "Eric is not seeking custody. What we want is reasonable visiting privileges." When Bank joined the meeting a few minutes later, Lenahan spoke a bit critically of his client, and of Elizabeth. "Both parties need a strong hand," Lenahan said. Bank, true to her conciliatory reputation, nodded in agreement. Kessler suggested that "both sides need to be educated" to act in Hilary's interest. He said there was probably no quick short-term solution and added that he hoped to come up with some sort of compromise.

In December, Kessler met separately with Elizabeth, Eric, and

Hilary. Eric told Kessler that he wanted a "fair and reasonable" solution. "I don't want to be just a man who puts out money and has no role in my daughter's life," he pleaded. "I want to make some contribution to her educational process. I want to enrich her life." During her interview, Elizabeth expressed her concerns about Hilary's well-being. "She's having a terrible experience with visits. She used to be a happy baby."

Kessler reserved judgment until he met Hilary, who at sixteen months was just beginning to speak. "Hilary was a very bright, lively, imaginative, engaging child, with a very strong basic personality structure," Kessler now recalls. "I deliberately saw Hilary twice, after she was brought by each of her parents, to observe how she did with each of them, and I concluded she was comfortable with both." Hilary played with a girl doll, then saw a soldier doll and said, "Daddy," and showed interest in the male as well as the female dolls. She playfully took a purse away from a grandmother doll. Kessler got a better impression of Hilary than he did of either parent. "I really didn't like either of them very much," he recalls, "but I do feel a lot of compassion for Dr. Foretich. My impression is that he would not abuse a child. I think he did care for Hilary, and for Heather too."

Kessler's negative feelings about Elizabeth—he found her manipulative—were apparently reciprocated. In *Custody,* Elizabeth describes Hilary's doll play in Kessler's office in a way that makes Kessler seem foolish. When Kessler remarked that Hilary was playing with the daddy doll, Elizabeth retorted: "This is a baby. Remember how old she is! She does not know a Daddy doll. She does not know a Mommy doll. She said 'Dada' to a giraffe on television last night. And a koala bear."

Elizabeth told Kessler that Hilary was still being harmed by the visits. Although there had been no more seizures, Hilary was, in her experience, an unhappy child given to fits of inconsolable crying.

Kessler decided that Hilary didn't have enough continuity in her relationships with either of her parents. A little child's memory is very short, and each time Hilary had a weekend visit she had to readjust to Eric's home and family, then adjust back to Elizabeth's. Kessler wondered if it might help to add some brief visits during the week to make Hilary more comfortable with the Foretiches. Kessler recommended overnight visits with Eric every other Wednesday. Bank wrote up a court order, and Superior Court Judge Eugene Hamilton signed it. In exchange, Eric agreed to shorten the extended Christmas vacation he was planning for Hilary.

The first Wednesday overnight was December 14. At four-thirty Friday morning, Kessler was awakened by the ring of the telephone. It was Elizabeth, and Hilary was screaming in the background. "You tell me. What am I supposed to do? You're her psychiatrist. You wanted me to follow your advice and keep doing this," came the desperate, beseeching voice. Although he tried to maintain his professional composure, Kessler was angry. He felt that his judgment was being attacked, and he also thought Elizabeth was using a moment of crisis to force his hand on his long-term recommendations for Hilary.

"We'll talk about the future another time," Kessler said. He suggested that Elizabeth deal with the immediate problem by giving Hilary a warm bath or rocking her. "I'm not her psychiatrist," he also blurted out, meaning that he had merely agreed to evaluate the parties, not provide therapy. He had only met Hilary once, and although he was genuinely concerned about her, he hardly knew her. At seven-thirty that morning, Kessler called Elizabeth back. Hilary was finally sound asleep, Elizabeth said. In *Custody,* Elizabeth blurred the details of Kessler's role. The statement, "I'm not her psychiatrist," coming from someone the reader is led by the narrative to believe *was* Hilary's psychiatrist, seems unfeeling.

Five days later, Elizabeth contacted Kessler again. "I should let you know that I decline to get involved with Hilary's visitation any further, and you'll have to work something else out with [Eric] for this coming Friday, that is the last day of December, and also for Wednesdays," she told him on December 20. She refused to permit any of the visits Kessler had scheduled. Eric had to go to Superior Court Judge George Revercomb on January 11 for a restraining order to compel Elizabeth to hand over Hilary at 9:15 A.M. on January 18, the following Wednesday. Elizabeth testified that Hilary had behaved "as if possessed by a demon" after the first Wednesday visit. Judge Revercomb nevertheless granted the order.

The designated day came, and Elizabeth still would not let Hilary go. On February 1, another Superior Court judge, Shellie Bowers, held her in contempt of court and ordered her to pay $175 in attorneys' fees. Elizabeth freely admitted that she had disobeyed the court order. This was the first time, but it would not be the last.

From Elizabeth's point of view, Kessler had failed to keep Hilary from the Foretiches, just as Daniels and Beal had failed before him. And Bank and Tucker, the highly recommended specialists, had failed too, just like Greenberg. It was time to find yet another lawyer.

Elizabeth finally decided that her brother Jim was right. As she explained in *Custody,* she had grown tired of dealing with an attorney who was a "make-you-feel-good artist" who would "give away" Hilary to Eric. To this day, Marna Tucker declines to discuss the Morgan case in any detail. But it was clearly a painful experience for her. She makes it clear that like Greenberg before her, she came to believe that Elizabeth's goal of shutting Eric out of Hilary's life was impossible and not in Hilary's interests. "I have very strong feelings about her," Tucker says now about Elizabeth. After five turbulent months, Tucker left the case. On February 7, 1984, a Superior Court judge granted her firm's motion to withdraw.

As 1984 began, Eric noticed that Elizabeth was becoming more dismissive and condescending to him. "As a result of yesterday's conversation (interrogation) during which you not only talked down to me but also spoke as if I were an irresponsible and feeble-minded child, the following statement is made," he wrote her, adopting the formal, stilted tone he often used with his ex-wife. "If during the course of any future conversation you assume a demeaning or otherwise belittling attitude toward me, said conversation will be abruptly terminated." Eric signed the letter "Hilary Foretich's father." Just a year before, his closing words to his ex-wife had been "Warm personal regards, Eric."

Elizabeth was in no mood for warmth. She felt she needed a real battler to champion her cause. Soon she had found someone whose credentials as a legal infighter were unquestioned: Hal Witt, a well-known Washington lawyer who, like Tucker, handles divorces of the rich and famous. Witt has a reputation for being more hard-nosed than Tucker. At the same time he was representing Elizabeth, for example, he was also representing John Fedders, the powerful head of the SEC's enforcement division, Washington's most notorious wife-beater of the year.

Witt, a major character in *Custody,* makes his appearance in a rather unusual manner. In the book, Elizabeth uses fictitious names for everyone except her parents, her brothers, and her secretaries. None of the false names she picked seems to have any particular meaning—except for "William Blackstone," the name she chose for Witt. The real Sir William Blackstone was, of course, an eminent eighteenth-century Englishman who was a judge, a member of Parliament, and a major codifier of the British common law. Elizabeth put Witt on a similar pedestal. "You are probably the only man in Washington who can save my daughter," Elizabeth told Witt. He was her new knight in shining armor.

Elizabeth's initial conversations with Witt made it clear that she had not changed her ultimate goal. "Ideally, I would want no regular overnight visitation until she is five," she told him. Witt presumably had heard from Tucker just how determined this new client could be and was prepared. He interrupted Elizabeth immediately. "If that is what you expect, I would prefer not to represent you. It is unrealistic and you will not get it."

Finally, Witt convinced Elizabeth that she had to limit her objectives, and she eventually agreed that Hilary should continue to maintain contact with Eric. She modified her goals slightly, deciding that she was willing to permit Eric one eight-hour daytime visit outside her home, every other weekend. No overnights, no weekends, no holidays.

There was still no final ruling in the custody case, and no one had any idea when one would come. Just before Witt entered the case, Elizabeth had shown up in court as her own lawyer and had convinced a judge to postpone the trial date from February 22 to May 2, 1984. At least four times after that, all the parties and their lawyers arrived ready for trial, waiting for a free judge and courtroom. But nothing ever opened up. Judge Pratt's temporary ruling of the year before continued to hold sway.

As the judicial process ground on, Hilary was growing into the toddler stage; her first word was "cook" for "cookie." Theodora Franke, Eric's office manager at the time, got to know Hilary because Doris and Vincent would often bring her to Eric's dental office on Fridays. "I kind of looked forward to the Fridays, because Hilary always was happy to come," Franke has testified. "She was a bundle of joy." Franke added that Doris would never directly say it was time to take Hilary home to Elizabeth. That always upset the child. Instead, Doris would spell out the word "H-O-M-E" so the little girl would not understand.

The uneasy truce between Elizabeth and Eric continued through the spring and summer of 1984—a year that, as measured by the volume of court filings, was by far the quietest in the convoluted history of the case. Eric and Sharon's divorce case, however, finally seemed to be reaching a conclusion. The court-appointed commissioner in Fairfax County had rejected Sharon's attempt to prove that Eric had committed "constructive desertion," wherein a spouse abuser is considered to have deserted his partner and to be at fault in the divorce (even though the abused spouse is the one who actually walked out). The commissioner had found no corroboration of Sharon's charges that Eric was physically abusive to her during their marriage. He found nothing to support the notorious allegation that he tried to pull out her IV tube. Under Virginia law, that meant Sharon had no legal claim to alimony from Eric. Sharon, still represented by Mark Sandground, appealed to Judge Lewis Griffith of the Fairfax County Circuit Court; but on April 9, 1984, Griffith rejected her arguments. The judge agreed that it was Sharon who had wrongfully deserted Eric, "contrary to the wishes of the husband and without provocation." Two and a half years after Sharon had left Eric, Griffith finally granted the divorce.

Under Judge Griffith's order, Sharon retained custody of Heather, which Eric had not contested. (Someone with an interest in sexually abusing children might have been expected to fight harder for custody.) Eric was ordered to pay $550 per month in child support and instructed to pay for Heather's reasonable medical and dental expenses and her tuition and books at preschool. He also had to pay $2,500 of Sharon's attorney's fee. In return, Eric got permanent visitation privileges: every other weekend, one Wednesday overnight a month, a two-week summer vacation, alternate Thanksgivings, and four days at Christmastime.

Eric also got the right to be consulted regarding the education of Heather, who was not quite four years old.

Sexual abuse was not mentioned in Griffith's opinion; it never came up in the case (apart from Sharon's passing thoughts about Eric bathing with Heather, thoughts that Eric denied and Sharon discounted). The divorce had been messy, however, replete with allegations of physical and mental cruelty. Had Heather given her mother the slightest basis to make an abuse charge, Sandground would almost certainly have made the explosive accusation.

That spring, Elizabeth briefly added a new accusation to her array of condemnations of Eric. At one point during a deposition, Elizabeth said she thought Eric might be dealing in illegal drugs and that she could provide a list of people with whom he dealt. She had gone so far as to report Eric to the FBI in 1983, she said, but the Bureau did not pursue the matter. Lenahan pressed her for the list, but she never provided it. Two years later, in another deposition, Elizabeth said she simply suspected drug dealing from Eric's behavior and income but that she never had any evidence against him.

To try to deal with her daughter's continuing emotional problems, Elizabeth started taking Hilary to a psychiatrist, Dr. Edward Beal. Beal, who trained at the Menninger Clinic in Topeka, Kansas, had testified unsuccessfully for Elizabeth at the *pendente lite* hearing, and Hilary saw him about a dozen times in the first half of 1984.

Elizabeth told Beal that sexual abuse was a possibility, at least in her mind, and he carefully observed Hilary at play to see whether she showed any of the symptoms.

Most child psychiatrists consider a child's free, unstructured play to be the best window into the child's psyche, and their offices reflect this. Normally, a portion of the doctor's office is partitioned into a playroom full of toys and games appropriate to children from the toddler stage through adolescence. Using these traditional play-therapy techniques, Beal concluded that Hilary was suffering from the typical conflicts attendant to divorce. He noted that Hilary expressed an unusual interest in undressing a male doll to see what was under the doll's pants. Elizabeth later made much of this as somehow indicating that Hilary had been abused; but the fact remains that Beal found nothing that he viewed as suggestive of sexual abuse.

Elizabeth thought Beal was helping Hilary. "The visits with the psychiatrist had increased her confidence," she wrote. "Her screaming fits had lessened." Hilary was still afraid of the dark, of thunderstorms, of running water, and of being by herself—she couldn't sleep alone and would crawl into Elizabeth's bed in the middle of the night. But Elizabeth was reassured that her daughter was now able to verbalize her fears. "I scared. Don't like it," Hilary would say.

Hilary seemed to be coming out of her shell. In the summer of 1984, when she was about to turn two years old, she was able to begin nursery school at the Metropolitan Methodist School across the street from Westover. Leora Graham would walk her there. Hilary started in the "Sandbox," a summer program at Metropolitan, and stayed at the school through three nursery years. Not all two-year-olds are emotionally ready for school, even for the few hours a week that they attend, but Hilary had no difficulties. Her teacher, Donna McClure, found her to be "a very loving child, very well adjusted, caring." At school, Hilary was never fearful or depressed. Apparently, she could put whatever was troubling her at home behind her and lose herself in play.

Tracy Gray, a woman whose daughter was Hilary's classmate and close friend, says Hilary was "a very sweet little girl" who was a delightful playmate. Gray, a licensed psychologist who works frequently with children, says she saw nothing about Hilary that "raised any red flags." But she did find Elizabeth "a little agitated." Another neighbor received the same impressions. "Hilary was a very normal, happy child," recalls Susan Bacon, whose son played and went to school with Hilary. Bacon says Elizabeth was "very attentive" to

Hilary. Once, she remembers, Hilary wanted something from a kitchen cabinet and Elizabeth went through every single cabinet to find it. Most mothers wouldn't have made the effort, Bacon said.

Despite the signs of progress, Elizabeth soon tired of Beal, deciding that he "had been nice but had little to offer." She broke off the relationship abruptly in June. Elizabeth later discounted what Beal had been able to do for Hilary, at least in part because he had not diagnosed her as a victim of sexual abuse. She blamed the failure of diagnosis on the fact that Hilary was not yet fully verbal.

Eric also took Hilary to a psychiatrist that same spring. He chose Joel Ganz, the doctor who had testified on his behalf at the *pendente lite* hearing. Eric was concerned that Elizabeth's overly possessive attitude toward Hilary might be preventing the child from developing properly. He also wanted to develop testimony that would help his cause at the final custody hearing. So, not yet two years old, Hilary was already seeing not one but two psychiatrists. Both agreed that her problems did not stem from sexual abuse.

Eric's behavior in connection with the psychiatrist is difficult to reconcile with the notion that he was sexually abusing his daughters. Eric *voluntarily* placed Hilary in a therapeutic setting where he intrinsically had no control. Physicians are required by law to report suspicions of child abuse to state police and social service departments. Moreover, Hilary was becoming more and more verbal; she could easily have blurted out details of abuse if it had been occurring.

That September, a Superior Court judge was finally ready to hear *Morgan* v. *Foretich*. At the start of the trial, John Lenahan asked Judge Bruce Mencher to order the courtroom closed to protect Hilary's privacy (if either party asks for the closing, the law requires it). This was the first of several court orders that kept information about the case from the public. (Contrary to later suppositions, the closing was not requested to conceal evidence of sexual abuse. No such evidence was produced at the custody hearing, and Mencher's ruling makes no reference to abuse.)

Elizabeth was utterly terrified that she would lose custody. "Could I accept a society that wrested a baby from its loving mother?" she asked. No matter how much Hal Witt tried to keep his client calm, she cracked under the pressures of the five-day trial. According to her account in *Custody*, she screamed out while trying to answer a question from her own lawyer, buried her face in her hands, and made an incoherent reply. She thought she had lost custody then and there. "To this day, only those who were present know what it was like. For two weeks, in that dark, sealed courtroom, I was forced to submit to psychological torture," Elizabeth wrote.

At that trial, Eric noticed Elizabeth frequently staring into space, rigid with anger and fear. On September 20, Judge Mencher announced that he had a ruling and would state it after a brief time away from the bench. The judge went to his chambers. Eric says Elizabeth got up and stood against the courtroom wall, seemingly paralyzed and mumbling to herself, for about forty-five minutes until Mencher returned.

Elizabeth was relieved by his ruling. "In a daze I heard him award me custody of [Hilary]," she recalled. Mencher explained his decision in Elizabeth's favor in a written opinion dated November 8, 1984. Hilary's best interests, he said, would be served by giving custody to Elizabeth and "substantial and liberal visitation" to Eric. Eric would have Hilary alternate weekends, from 10:00 A.M. on Friday until 4:00 P.M. on Monday, and six weeks every summer; he and Elizabeth would take turns being with their daughter on Thanksgiving, Christmas, and New Year's Day in alternate years. The judge calculated that Eric would have a total of 112 days with Hilary each year, slightly less than one third of the year. The decision also stipulated that Eric was to pay $450 a month in child support.

Mencher explained that Elizabeth had "a truly deep and abiding attachment" to Hilary. In her favor, he counted her move to Westover Place (near a preschool and plenty of friends for Hilary); the "stable and nurturing" environment Elizabeth provided at home, including Antonia's presence; and Elizabeth's employment of a full-time housekeeper. William Morgan was not mentioned.

On the other hand, Mencher noted that Eric, despite his excellent academic background and his professional accomplishments, had "a tenor of instability" in his life. The judge recited the litany of Eric's failed marriages and his ill-fated plan to divorce Sharon in Haiti. Eric had yelled at Sharon at his office in front of Heather. He had let his messy divorce with Sharon spill over into his professional life, and he "had revealed a disturbing tendency to blame his problems on others rather than confront them himself."

The decision, however, was by no means one-sidedly in Elizabeth's favor. Mencher explained that there were many positive aspects in Eric's life. "As with the mother, the Court was impressed with [Eric's] love and concern for his child. His parents have moved in with him. The grandparents greatly impressed the Court and should have the opportunity to build a substantial relationship with Hilary. Moreover, Hilary has developed a meaningful sibling bond with her stepsister, which should be fostered and encouraged."

Mencher contrasted Elizabeth's family, who he said appeared to be "more restrained and emotionally sedate," with Eric's parents, who were "more warm, outgoing and openly emotional." (This is a fair contrast between Antonia Morgan and Doris Foretich. Vincent Foretich, however, leans almost as much toward emotional restraint as Doris does toward effusiveness.) Mencher, in any case, said Hilary should have the opportunity to "experience this interesting and beneficial contrast of personalities."

Mencher also noted Elizabeth's "consistent and unjustifiable intransigence" regarding visitation and her "unwillingness to allow the father any significant role in bringing up this child." This, he said, represented a failure by Elizabeth to act in Hilary's best interests. The only substantial visitations Eric ever received, Mencher pointed out, were by court order. The Morgans made the visits into "rude ordeals" by placing Hilary on the steps and by following Eric around with a tape recorder held close to his face. Mencher, however, continued to hold out hope for a peaceful solution. He said that Elizabeth had tried to encourage Hilary to love her father and that Hilary's "positive reactions towards her father . . . indicate that Hilary has developed, under the care of her mother, a healthy affection for [Eric]. . . . The difficulties during the visitation exchanges have begun to dissipate."

Elizabeth had won before Mencher, just as she had won the previous year before Pratt. But the decision, like all decisions in family court, was neither absolute nor final. Elizabeth had custody of Hilary—but Mencher said that custody was granted on the basis of some key assumptions. He assumed that Elizabeth would not stand in the way of Eric's visitation, that she would consult with Eric regarding important decisions in Hilary's life, and that there would be a "free and full flow of information" between the ex-spouses concerning Hilary. Sounding an unmistakable warning note to Elizabeth, Mencher referred to a legal precedent that permits a court to change custody if one parent is found to be denying "full and fair visitation" to the other.

Eric and his parents were relatively pleased with Judge Mencher's order. Although Elizabeth still had custody of Hilary, their message had gotten through; the judge had spoken to the issue of Elizabeth's improper interference with Eric's visits. Perhaps the "rude ordeals" would finally give way to civility and order, Doris thought. And 31 percent of Hilary's time would give them the opportunity to enjoy the little girl and to help her grow up.

Elizabeth's feelings were much more complicated—"grateful and bitter," she wrote. Although she was relieved to retain custody of her daughter, Elizabeth was torn apart by the experience of testifying in court. Why, she asked, did she have to fight at all to keep "what was rightfully hers—her child?" After Mencher's verdict, Elizabeth cried for two hours. It was days before she could sleep.

Elizabeth's emotional collapse may explain Hilary's anxiety, which continued. She was still throwing crying fits that Elizabeth couldn't stop. Beal had failed, Elizabeth thought, so she looked for another psychiatrist for her two-year-old. "She and I needed help together," Elizabeth said in *Custody:* Hilary needed help to allay her fears, and Elizabeth needed to heal the damage that the legal system had done to her. "I had been the victim of a brutal psychological assault," Elizabeth wrote. "I was afraid I had been destroyed, afraid that the system had given her to me after letting me be scarred, battered, broken, and rendered unfit to be a mother."

Elizabeth started doctor-shopping. She rejected four therapists, one on the grounds that he "was condescending and didn't believe what I told him."

Eric objected to one of them, Dr. Joseph Novello, because he had earlier testified in favor of reducing Eric's visitation with Heather. As a favor to Eric, Elizabeth agreed not to use Dr. Novello.

Eric was perplexed about why Elizabeth was making such a to-do about therapists. In a letter he wrote her on December 1, 1984, he noted that Elizabeth was concerned that Hilary was afraid of strangers, the dark, taking a bath, and having her hair washed. None of these are unusual fears for two-year-olds.

"Admittedly, Hilary sometimes, but not always, dislikes the thought of a bath," Eric wrote. "However, other parents have told me that their children had a similar fear for several years. As to darkness, I have never known a child who liked being in the dark. We usually keep a low-wattage night light in her room. As to strangers, I have noticed no particular problem here. Frankly I do not share your belief that a psychiatrist is required or even desired." This sounds like common sense.

Elizabeth also decided it was time to change housekeepers again. She came to believe that Graham, whom she had viewed as "Mary Poppins" a year before, was better with a baby than with a bright, verbal two-year-old. (Actually, Graham's background was not so limited. She had worked with children up to about the second grade and had also been a nursing aide for the elderly.) Searching for a replacement, Elizabeth heard from Janice Urich, the wife of her brother Rob, about Fran Walton, a middle-aged Washington woman who had worked as a child-care provider for more than twenty years. Walton is a bright, vivacious black woman in her early sixties. She comes across as a person who takes herself seriously but maintains a lively sense of humor. She impressed Elizabeth, and in December 1984, Elizabeth hired Walton as her new housekeeper. Her hours were weekdays from 8:00 A.M. until 5:00 P.M. Elizabeth had cut back her medical practice somewhat, but it was still Antonia who relieved the housekeeper at the end of the day. Like Graham before her, Walton was Hilary's main caretaker. She bathed and diapered Hilary and walked her across the street to nursery school.

What Elizabeth did not know—not that there is any reason it should have affected her decision to hire Walton—was that more than fifty years before, as a three-year-old, Walton had been sexually abused. Like many victims of abuse, Walton had almost completely suppressed the memory. But it lingered somewhere in her subconscious mind. That long-ago event would soon have its effect on *Morgan* v. *Foretich*.

CHAPTER 5

January 1985 through May 1985

One morning in early January 1985, just after she started working for Elizabeth, Fran Walton was bathing little Hilary, following her daily routine. As usual, Hilary was squirming in the bathtub, a habit that Walton found exasperating. When she reached down to clean the little girl's vagina, Hilary burst into a crying fit. For reasons Walton still can't fully explain, she asked Hilary if anyone had been touching her there. Walton says Hilary nodded yes. "Who did it?" she went on. "Papa. Papa was taking sand out of my vagina," Hilary replied.

That evening, Walton told Elizabeth what had happened. (Antonia was out of the country on an extended vacation.) "Oh, my God," Elizabeth responded. Walton got the impression that this was the first time Elizabeth had thought of Hilary being abused. "I was the one who opened up the can of worms," Walton said in a deposition. The idea, though, was not as new to Elizabeth as Walton suspected. In the back of her mind were Sharon's suspicions from 1983 about Eric bathing with Heather.

According to Elizabeth's consistent retellings of the story, Hilary identified the person who had touched her as "Papa," and Walton emphatically agrees. Eric, Vincent, and Doris assert, and neutral sources confirm, that "Papa" was not the name Hilary used for Eric (whom she called Daddy), or Vincent (whom she called Gramps). Elizabeth says Hilary called Vincent, but not Eric, by the name "Papa." But in recent interviews, Walton says that "Papa" was a name Hilary had occasionally used to refer to William Morgan.

This does not necessarily imply that Hilary was identifying William as a sexual abuser. He had not lived at Westover Place for more than a year and had spent relatively little time with Hilary. But Hilary's use of "Papa" adds uncertainty about whom exactly she was identifying, an uncertainty magnified by the fact that the little girl was not yet two and a half years old. Further uncertainty is provided by the reference to "taking sand out," which may point to a normal, non-abusive act of child care.

Elizabeth recalls that Hilary was doing and saying other things that suggested sexual abuse. On the morning of January 15, 1985— Elizabeth is not clear about whether she was diapering Hilary or putting on her snow boots at the time—Hilary told her mother she had "seen her daddy's heinie" ("heinie" was the Foretich family word for the genitals). "Does he have his clothes on?" asked Elizabeth. Hilary said he did not, and then, according to Elizabeth, the little girl made licking noises with her tongue and mouth. Although Hilary did not spell out the connection between the licking noises and the "heinie," Elizabeth decided that Hilary was describing oral sex with her father. Suddenly, it all came together. She had always believed something was terribly wrong with Hilary; but her suspicions, which no doctor had been able to confirm, were finally substantiated, at least for her. She thought she knew why Hilary had been such a difficult child.

Elizabeth had just found a new psychiatrist for Hilary. She had been referred to Dr. Joseph Noshpitz, then a senior attending staff psychiatrist at Washington's Children's Hospital. Noshpitz is revered as the grand old man of Washington child psychiatry. Elizabeth called Noshpitz quickly after her talk with Hilary. She told him, as she had planned to all along, that Hilary was a troubled child with a lot of fears and anxieties. She added that there was a possibility that sexual abuse was involved. Since physicians are required to report possible abuse to the authorities, Noshpitz notified the sexual-abuse team at Children's Hospital immediately after his first interview with Elizabeth.

On January 29, Elizabeth took Hilary there for a physical examination by Dr. Mireille Kanda, then a pediatrician in the sex-abuse unit and now the director of the hospital's child protection group. Kanda found nothing out of the ordinary. Thirteen days later, a doctor at Georgetown University Hospital, conducting a separate examination, found no bruises or lacerations in Hilary's vaginal or rectal areas. Her vaginal area was somewhat inflamed.

Physical examinations of the genital and anal areas of little children are routine in sexual-abuse cases. But such examinations are not definitive—either in identifying sexual abuse or in ruling it out. Many sexual acts that constitute abuse, such as fondling of the genitals, do not ordinarily leave identifiable marks. Conversely, symptoms that some pediatricians believe indicate sexual abuse, such as scarring around the vagina or an enlarged hymenal opening, are very difficult to distinguish from congenital conditions or accidental injuries. Without the presence of semen or of a venereal disease (neither of which was found in Hilary's case), it is impossible to substantiate abuse without some margin of error.

Since the abuse had allegedly occurred in Virginia, not in Washington, the Children's Hospital specialists called the matter in to the Fairfax County Department of Social Services (DSS) on the department's "hot line" for child abuse and neglect.

On January 30, Daisy Morrison-Gilstrap, a social worker for the department, opened an investigation of possible sexual abuse by Eric Foretich. The purpose of informal social service investigations like Gilstrap's is not to punish wrongdoers—that is left to the prosecutors and the courts—but to identify children and others who may need help.

Gilstrap began work immediately by reviewing the Children's Hospital records. She made a list of the people she had to talk to— obviously beginning with Eric, Elizabeth, and Hilary. But things moved too slowly for Elizabeth, who got nervous when Gilstrap canceled a couple of appointments. Elizabeth wanted to make sure that the Fairfax social workers understood how serious Hilary's problems were.

She soon thought of a way to show them. On the evening of February 6, according to Elizabeth, Hilary began to masturbate in front of her with a tiny saltcellar spoon. Elizabeth viewed this as further evidence of abuse by Eric. She decided it would help her case to take pictures of Hilary to show that the girl knew her body parts and that her descriptions of abuse were credible. Elizabeth and Hilary drove to Elizabeth's McLean office—Antonia was still out of the country and unavailable to baby-sit—and fetched the Polaroid camera that Elizabeth used to take medical pictures of her plastic-surgery patients. Around eight-fifteen, when they returned to Westover, Elizabeth took eight Polaroid shots. In seven of them Hilary is clothed; in the eighth she is wearing only a T-shirt and is pointing to her vagina with the spoon. Her face is not visible. When Elizabeth gave Hilary the photos to play with, she urinated on them. "I'm bad, Mother," she said. "You're bad. You will go to jail."

Elizabeth later believed that Hilary urinated on the pictures because she associated urination with ejaculation.

The next evening, according to Elizabeth's diary, Hilary asked her mother to kiss her in her mouth "like her daddy." Elizabeth explained that this was not right for Eric to do. Then she took three pictures of Hilary kissing and blowing kisses, to prove that the little girl knew the difference.

During this same time, as she was building her case against her husband, Elizabeth was taking a conciliatory tone in her letters to Eric, who knew nothing of her suspicions. In a January 24, 1985, letter, he had suggested that for Hilary's sake, he and his ex-wife "put the onerous and disruptive events of the past three years behind" and try to achieve a rapprochement.

Elizabeth replied on February 8 that although she was once very much in love with Eric, and found the failure of the relationship very painful, she wanted to wait a little while so that Eric's anger could cool. Then, and only then, could they begin a friendly relationship.

A few days later, Gilstrap and Elizabeth set a date and place for Gilstrap's interview with Hilary. This meeting was set for Elizabeth's home on February 15. That day, Gilstrap sat in one room with Hilary, while her DSS colleague, Beth Iddings, sat in another room with Elizabeth, who described what she had seen and what she suspected. Hilary didn't answer Gilstrap's direct questions about sexual abuse, so Gilstrap brought out a set of anatomically correct dolls. "These are my babies, and we came here to find out what happened to Hilary," Gilstrap said.

Anatomically correct dolls are designed to elicit responses in children too inarticulate or fearful to verbalize events. They come in male and female versions, adult and child, and are intentionally built with larger-than-life genitals in order to help children recall suppressed memories of abuse. The dolls are standard equipment for sexual-abuse investigators, but many experts say they are too suggestive and can, because of their design, lead to "sexually oriented" responses from children who have not been abused. These experts contend that almost any effort to put the dolls together in play can easily be seen as some sort of sexual act.

"There is just about one game to play with these dolls: sex," a leading child psychiatrist wrote in a 1988 article. Current consensus is that the dolls can be helpful if used carefully by well-trained professionals. In the hands of less experienced persons, the risk of a "false positive" (a child misidentified as abused) is too great.

Gilstrap had a bachelor's degree in social work and four years' experience as a child-abuse investigator.

Hilary looked at the male doll and giggled. "Heinie," she said. "Daddy's heinie." In response to a direct question by Gilstrap about whether she had seen "Daddy's heinie," Hilary did not answer. "Daddy's heinie. Daddy's heinie," she repeated, but didn't act out any sexual scenarios with the dolls. So Gilstrap decided to trade places with Iddings. She talked with Elizabeth while Iddings sat down with Hilary. Then everyone shared a snack, and Iddings and Gilstrap tried again; they still couldn't get Hilary to say anything. Finally, Hilary took cover under a blanket on a sofa, putting her mouth on the male doll's genitals and repeating, "Daddy's heinie." Then she threw the doll across the room and hid under her blanket. The interview was over. Gilstrap had the feeling that something was going on, but Hilary had been too "nonverbal and noncommunicative" to make any definitive finding at that point, she reported.

The standard procedure of the Fairfax DSS is to involve the county police in abuse investigations if there is any possibility that a crime has been committed under Virginia law. The police had been too short-staffed to send someone to the February 15 meeting. After the meeting, however, Gilstrap, following procedure, asked the police to assign an officer. The assignment went to Daniel Gollhardt, who has made abuse cases his specialty. At the time he was assigned Hilary's case, Gollhardt had been pursuing sexual abusers for ten years. He had also spent six weeks at Children's Hospital learning how to interview sexually abused children, and he himself had taught techniques of interviewing in sexual-abuse cases around the country.

A few days later, on February 20, Eric received a telephone call at his dental office. He didn't usually interrupt his work to take personal calls, but this one sounded important—and ominous. "It's about your daughter," his secretary told him.

It was Gilstrap, informing him that he was under investigation for "sexual molestation" of Hilary. The social worker suggested it would be a good idea to suspend his visits with Hilary until the matter could be cleared up, but Eric flatly refused. "Part of me was shocked," Eric recalls, "while part of me said that's just what Elizabeth would do."

Two days later, Eric told Elizabeth in a six-page letter what he thought of her strategy. "The real problem with Hilary," he wrote, "is that she relishes it here with us and does not want to go home to you. I am sure we show her more love in one weekend than you are capable of in an entire month.

"Last year," he continued,

> you accused me of being a drug dealer, this year a child molester! . . . With this latest malicious fabrication you have sunk into a smelly abyss. While you were busy writing me three letters in two days, you had already initiated an investigation of me as a child molester. A molester of my own 2 1/2 year old daughter! The letters were clearly a sinister cover-up to your obvious intention to eliminate or severely restrict my access to Hilary—at any cost! If you are capable of this low a deed, what else are you capable of—murder? I don't believe you will stop your relentless goal to have Hilary all to yourself—and also meanwhile collect child support from me. . . . I have to believe your obsession with eliminating my role with Hilary is based upon mental sickness and not satanic influences. Nevertheless, I will pray for you! Meanwhile, for Hilary's sake, please seek treatment!

On February 26, Doris wrote Elizabeth an eight-page letter about what she viewed as a false and malicious accusation against her son:

> In regards to your efforts to keep Eric from his daughter because of your most recent mental aberration, I must (as a grandmother and mother) protest. The using of one's own innocent in order to obtain one's objective is really vile. We are quite aware of your timing. In a year or perhaps less, Hilary would be old enough to know what really is happening and thus could not be so easily manipulated. . . . In the first place, it is I who looks after Hilary's needs as to hygiene etc. I bathe and dress her, change her dirty diapers and put her to bed with her sister in their own room! . . . Vincent rocks her when she is tired or cross, and as to Eric, when he can be home, he takes his children for walks up and down our road, takes them back to our fence to look at the horses, helps me feed Hilary, takes them to the zoo and shopping. He dearly loves his little girls and would never do anything deliberately to undermine their well being. . . . What are you afraid of, Elizabeth? What inner demons haunt you? . . . My God, I would be afraid of divine retribution, but then perhaps you don't feel the need to believe in anything but your own machinations. . . . You really ought to be quite ashamed of yourself. . . . I know something must be wrong with you as I just cannot believe that you are this bad a person.

Eric and his parents were glad that they had received Bob Machen's advice eighteen months earlier and that they had taken so many precautions to counter an abuse accusation. But despite all their efforts, Elizabeth had gone ahead with the charge. Now the Foretiches had to devise a strategy to refute the charges, which they thought reflected Elizabeth's neurotic obsession with keeping Hilary to herself.

During the next visitation, Doris and Vincent took Hilary to her regular pediatrician, Elizabeth's friend Voja Russo, and told her that their son was being charged with sexually abusing his daughter. Russo's office is in Great Falls, a few minutes from Eric's home. Doris and Vincent asked Russo to examine Hilary after every visit in order to satisfy herself, and presumably Elizabeth, that Hilary was not being abused. "I don't want to be drawn into this," the Foretiches recall Russo saying.

She agreed to do one examination only. "They wanted [Hilary] to be examined and rule out fondling and/or sexual child abuse," Russo wrote in her March 11 notes. "Exam of vaginal and rectal area appeared within normal limits. No redness, discharge, or irritation noted in vaginal and/or rectal area. Introitus [the opening of the vagina] appeared intact." Russo told Doris she thought Hilary was "in very good shape."

Dr. Russo has declined to discuss the Morgan-Foretich case publicly, and Elizabeth has never identified Russo—her trusted friend, Hilary's first pediatrician—as a doctor who would substantiate her charges. Russo told Elizabeth and Eric that she did not want to get involved in the case, and neither ever called her to the stand.

What Doris and Vincent did not know when they brought Hilary to Russo was that Elizabeth was in the process of dismissing Russo as Hilary's pediatrician. On January 11, a few days before Elizabeth's first conversation with Hilary about the alleged abuse, Elizabeth had written Eric to suggest that since Russo was her friend, it might be a good idea for her to look for a new pediatrician. She did not want Eric to suspect Russo of seeing things only Elizabeth's way, she said. A week later, Elizabeth wrote that she had found a new doctor: Dr. Ann Richmond, an assistant professor of pediatrics at Georgetown University.

Eric had never had any particular problem with Russo, and he wondered why Elizabeth was making such a fuss just then about changing doctors. When he heard about the sexual-abuse charge, he thought he understood. As he told Elizabeth in his February 22 letter, it had dawned upon him that Elizabeth might be trying to draw in "other professionals, those who do not know me or the history of my struggle with you, to unwittingly cooperate with your malfeasance."

By late February, Eric and his parents had put together their own strategy. Hilary was not yet three years old and could not always speak in a manner that could be reliably understood. But Heather was two years older and had been present at almost all the visits. Heather, Eric thought, would be able to clear his name. Eric, about to leave on a long-scheduled ski vacation, asked his father to suggest that Gilstrap talk to Heather. Gilstrap was out of the office when he called her: "There is another child involved," Vincent's message read. "If you want the right answers, go and talk to the child."

Gilstrap called Sharon and explained the situation. Except for the story about bathing with Eric almost two years before, Sharon had no indication that there was any problem with Heather, a healthy, blond-haired kindergartner. "As far as I was concerned, she was a very well-adjusted child," Sharon recalled. Heather had never said anything about sexual abuse. Sharon told Heather to make sure to tell the truth when Gilstrap and Gollhardt came to their apartment.

On February 28, the day before they were to visit Sharon, Gollhardt and Gilstrap met with Elizabeth—without Hilary—at Elizabeth's medical office. Elizabeth showed Gollhardt the pictures she had taken of Hilary, but he told her they were useless in a criminal investigation; they indicated nothing. There are sharp differences about what happened next. Elizabeth says Gilstrap and Gollhardt both encouraged her to take explicit photographs of Hilary again, but this time to make sure to include her face so that the photos could be admitted for evidence. Gollhardt and Gilstrap both emphatically deny suggesting that Elizabeth take more nude pictures of her child.

After two interviews on two separate days, Heather came forward with a story that shocked Gilstrap—and Sharon. Gilstrap and Gollhardt's March 1 interview was unproductive; Gilstrap returned on her own on March 2. That day, Heather told the social worker that her father had "opened her heinie and put his heinie in her heinie." Using the anatomically correct dolls, she demonstrated an act of intercourse between an adult male doll and a little girl doll. Heather said that it had hurt and that it had happened three times. In response to a direct question from Gilstrap, Heather said she was not fibbing and was telling the truth.

Gollhardt later tried to follow up on Heather's statements to Gilstrap. But in repeated interviews, at some of which Gilstrap was present, Heather never repeated the statement that she had been abused. (Gilstrap says she recorded some of Heather's statements on tape, but Gollhardt says that when he tried to play the tape, he found that it had been erased.)

Gollhardt later testified that Heather repeatedly denied that her father had ever touched her vagina in any way. To Gilstrap, however, it seemed much more likely that Heather had been abused than Hilary.

A little more than a week later, on March 8, Gilstrap and Gollhardt met with Eric and John Lenahan in Gollhardt's office. Eric, cornered and defensive, lashed out at the investigators. Gilstrap says Eric angrily condemned his wives for their lack of concern for him. "Can you imagine, she attended Harvard," she recalls him saying sardonically about Elizabeth. (Eric says he was distraught but denies talking about Elizabeth's educational achievements.) In a DSS report, Gilstrap described Eric as "a very anxious, distraught and persecuted man," who "appeared to be very concerned about his reputation in the community."

Gilstrap asked Eric to suspend visitation temporarily until her investigation could be completed, and again he said no. Eric told the social worker and the police officer that his parents lived with him and could verify what he had told them. Gollhardt and Gilstrap later went to the Great Falls house unannounced and found that Doris and Vincent did indeed live there.

That same day, March 8, Elizabeth tried to achieve by court order what Gilstrap could not achieve voluntarily. Hal Witt, her lawyer, went before Judge Henry Kennedy of the D.C. Superior Court to try to suspend the visitations with Hilary on the grounds that Eric was abusing his daughter. The DSS investigation was incomplete, and Gilstrap refused to testify on Elizabeth's behalf. The hearing, scheduled on a Saturday (Witt had convinced Kennedy that it was an emergency), didn't go as Elizabeth had planned. Kennedy turned down the request. He wasn't convinced of the abuse. Sharon also asked Judge Barnard Jennings in Fairfax County to stop the visits; but rather than make a decision, Jennings turned the matter over to the county's Juvenile and Domestic Relations Court, a specialized family court.

Apart from Heather, all Gilstrap had against Eric was Elizabeth. Moved by Elizabeth's insistence, Gilstrap decided to reinterview Hilary, and returned on March 15 with Gollhardt to Westover Place. This time, Elizabeth was not there—Hilary was alone with Fran Walton. Gollhardt sat on the floor with Hilary and colored a drawing with her. Then they took a tour of the house. The police officer, with Gilstrap present the entire time, asked Hilary whether she showered with her father. She responded that she showered with her mother.

Gilstrap took Hilary into a bedroom to try to get her to relate a "bedroom scene" of abuse. Hilary did nothing of the sort. Instead, she took Gilstrap back into the bathroom and gave her doll a bath. Gilstrap says that Hilary gave no indication that any of the play represented anything that had happened to her. "There was nothing that I could apply to the investigation," Gilstrap concluded. Gollhardt returned and saw Hilary two more times but again found no evidence of abuse.

Eric had won in the D.C. court and Fairfax County courts, at least temporarily, but his strategy looked weak. Dr. Russo, quite understandably, did not want to take either side of the dispute; and Heather, rather than support Eric's version of events, had said enough about abuse to keep the DSS investigation going. (Eric blamed Sharon for Heather's statements, taking the view that she had prompted Heather to make her "disclosures.")

Eric told Lenahan he had two more ideas: He would send Heather to a therapist for a full professional evaluation, and he would take a lie-detector test. These steps were to prove more effective.

Eric took Heather to Dr. James McMurrer, head of the child psychiatry department of Fairfax Hospital. Eric had consulted McMurrer about Heather in early January, before he learned of the abuse charges, and asked him to evaluate her to support his request for more liberal visitation rights. He was concerned about Sharon's parenting abilities; Heather was frequently late to school. He did not seem worried that an evaluation of Heather would reveal any secrets. At that time, Heather told McMurrer that she wanted to continue to live with her mother but expressed no negative feelings about her father.

After the charges, Eric asked McMurrer to conduct a full sexual-abuse evaluation. In three sessions in March and May, McMurrer used anatomically correct dolls with Heather but found no evidence of abuse. He also saw no evidence that Heather had been coached by her mother or anyone else. On one of those three visits, Sharon informed McMurrer that Heather had been seen by Cora Lynn Goldsboro, a psychologist who happened to be an old colleague of William Morgan's from the Virginia Psychological Association. She had found no evidence of sexual abuse.

Most of the time, Heather said nothing to indicate abuse—at least not to Gollhardt or McMurrer. Nor did she speak to Goldsboro or her mother about the abuse. In fact, as late as June, Sharon told a DSS worker that she was uncertain about whether Heather had been abused. She asked for more persuasive evidence.

But Heather's statements bothered Gilstrap. If Heather had not been abused, Gilstrap wondered, why did she say even once that she had been? Coaching from her mother, Gilstrap knew, was a possible explanation, but McMurrer did not see evidence of this and Sharon denies it.

Doris Foretich believes that Heather's lively intelligence and imagination may have been engaged by Gilstrap's questions. With more than a trace of revulsion, Doris explains that Sharon used to leave Heather with a fifteen-year-old babysitter who would play "doctor" with her and describe in some detail to the five-year-old what she did with her boyfriend. Once, Doris recalls, Heather told her that the babysitter had introduced a game of "I'm having a baby." During this game, she would "open Heather up."

From Eric's point of view, McMurrer helped dispel the accusations, and the polygraph helped even more. The test was administered at Eric's insistence. Lenahan had advised his client that although the results of polygraph tests are not admissible in court, they count very heavily in police decisions on whether to go forward with a case. Lenahan advised Eric to take a private polygraph first; then if the results cleared him, to go ahead and take the police test. The private test came out fine, so on April 8, Eric took the police test. He denied to the examiner that he had sexually abused either of his children, and the results showed no deception.

Elizabeth denigrated the importance of the polygraph. Seventy percent of habitual child molesters pass the test, she claimed, because they tend to be educated and middle class and cannot easily be intimidated by the machine.

Jim Wilt, a polygraph expert whose clients have included Albert Hakim in the Iran-Contra affair and former Attorney General Richard Kleindienst, disagrees. Wilt says intelligent people with professional degrees are the easiest to catch with the polygraph. "If you explain to a doctor what the physiological changes are that accompany a lie, and he's guilty, he'll normally either confess on the spot or refuse to take the test," Wilt says.

After the polygraph test, the criminal investigation of Eric Foretich seemed to lead nowhere as far as Gollhardt was concerned. Probably in early April, he called Elizabeth and told her there was no evidence of any abuse. "The mother has coached the child," Elizabeth recalls him saying.

When Gollhardt called, he had already talked the case over with Corinne Magee, a young, aggressive prosecutor in the Commonwealth Attorney's Office. Like Gollhardt, Magee specialized in putting sex offenders behind bars and had become very good at it. Magee takes child abuse very seriously, so seriously that she refuses as a matter of principle to defend people accused of molesting children.

Magee agreed almost at once that there was essentially no case to be made against Eric. "We had no statements whatever, after very careful questioning by two people, that anything had happened, and Dan Gollhardt is one of the best investigators in the country. There were no politics, no public outcry. I just looked at the case as an experienced prosecutor," Magee recalls. "We had no eyewitnesses, we had an alleged victim who was under three, and we had a police polygraph conducted by one of the best operators we had."

The criminal case was soon brought to a close. But Gilstrap still had to present her findings to the DSS. On April 22, 1985, she decided that the allegations involving the sexual abuse of Heather were, in DSS terminology, "founded." This result was not the equivalent of a criminal conviction or a police arrest. As Gilstrap's supervisor, Meredith McEver, explained in a deposition, the "founded" designation meant that the department felt there was enough evidence of abuse to provide counseling to Heather. The determination also meant that Eric would be listed permanently by the state on the confidential registry of child abusers it keeps in department headquarters in Richmond.

McEver said, "This is what happens in every [founded] case. Services were offered to Mrs. Foretich. She accepted them. An ongoing worker met with Heather on a regular basis."

In DSS jargon, an "ongoing worker" is a social worker who provides counseling and other services to a client on a continuing basis. Kimberly Carr was assigned in June 1985 in order to monitor Heather's progress in therapy and to help Sharon deal with the situation. Heather was also placed in therapy geared to victims of sexual abuse. Her therapist was Jean Albright, a social worker at the Chesapeake Institute, a small institution in Wheaton, Maryland, that conducts research and counseling in sexual-abuse cases.

The case involving Hilary was termed "unfounded with reason to suspect." This confusing term means, according to Gilstrap, that there was "no concrete evidence, but enough behavior or indicators to lead us to believe that something had happened, but we didn't know exactly what." Elizabeth was given notice of this predominantly negative finding and was given the right to appeal within forty-five days. Gilstrap told her it was probably a good idea to keep Hilary in therapy with Dr. Noshpitz.

Gilstrap told Elizabeth that the finding would remain in the central registry for a year; after that, Virginia law required that all record be purged from the system to prevent unfounded charges from remaining on the books. With the "unfounded with reason to suspect" ruling, the DSS case involving Hilary Foretich was essentially closed.

Under Virginia law, when the DSS concludes after an investigation that a child is in immediate danger of harm, the department has the power to petition the Juvenile and Domestic Relations Court to protect the child from the abuse. No one from the department ever appeared in court to make such a petition on behalf of either Hilary or Heather Foretich.

Gilstrap's ruling satisfied no one. Eric asked Lenahan to begin the laborious internal appeal process at once. Not surprisingly, he wanted to erase the charges from the books. Elizabeth was also disappointed; Hilary, she complained, was still not acting normal—although Eric, Doris, Vincent, and Hilary's preschool teacher noticed nothing unusual. Elizabeth reported that from time to time Hilary would crawl under the table and masturbate. She also said that Hilary acted strangely after visits with the Foretiches. She would run around the room and throw things. She would try to insert bacon, lettuce, and other foods into her vagina. Elizabeth believed that all Hilary's problems resulted from sexual abuse. She was shaken. "I saw that every action I took to protect my child, through the psychiatrist, who proved to be ignorant of the problem, through the social services departments, proved to be . . . for some reason unable to protect an abused child," Elizabeth recalled in a 1986 deposition.

By the time of Gollhardt's March 15 interview with Hilary, Elizabeth was convinced that she would never get what she wanted—the termination of all visitations—from the police or from the Fairfax DSS. The February picture-taking session had not produced the desired result, and she decided it was time to get definitive proof of the abuse in the form of more pictures. According to Elizabeth's diary, on March 25, 1985, after Gollhardt and Gilstrap's visit but before the formal finding of "unfounded with reason to suspect," Elizabeth happened to be photographing bruises on Hilary's right leg and hip. During that session, Hilary began to insert her finger in her vagina repeatedly. She said, "My daddy do this," while she was masturbating in that way, and Elizabeth took a picture that included the masturbatory act.

This session may solve a mystery about the photographs. In her deposition and court testimony and in documents given to the media, Elizabeth has generally referred to only two occasions on which she took explicit pictures of Hilary: one on February 6, before she met with Gollhardt and Gilstrap; and one on April 30, after she received notice that her case was unfounded. Both dates are based on Elizabeth's journal, which is extremely reliable, often to the precise minute, as a chronology of events in her life. Sessions on those dates do not explain, however, the existence of an April 4 letter to Elizabeth from the Kodak developing laboratory, declaring that fourteen negatives were being withheld because they depict sexually explicit conduct. The laboratory, in fact, said it would destroy them rather than risk a prosecution for obscenity. Nor do they explain Elizabeth's written reply to the laboratory (asking that the photos be sent directly to Gilstrap) nor an April 21 letter from Elizabeth to Gilstrap explaining to the social worker what she was going to receive.

Perhaps the photographs rejected by Kodak because of their explicit sexual nature were those taken on March 25; however, it does not appear from Elizabeth's diary that as many as fourteen explicit pictures were taken that day. Alternatively, perhaps the April 30 date is incorrect. (One chronology compiled later for Elizabeth's attorneys puts the April 30 events on March 30, three weeks before the formal DSS finding.) In either case, it seems possible that Elizabeth took graphic photos of Hilary on *three* separate occasions, not two.

The April 30 session, which Elizabeth has discussed in detail, would have taken place after the DSS finding. That evening, as Elizabeth recalls it, the telephone rang while she was giving Hilary a bath. After Elizabeth went to answer the phone, Hilary got out of the bathtub and ran upstairs to Antonia's room on the third floor of the townhouse. There she saw a box of crayons that Antonia kept for her to play with. She sat on a towel and, "almost trance-like," started inserting the crayons inside her vagina. Antonia, who by then had returned from her trip, was talking on the telephone. Hilary ran up to her and sat down at her feet. Antonia was shocked to see what Hilary was doing. The two women let Hilary continue for fifteen or twenty minutes.

Elizabeth got her Canon 35-millimeter camera and took a few pictures of the naked girl. But upon rewinding, she thought the film might not have been properly placed in the camera. So she left Hilary with Antonia and drove to her medical office to get her Polaroid camera. (Elizabeth says this took 20 to 25 minutes round-trip; a better estimate of the time would be 40 to 45 minutes.) Upon her return, Hilary had stopped her acting out. Elizabeth asked Hilary to put the crayons back where they had been before she left. "She looked unhappy, and then when I had the camera it was like this was a game," Elizabeth said in 1987 court testimony. "And at first she wouldn't do it and I was going to put the camera down, and then she did it and that's when I took the photographs." Elizabeth took six pictures with her Polaroid. That day's photographs, later introduced as part of the court record, show a smiling, almost flirtatious naked child. In one of them she is putting her hand up as if in a futile attempt to block the camera's view.

In materials that appear to have originated from the Morgan camp, Elizabeth is quoted as explaining: "Each time, it was unpleasant and upsetting for all of us. . . . They were to me like medical photos of a bad accident—unpleasant but necessary to help the victim in court." Elizabeth expected that the photos would induce the DSS to reopen the investigation. She had gotten just the shots she wanted.

But nude photographs of little girls, especially ones that show acts of sexual gratification, are not usually taken by parents who want to protect their children from abuse. Meredith McEver, Gilstrap's supervisor when the investigation began, had never seen a parent do anything similar in a case of alleged sexual abuse. In fact, McEver concluded that the pictures proved nothing about Eric and showed only that Elizabeth "was encouraging [Hilary] to stick crayons in her vagina."

In June 1985, Gilstrap, who had received the pictures from the developer, was shocked at their graphic content and showed them to Meriam Rogan, her DSS supervisor at the time, and to Gollhardt. Gilstrap inserted the photos into the official DSS file, but, contrary to Elizabeth's wishes, did not reopen the investigation. In fact, because the inquiry had been closed as unfounded, Gilstrap never contacted Elizabeth again. A few months later, Gilstrap left the DSS to move to the Chicago area, where her husband had been transferred. She had no further involvement in the Morgan-Foretich case.

Also leaving the scene that spring was Fran Walton, whose tenure as Hilary's babysitter ended in May 1985 after four months. Elizabeth says the decision was mutual: "That was the period that it became obvious that [Hilary] was being sexually abused and I don't know whether that was a factor for Fran, but it was very upsetting for everybody looking after Hilary, and one morning Fran just didn't come, and we talked on the phone. She and I agreed that she'd be happier in another job."

Walton, on the other hand, says Elizabeth called her one evening and said, "Fran, you're fired. Don't bother to come to work to-morrow. We won't be needing you anymore. It's your attitude." Walton, who had always gotten along very well with Elizabeth, assumed her firing was Antonia's doing; her outspoken style clashed with Mrs. Morgan's British reserve. She couldn't find any obvious cause for her dismissal. Only later did she suspect that Elizabeth may have preferred a less independent thinker who would go along with her interpretation of Hilary's problems. On May 21, Elizabeth hired a new babysitter—Narcisa Ramirez, a nurse from the Philippines. She was Hilary's fourth full-time caretaker in just over two years.

Hilary continued in therapy with Dr. Noshpitz all through that spring and summer. During an interview about her marriage and Hilary's troubles, Elizabeth told Noshpitz that she strongly suspected Hilary was being sexually abused on a regular basis. In the therapy, Noshpitz tried very hard to get Hilary to talk about the alleged abuse. He asked some leading questions, wondering aloud to Hilary whether her "heinie" was involved in her problems; when he got no response, he tried to get Hilary to act out abuse scenarios with puppets on the floor. (Like many psychiatrists, Noshpitz did not use anatomically correct dolls.) While playing with Hilary, Noshpitz saw her exhibit a "very general, diffuse aggression," hitting and attacking all the puppets and hitting him as well. He thought that Hilary had a lot of anger to act out.

Elizabeth told Noshpitz about Hilary's abnormal behavior. On the evening of May 20, 1985, for example, while Antonia was in the tub, Hilary and Elizabeth followed her into the bathroom. Elizabeth reported that Hilary took off her clothes and said, "My Papa gets in the bath with Heather and with me." That same evening, ac-cording to Elizabeth's diary, Hilary told her that she and Heather each had a "fucker," pointing to her clitoris. What was more, Heather used to hit her on the face with her "fucker" because Daddy tells her to. "It's bad," Elizabeth replied, "but I won't tell Daddy or Papa. You just tell me and Mama and Dr. Noshpitz." The diary is replete with similar conversations.

On three occasions—March 6, June 26, and August 26, 1985—

it was Eric who brought Hilary to Noshpitz for therapy. At the June 26 session, Eric—who blamed Noshpitz for touching off the DSS investigation by reporting Elizabeth's suspicions—told the psychiatrist he was going to sue him for trying to ruin his reputation. "You are just another instrument Elizabeth is using to achieve her ends," Eric said. Noshpitz explained that the referral was required by D.C. law in all cases of suspected abuse. By the end of the hour, Eric had apologized.

Noshpitz found Hilary's play in Eric's presence, on all three occasions, to be "substantially the same as it had been when the mother was present." His notes reflected that Hilary's behavior with her father "was rather affectionate and clean, and not otherwise remarkable." Hilary was "attached" to Eric, and "tended to cling to him," Noshpitz reported. During the therapy, Elizabeth professed support for Noshpitz's efforts. On September 5, Elizabeth wrote to Eric that Noshpitz had been "very helpful" in dealing with Hilary's problems, which she said consisted of deep anxieties and fears.

CHAPTER 6

June 1985 through February 14, 1986

Now that the DSS investigations were over, Doris and Vincent Foretich sensed a temporary lull in the separate legal cases involving their granddaughters—Hilary's case in the D.C. Superior Court and Heather's in the Fairfax Juvenile Court. Hilary had grown out of the baby stage and had become a happy, verbal girl of almost three. Her visits with Eric were continuing to go well, the Foretiches say. Eric loved to take his daughters to the park and the zoo and to romp with them in the backyard. According to them, Hilary was so happy at Eric's house that she had to be coaxed to the phone when Elizabeth called. All she would say, according to Doris, was "Hello, Mama, I'm playing. Goodbye."

By June 1985, Doris and Vincent decided that the crisis had passed. They could finally go back to Gloucester and pick up the strands of their life there. Two years before, when they had told Judge Pratt they would move to Great Falls to help Eric with Hilary, they had never thought they would see their son accused as a child molester. Now they missed their friends and family. Their home in Gloucester needed maintenance. And Doris's mother had just turned ninety and was becoming more dependent on her children.

Doris and Vincent, however, could not put Eric and his problems fully behind them, nor did they wish to. They still planned to be with Eric for every court-ordered visit by the children. They told Eric they would make the three-hour drive every other weekend to spend time with their son and his daughters.

In the spring and summer of 1985, Sharon often acted as if she believed the DSS was wrong about Heather. According to Kimberly Carr, the social worker assigned to her case, Sharon repeatedly asked whether Carr really had evidence of Heather's abuse. Carr said her job was to provide "ongoing services" for the DSS, not evidence. She was not supposed to investigate the allegations but merely to provide play therapy for Heather and encourage Sharon to keep sending Heather to Jean Albright, the therapist at the Chesapeake Institute. Sharon, who had never had a particularly well-organized life, repeatedly broke appointments with Albright, and Carr frequently had to remind her that the DSS felt the therapy important for Heather.

According to Eric, Sharon began to view the abuse allegations as a way to wrest some more money out of him. After the final divorce decree in the spring of 1984, Sharon had filed a lawsuit against Eric to get a larger chunk of their joint property. Theodora Franke, Eric's office manager, has testified that in March 1985, Eric asked her to listen in on a phone conversation with Sharon. According to Franke, Sharon told Eric she would stop the DSS investigation if he would give her full title to the couple's Monte Carlo, their grand piano, and their condominium in the Regency. (Sharon could not stop the investigation by herself, but she could withdraw her accusation that Heather had been molested.) She also wanted him to pay for Heather's private schooling through high school. Heather, Sharon complained to Eric, had been forced to reduce her standard of living after the divorce.

Around this time, Doris confronted Sharon and asked why she persisted in pursuing allegations that she didn't really believe. "I don't believe Eric would do anything to hurt his child. I don't believe that, but I have my needs," Sharon replied, according to Doris. Sharon may well have felt a financial squeeze. She was used to the income of a successful dentist; she had no career of her own; and she had never received a cent of alimony. Sharon has denied that she pursued the abuse charges in order to exact money from Eric.

In August 1985, Eric was awarded an extended three-week vacation with Hilary, the longest continuous stretch of time he ever had with her. Doris and Vincent drove her to Gloucester. Eric had arranged with Sharon that Heather would share a week of the vacation with her sister. Eric and Heather spent some time in Great Falls—in the company of Evie Dimageba, a Filipino housekeeper Eric had hired as a live-in caretaker—and then drove down to Gloucester to see Doris and Vincent. There, Eric and both girls met Eric's cousin Bill Hale and Bill's wife and children for a few days at the Busch Gardens amusement park near Williamsburg. Eric remembers Hilary particularly enjoying a speedboat ride with one of his uncles.

On August 9, according to Doris and Vincent, Heather and Hilary were visiting their grandparents in Gloucester, along with Eric and Pamela Nader, a concert pianist Eric was dating that summer. According to Doris's later testimony at a custody hearing, five-year-old Heather, her face blanched with embarrassment, suddenly told Doris she had "done something bad." She had told a lie to "that black lady," meaning Daisy Gilstrap. With her gaze fixed firmly down on her shoes, Heather said she had not told the truth when she said her father had let her touch him. Her grandfather, Cornelius Sullivan, had told her to tell the lie, she said. Doris also testified that Heather told her that Grandmother Sullivan and her mother knew about it.

"Heather," Doris replied, "don't ever let anybody get you to tell a story, because you know it is wrong and it makes you sad, and remember what I told you about the angels, they dance and sing when you tell the truth." Heather seemed satisfied with her grandmother's admonition and walked off to play in the wading pool with Hilary.

On the last day of the three-week vacation, Eric, setting the facts on the record for his ex-wife, wrote to Elizabeth that Hilary had developed a slight cold but had otherwise shown no signs of illness while she was with him. When Hilary returned to Washington the next day, August 22, Elizabeth took her to Dr. Mireille Kanda at Children's Hospital for another full sexual-abuse work-up. The result of the exam, indicated on the hospital's Clinical/Laboratory Assault Form, was again negative: no evidence of abuse. No follow-up was recommended, except that Hilary ought to continue seeing Noshpitz. (Hilary cooperated willingly with the exam, and when she was asked whether anyone besides herself had touched her "heinie," she cheerfully replied no.)

Elizabeth kept trying. On Tuesday, September 10, the day after Eric returned Hilary from the next regular weekend visit, Elizabeth had Antonia take her right back to Children's for yet another checkup. When asked if anyone had put anything in her heinie, Hilary told Kanda that her father had put a "fucker" there. She also said he had put something in her rectum but was unable to specify what. Again, the physical examination was completely normal. Kanda's report reveals an "alert, very articulate young girl in no distress. Very cooperative." Hilary's vaginal area was pink, with no discharge visible, and her hymen was intact. The introitus, the vaginal opening, varied from pinpoint diameter to a diameter of 2 millimeters. A rectal examination showed that the sphincter tone was normal. Cultures for sexually transmitted diseases also proved negative. Dr. Kanda did not prescribe any treatment for Hilary, who must have found the constant visits to doctors and hospitals more than a little confusing. The only reference to possible sexual abuse in Kanda's report are the words "SA by Hx," i.e., "sexual abuse by history." This means simply that Elizabeth had told Kanda that she believed there had been abuse.

But because Hilary had said something that indicated possible abuse, Kanda asked Ruth Sihlangu, a Children's Hospital social worker, to meet with Hilary. Sihlangu gave Hilary two anatomically correct dolls to play with. She asked the girl what she was doing with the dolls that her father had done to her. Hilary replied, "He put sun cream like that." When asked how her father had "hurt her heinie," Hilary said, "I don't know." Hilary, Sihlangu concluded, "is unable to indicate any consistent information or behavior in play therapy indicative of possible sexual abuse."

None of the negative findings mattered to Elizabeth, and her lack of faith in the tests had a certain logic: Some types of sexual abuse leave no physical scars, and Hilary may have preferred to discuss the abuse only with certain people in certain situations. But Elizabeth did tend to support the results of medical examinations when they confirmed her views.

Elizabeth wrote no less than three letters to Eric on September 11, the date of Hilary's last visit to Children's Hospital. None mentioned her continuing suspicions or her trip to Children's. Instead, she berated Eric for shouting obscenities at her on the phone; for disregarding Hilary's welfare by taking her to Gloucester with him on a Friday and returning the following Sunday; and for taking Hilary to the Fairfax courthouse on September 9 to a hearing on Heather's case. (Eric says he and Elizabeth had testy conversations but denies that he ever yelled obscenities at her.)

Heather's case was getting bogged down; the five-year-old kept changing her mind. After months of denials that she had been abused, she began to speak, during her therapy with Jean Albright, about sexual contact with Eric. On her tenth visit, in August 1985, she said she had touched Eric's penis while he was wearing only a T-shirt. When she spoke about this in the social worker's office, she was sitting on Sharon's lap. Heather also described another occasion on which Eric had asked her and Hilary to lift up their dresses and had touched them on their underclothes. She testified about this at a September hearing, and a juvenile judge ordered Doris and Vincent to supervise Eric's visits with Heather. (Heather never implicated Eric's parents in any of the abuse she described.)

While Heather was seeing Albright, Eric had also received court permission to keep Heather in therapy with James McMurrer, the psychiatrist he had consulted at Fairfax Hospital in January. On Saturday morning, September 21, Eric and Vincent took Heather to McMurrer's office, and Hilary went along for the ride. During therapy, Heather told the psychiatrist that she had once touched Eric's penis, and in the corridor, McMurrer told Eric what she had said. As the four were leaving, Sharon arrived uninvited during Eric's visitation period, presumably to help Heather talk about the abuse. (Heather had been talking about "touching" with Albright, and Sharon thought that with enough emotional support, she might discuss it with McMurrer too.)

A loud shouting match broke out between Vincent and Sharon. Sharon called Vincent "scum" and Vincent called Sharon a "shanty Irish half-breed." McMurrer was forced to leave his office to break up the yelling, and both girls cried. The Foretiches recall that as soon as Heather got into the car with Vincent and Eric, though, she told them she had told another lie about her father. "You told your nanny just a month ago that you would never do that again," Vincent said.

Eric and Vincent decided to take Heather back so she could tell her new story to McMurrer. They wanted to wait until Sharon left, so Eric first saw two patients in the hospital. When they returned to the psychiatrist's office two hours later, Heather told McMurrer that she had not told the truth before and that her grandfather had coached her. McMurrer realized that the coaching might also have come from Eric and Vincent. He tried to sort it all out: at the end of his sessions with Heather, he came to the conclusion that there was no evidence of penetration but that there had been "touching." He could not establish the circumstances of the touching—in his words, whether the touching was "accidental or contrived."

A few days later, Kenneth Ison, a dentist friend of Eric's, also heard Heather recant. As Ison recalls it, Eric had hoped Heather might talk about the abuse with a trusted family friend—someone who was neither a relative nor a psychiatrist. Ison's daughter is about the same age as Heather, and the girls occasionally played together. According to Ison's later testimony at a custody hearing, Heather told him that her grandfather Sullivan had told her to "make up stories or whatever" to the effect that "her father had touched her."

That fall, Sharon had developed the habit of calling Eric at home quite frequently while Heather was visiting. One afternoon, Sharon asked Heather, "Have you told her the important stuff?" (By "her" she was referring to Kim Carr, the social worker who was there that day to check on the visit.) Heather said sheepishly that she hadn't said anything. Sharon chided her. "I told you to. You didn't forget, did you? You just don't want to." Hoping to please her mother, Heather said she had mentioned "one thing" to Carr. "What was it?" her mother asked anxiously. "I forgot it," Heather whispered.

Elizabeth's efforts to build a case against Eric were also being frustrated that fall. Dr. Noshpitz, Hilary's psychiatrist, concluded after seven months that Hilary was a troubled but not an abused child. The doctor reasoned that if Hilary had anything to say about abuse, she certainly had had the opportunity: she had just had three solid weeks with her alleged abusers. Noshpitz told Elizabeth that Hilary's problems had nothing to do with sexual abuse, for which he had found no evidence. Rather, the stress originated in what he diagnosed as an "adjustment disorder." Hilary, he believed, was having difficulty mainly because she was a child of divorced parents who hated and distrusted each other. He said that during play therapy, Hilary had imagined herself as "the thing that was being held or passed back and forth between [her parents]."

At the age of three, Hilary was being used as a pawn in an angry custody battle, Noshpitz decided. She was being asked, openly or covertly, to choose sides between her parents. This was an untenable burden on the little girl. Noshpitz's proposed solution was elegantly simple: Let Eric and Elizabeth work together to reduce the tension.

Noshpitz called Elizabeth in and told her what he had found. Two weeks later, she dismissed him; he had not come up with the diagnosis she thought was correct. Instead, he had said that Elizabeth herself was part of the problem, and that she could help her daughter by making peace with someone she deemed an abuser. This was unacceptable. Speaking "mainly as a mother," Elizabeth concluded after the diagnosis that Dr. Noshpitz had done little for Hilary. "It seemed to be an hour of her roaming around his toys and then hitting him until he says she should stop and then serving a tea party," she testified. Later, she concluded that Noshpitz had lied about his credentials by telling her he was qualified to treat abuse cases. (Noshpitz has maintained that he is competent to handle child-abuse cases.) It was time to find a new therapist.

John Lenahan, still pursuing his appeal of the DSS findings, asked Noshpitz to furnish a letter on Eric's behalf. Noshpitz relayed the request to Elizabeth, who forbade him to tell anyone about his treatment of Hilary.

On October 3, just after she fired Noshpitz, Elizabeth wrote the most disingenuous of her letters to Eric. In that letter, she suggested to Eric that she had dismissed Noshpitz in response to Eric's concerns. (In his August 21 letter, Eric had asked Elizabeth to explain "specifically why [Hilary] is seeing the psychiatrist.") Elizabeth went so far as to ask Eric if he could suggest a female therapist for Hilary. Eric refused to help.

The girls' next visit to the Foretiches, on the weekend of October 5, was seriously marred by events involving Heather and Sharon. Doris had given a wedding shower for a niece on Friday and had not driven up to Great Falls with Vincent. She was planning to take the bus into the Washington area on Saturday. Vincent decided to drive down to Gloucester at seven that morning to pick up his wife; she had had a colon operation the year before, and Vincent didn't want her to undergo the stress of a long bus ride. By the time Vincent and Doris returned to Great Falls six hours later, Heather was gone. They learned that Sharon had called Eric's home to talk with Heather and had found that the only people there were Heather, Hilary, and Evie Dimageba, the housekeeper. (Eric was seeing patients at the hospital.) Vincent and Doris, the court-appointed supervisors, were not present and were technically in contempt of court. Dimageba was not a court-certified supervisor. Sharon asked the Fairfax County police to go and pick up Heather, and they brought her home in a police car.

It must have troubled Hilary to see her older sister, whom she idolized, taken away by the police. (Elizabeth wrote Eric a week later that these kinds of scenes were disturbing to Hilary.) After this episode, the Fairfax County juvenile judge decided to appoint Joan Beach, a private investigator and former probation officer, as a professional supervisor for Heather. Beach was required to be present at every visit as long as Eric had visitation rights with his older daughter, and Eric had to pay her fee of $50 per hour. "The antagonism in the case was very unpleasant," Beach recalls. "But I do recall Hilary. She was a bright, precocious, beautiful girl. She seemed comfortable in that house with her grandparents and her sister."

That fall, the same judge also ordered evaluations of Eric and Sharon by a clinical psychologist. The psychologist, Dr. Nancy Fretta, interviewed them and administered the Rorschach Inkblot Test and two standard personality tests, the Thematic Apperception

Test (TAT) and the Minnesota Multiphasic Personality Inventory (MMPI). She was struck by the way in which Eric, while denying the charges of sexual abuse, seemed to focus on the possible loss of his reputation and dental practice rather than on any negative consequences for Hilary from the charges. She also noticed his anger at both Sharon and Elizabeth, as well as his suspicions that Sharon was using him for money. He thought Elizabeth was using him too— as a sperm bank and as a source of material for her books.

Fretta found that Eric gave overly intellectualized answers to her questions and that he "tested as an individual who attempts to have tight intellectual control over emotions he cannot integrate." She thought his problems might have originated in those long-ago days when the family was adjusting to the death of his sister in infancy and to Craig's death during his college years. "At the deaths of both his siblings, Dr. Foretich had to assume the role of arranging for the funerals, even to the selection of the burial sites," Fretta pointed out. She thought he had never worked out his own emotional reactions and had therefore developed "a rigidity and fragile defensiveness around exploring his emotional needs."

Fretta, like all psychologists who administer test batteries, cautioned that the tests cannot determine whether a person has engaged in a particular behavior pattern such as child abuse. The MMPI results, however, showed that Eric was "somewhat immature and impulsive, a high risk taker who may do things others do not approve of just for the personal enjoyment of doing so." Eric also tended to be "somewhat selfish, pleasure-oriented, narcissistic, and manipulative." On the other hand, he showed no neurotic or psychotic symptoms and appeared to have "no sex-role conflict." Fretta's conclusion after evaluating Eric and Sharon was that they both needed help to become better parents. Both were too wrapped up with their own emotional needs to give themselves unselfishly to a child.

Evie Dimageba, the new housekeeper at Great Falls, had fewer doubts about Eric. She has testified that Hilary was very affectionate to Vincent, Doris, and Eric, and always seemed to be having a good time. She never seemed nervous or frightened, says Dimageba, who adds that it would have been extremely unlikely for Eric or anyone else to have slipped into the bedroom at night and abused either girl. Dimageba slept in the children's bedroom with both girls, and the door had a pronounced squeak. She never noticed anyone trying to open the door at night. Moreover, Dimageba says, when Eric hired her, he immediately told her about the abuse charges. He denied they had any basis in reality and told her she was free to look at all the court papers that were piling up in various corners of the house.

Joan Beach, the neutral supervisor, quickly learned how difficult it was to avoid taking sides in the controversy. Doris recalls vividly that in November or early December 1985, Hilary woke up suddenly around 4:00 A.M., crying, "Crayons, crayons. They hurt me." Doris asked, "Who hurt you?" Hilary replied, "Antonia. She put crayons in my heinie. My mother took the pictures." While the event may have seemed vividly real to the three-year-old, Antonia had been merely an interested observer when Hilary used the crayons. Still, Doris was concerned. Eric was in Switzerland at a dental conference and Doris called him at daybreak, Washington time. Eric was shocked. He suggested to his mother that she try to get Beach to listen to Hilary. Beach did talk to Hilary but, to the Foretiches' chagrin, was unable to understand exactly what she was saying. "She was only three years old," Beach recalls. "I just didn't feel that the child was telling me enough. I would have called DSS if I had anything concrete, and I didn't have enough to call DSS." Vincent says he and Doris thought about calling the DSS but did not. They knew Eric had a continued disdain for the agency because of Daisy Gilstrap's investigation, which he considered shoddy.

Dr. Norman Coleman, a Virginia dentist with Eric in Switzerland, has testified that Eric told him he was troubled because Hilary had "awakened, claiming she had been hurt." And a few weeks later Elizabeth noted, in a letter to Eric, that he and Doris had told her that Hilary was waking up screaming that "someone is putting crayons in [her] vagina and rectum." Elizabeth asked Eric if he did not think further evaluation at the Chesapeake Institute would be helpful.

Although Elizabeth had received no help from Eric in finding a new psychiatrist for Hilary, her connections in the medical community permitted her to find plenty of therapists on her own. In November, Elizabeth took Hilary to Dr. Sandra Herschberg, a well-regarded Washington psychiatrist. Elizabeth, possibly treating Hilary too much like an adult, thought the problem in the past might have been that Hilary had refused to confide her sexual secrets to a male therapist. As is normal practice, Herschberg consulted with Joseph Noshpitz, Hilary's previous psychiatrist. Then, after one session with Hilary, she told Elizabeth she saw no evidence of sexual abuse.

According to her trial testimony, Elizabeth decided then not to

continue the therapy. Herschberg wasn't telling her what she wanted
to hear, and besides, it was necessary to take an elevator to her
office. Hilary was afraid of elevators. Elizabeth also met with Dr.
Kent Ravenscroft, another top-flight Washington psychiatrist, but
rejected him because his office was in a gloomy basement area of
his building.

Elizabeth's efforts to amass evidence of abuse culminated in November 1985 with another hearing in the D.C. Superior Court—her
first court date since her unsuccessful attempt to obtain an injunction
from Judge Henry Kennedy in March. This time, Hal Witt's arguments that Hilary was being repeatedly abused by Eric during visitations were heard by a judge who was new both to the case and
to the Superior Court. The judge was Herbert Dixon, Jr.

Like several of the other Superior Court judges, Dixon was a
product of the "Carl Moultrie pipeline." In the early 1970s, the late
Judge H. Carl Moultrie became an almost legendary figure in the
District of Columbia as the first black chief judge of the Superior
Court. Lawyers who clerked for Moultrie, many but not all of whom
are black, still view themselves as something of an elite in the District's trial bar. Dixon was one of the first of those clerks. Born in
1946 in Savannah, Georgia, the son of a postal employee, he grew
up in the segregated South of the 1950s and early 1960s, as the civil
rights movement emerged. Rejecting street protests, Dixon nur-
tured his ambitions quietly by trying to get the best education possible and make the best connections he could. For him that meant
Washington's Howard University, where he received a bachelor's
degree in electrical engineering in 1970, and the Omega Psi Phi
fraternity. Moultrie was, at one time, the fraternity's national ex-
ecutive director.

After graduating from Howard, Dixon entered the Georgetown
University Law Center, and upon his 1973 graduation and his year's
clerkship, launched a small general law practice in Washington. One
of Dixon's biggest clients was the D.C. Public Service Commission;
another specialty was domestic relations law.

"Domestic relations matters take a special type of temperament
because of the emotions involved," Dixon said, more prophetically
than he realized, during his Senate confirmation hearings in April
1985. Dixon represented both husbands and wives, as most family
lawyers do, but he also occasionally took on the difficult task of
representing children in domestic disputes. He and his wife Phoebe
raised two children of their own, and his law practice blossomed.

Still, Herbert Dixon, Jr., a soft-spoken, slight man, was hardly a

household name even in legal circles when, on January 11, 1985, he
was nominated by President Reagan as a judge of the Superior
Court. Those who knew him were impressed. "I've never seen him
lose his temper," says Frank Carter, an ex-partner who is a distinguished criminal defense lawyer in Washington. "One of his first
assignments was family court motions. At the time, it was unheard
of that a judge would get to everything on his docket. To the amaze-
ment of the court clerks, he heard the entire docket in one day."
One of the matters that came before Judge Dixon in his motions
assignment in the fall of 1985 was the unusual family-law case of
Morgan v. *Foretich*. The judge was only thirty-eight years old.

The immediate matter before the judge was a request by Elizabeth
to suspend Eric's visitation rights until she could take Hilary to be
evaluated at the Chesapeake Institute, where Heather was also being
treated. Elizabeth had first heard about Chesapeake from a patient
of hers who was a sex-abuse investigator, and Sharon had also told
her about it. (From time to time, Eric's ex-wives had been talking
on the phone, comparing notes about their daughters' progress in
therapy.)

Eric opposed Elizabeth's motion. He thought Chesapeake was
"full of incompetents" and felt that Albright, Heather's therapist,
had given the abuse charges too much credence. He was afraid that
the Institute would rubber-stamp Elizabeth's accusations and treat
Hilary for sexual abuse that had not occurred. So he made a motion
of his own before Dixon, asking him to prohibit Elizabeth from
taking Hilary to Chesapeake.

On October 23, 1985, Noshpitz had reported his findings about
Hilary to Barbara Dunlap, a Chesapeake social worker, in the same
way as he had told them to Herschberg. "On no occasion did Hilary
enact any discernible version of sex play," the psychiatrist wrote to
Dunlap. "She did seem to be a troubled youngster with a great deal
of suppressed anger. . . . The best thing that could happen to Hilary
would be if mother and father could find a way to talk together
about her that was less tinged with anger and tension." But on
November 4, Dunlap wrote to Hal Witt that the material before her
(Elizabeth's and Antonia's accounts of Hilary's statements, the negative reports from Children's Hospital and Dr. Noshpitz, and Ruth
Sihlangu's reports of her brief therapy for Hilary) was "strongly
indicative though not conclusive" that Eric was guilty.

Eric was becoming angry with what he saw as Elizabeth's two-
faced approach and with her incessant search for a therapist who
would indict and convict him as a child molester. (In letters written
at the time, Elizabeth told Eric that it was "essential" for Hilary to

maintain a relationship with him and that she hoped he would participate in the therapy at Chesapeake.) Eric tried to use her behavior against her, asking Dixon to reverse Mencher's custody order and switch custody to him away from Elizabeth. But Elizabeth was clearly Hilary's primary parent, and Eric had a tough job ahead of him if he wanted to get custody.

Judge Dixon decided to deal with all the motions at one trial. At a three-day hearing in mid-November, Antonia and Elizabeth—the chief witnesses on Elizabeth's side—testified about Hilary's descriptions of various sexual acts to which she said Eric and Vincent had subjected her. By this point, Elizabeth was convinced that horrible abuse was occurring on each and every visitation. At Witt's suggestion, she had been keeping a diary of what Hilary was saying and doing. "My daddy puts his fucker in my heinie. My daddy puts his fucker in my mouth. He pokes me in the behind. He licks my heinie." Elizabeth also introduced the sexually explicit pictures she had taken of Hilary. And Barbara Dunlap of the Chesapeake Institute took the stand to explain Chesapeake's procedures, which included a five- to seven-week period of evaluation.

Eric, Doris, and Vincent testified that Hilary was not being abused. But for Dixon, the key witness seemed to have been Noshpitz. He testified that he saw no evidence of sexual abuse and that Hilary seemed to be a child torn between two loving parents. Like Pratt in 1983 and Mencher in 1984, Dixon decided that Hilary's interests would be best protected if Eric and Elizabeth each won a little and lost a little. Dixon concluded that what Hilary needed was one parent, Elizabeth, who would clearly be the custodial parent—and one parent, Eric, who would have a secondary role. That way, Dixon hoped, Hilary's anxieties would dissipate. Since Elizabeth had already been the custodial parent, she was the logical candidate. Dixon found that Eric had a good relationship with Hilary but felt him best qualified for the role of visitational parent.

Instead of Friday morning through Monday afternoon, as Mencher had ordered a year before, Eric would have Hilary with him only from Friday afternoon, when her preschool day ended, until Sunday evening at 8:00 P.M. Dixon turned down Eric's move to prevent Hilary from being treated at Chesapeake, as well as his motion for a change in custody. Based on what Noshpitz had said, he found that the continued litigation itself had had an adverse impact on Hilary, and that in all future psychological evaluation and treatment of Hilary, it would be essential to ask whether the process of evaluation itself was part of the problem.

Elizabeth's only defeat was that Dixon refused to suspend the visits pending the evaluation at Chesapeake. The evidence of sexual abuse, he said, was "at most inconclusive."

Looking at the decision as a whole, Eric was disappointed. He felt that as an inexperienced judge, Herbert Dixon hadn't had the guts to decide the case either way. The judge hadn't accepted Elizabeth's story, but had still taken away a good deal of Eric's time with his daughter.

Elizabeth was also disappointed. She had won more than she had lost. But that was not enough; her accusations of abuse had not been validated by the courts. The police, the social services department, at least five psychiatrists, Hilary's pediatricians, and the experts at Children's Hospital—none of them had been convinced by her evidence.

But was the evidence so unconvincing? How would a child invent descriptions of sexual acts of which non-abused children are presumably unaware? Some researchers take it as a given that "children don't lie" about these matters, on the theory that someone who had not had the experience could not invent it. Psychiatrists, however, set forth a number of ways to account for these stories. One is unconscious reinforcement. The charges had begun the winter before with statements by Hilary that were at best unclear. According to the unconscious reinforcement theory, Elizabeth could have unintentionally cued and rewarded Hilary for saying all sorts of things that did not necessarily correspond with reality. Hilary was not yet three years old, an age at which children do not always distinguish between reality and fantasy. After enough time, having received enough reinforcement from Elizabeth when she talked about abuse, Hilary may have come to believe, at least while she was speaking with her mother, that Eric and his parents had actually abused her.

As psychiatrists Elissa Benedek and Diane Schetky pointed out in a 1985 article in *Psychiatric Clinics of North America,* a medical journal, "Very young children who cannot think for themselves and are totally dependent on the custodial parent may be particularly susceptible to brainwashing and come to believe that the horrible things one parent says about the other are true. The parent, meanwhile, succeeds in binding the child to himself or herself while punishing the other parent." The psychiatrists were writing from their clinical experience and were not discussing the Morgan case, with which they were unfamiliar at the time.

In another article Benedek and Schetky said that this process is possible because a child's "primary psychological bond may be with the parent who alleges sexual abuse and has custody of the child."

A year later, Benedek found that just after Hilary's reports of abuse, Elizabeth would ask leading questions like "What do they put in? Do they put their finger in?"

Over time, Hilary's descriptions of the abuse became more and more lurid. In a deposition describing this period, Elizabeth has stated:

> There were times when she's described to me her father assaulting her alone, her father assaulting her with Heather, her father and her grandfather assaulting Heather and Hilary, her father and his mother assaulting her, his mother preparing Heather and Hilary for sexual assault, and then telling the men that the girls were ready and letting them in.
> [She was] in the elevator in her father's office and Vincent was with her and Eric was with her. She said that her daddy took her panties off and unzipped his trousers, put his fucker in her heinie and Vincent stood there and laughed at her. She said there's another time, at night, or evening, outside the house at Great Falls. She and Heather and her daddy and Vincent were out in the garden, by the bushes, and they unzipped their pants and they took off their panties and they put their fuckers in their heinies and she and Heather cried and they [Eric and Vincent] laughed.

During years of repetitive questioning, Heather, two years older than Hilary and presumably present at most or all sessions of alleged abuse, *never* named Vincent or Doris Foretich as playing any part in the abuse. Sharon's lawyers never accused Vincent or Doris of anything. If Doris and Vincent were not involved—and one can wonder how three people simultaneously developed similar sexual deviations well into adulthood—could Eric have been involved? If Doris, who was responsible for Hilary's day-to-day care, had suspicions that her son was having incestuous relations with his infant daughter, why didn't she blow the whistle? And if actual penetration—"fuckers in heinies"—had occurred, wouldn't the physical evidence have been less equivocal?

Eric's dental office, then and now, is in a low-rise suburban medical building. The elevator stops at only three floors. Hilary did spend time at the office on Friday afternoons after Eric picked her up for the visits. Conceivably Eric might have taken her there if he had patients to see on a Saturday, although it is more logical to assume that he would have left her home with his parents. But is it even conceivable that with the police and DSS investigation fresh in his mind, with his paramount concern for his reputation, Eric would do anything even suggestive of abuse in a public area of his office building where he could be recognized?

A phone conversation between Eric and Elizabeth not long after Dixon's decision gave Eric another chance to deny the allegations— and gave Elizabeth another chance to convince him that an evaluation at the Chesapeake Institute would be in his interest. "I've never touched her," Eric told Elizabeth indignantly, "but she tells me that your mother stuck crayons in her vagina, or something like that." Elizabeth took the conversational gambit. "If you think that happened," she recalls saying, "then she's been sexually abused, and we ought to look into that. Let's investigate it." Eric hung up on her.

Six weeks after Dixon's hearing, on the last day of 1985, Elizabeth and Antonia made the half-hour drive from Westover Place to Wheaton, Maryland, to meet with Mary Froning, who was at the time a staff psychologist at the Chesapeake Institute. "Hilary has never told any man anything," Elizabeth told Froning. "Dr. Noshpitz didn't ask about anything. The court in D.C. was sympathetic. The judge wouldn't suspend the visits, but he did decrease them."

Chesapeake's policy was that therapy for victims of sexual abuse should not proceed unless the child had first been removed from all contact with the alleged abuser. Froning and her supervisors at Chesapeake—who, despite the result of Dixon's hearing, believed abuse a likely possibility—had therefore decided that Eric had to be kept away from Hilary for three months if the therapy was to have any chance of success. The theory was that Hilary would not begin to speak frankly about the alleged abuse unless she was no longer seeing Eric. What would happen after that would depend on what happened in therapy. If the professionals at Chesapeake were convinced Eric was an abuser, they would recommend that all contact stop permanently.

Froning received a doctor of psychology (Psy.D.) degree, not the clinical psychologist's traditional Ph.D. in psychology, from the Illinois School of Professional Psychology in 1982. At the time, her school had not yet been approved by the American Psychological Association (it is now approved), and Eric's lawyers often questioned Froning's credentials. Psy.D. degree programs tend to emphasize clinical practice more than Ph.D. programs, which are heavier on theory, but people with the Psy.D. are generally considered qualified to provide therapy.

Froning first met with Hilary on January 7, 1986, for the first of what would eventually total eighty-seven sessions. Very soon after the therapy started, Elizabeth recalls, she asked Froning whether she ought to continue letting Hilary go on the court-ordered visitations. Froning, following Chesapeake's routine, said that it was against good mental-health policy to send Hilary "against her will." On January 16, Eric called Froning. Irate at what he called Chesapeake's "unprofessional" procedures, he told Froning his life had been "decimated" because of "something I never did . . . I'm tired, I'm ready to give up [legal rights to] my children."

On February 11, Froning left her secretary a message for Eric if he called again to ask about Hilary. It read in its entirety:

> Dr. Froning has asked me to convey to you her regret that she is unable to speak with you for the time being. Hilary has asked her not to speak with her Daddy. In order to build trust, she has agreed with her request. Dr. Froning is sure you will understand the importance of this to Hilary. Any information that you feel Dr. Froning needs could be sent by mail.

Although Mary Froning did not allow Eric to participate in the evaluation and treatment of his daughter, she later offered to see him for the purpose of evaluating him. Eric politely declined this offer. As soon as Hilary began to see Froning, Eric asked the therapist for copies of her records; Elizabeth did not permit Froning to release them.

Hilary's visits with the Foretiches since the hearing had seemed as pleasant as usual. Elizabeth, however, had begun to report that Hilary complained bitterly before Eric or his parents arrived to pick her up. Though she used to jump into Eric's arms, Hilary now seemed fearful and shy. None of this is inconsistent with Noshpitz's diagnosis of Hilary as a child suffering stress because of the conflict between her parents. By this point, one could suggest, Hilary had intuited the idea that she was supposed to dislike and distrust her father.

Eric's relationship with Pamela Nader, the concert pianist, had ended in the early fall, and he began dating a woman named Patsy, a thirty-three-year-old dentist whom he had met at a convention. (Her maiden name is omitted at her request.) Eric quickly brought Patsy into his life and invited her to the Great Falls house for almost every visitation. Around the time of their second date, Eric told Patsy about the accusations against him, which he strenuously denied. She believed he was telling the truth.

"The more often I saw them together and the more I got to know

Eric, I knew it wasn't even possible," Patsy has testified. "Eric was a very good father, very devoted. He said, 'At no time, don't ever let me be alone with her, because it won't look good.' "

Patsy got along very well with the Foretich family. In her testimony, she described the weekend of January 19, 1986, when she, Eric, and Hilary took the train down to Gloucester to visit Vincent and Doris. On the way, Patsy took a picture of Eric dozing off in the train with Hilary sitting on his lap, dozing off as well. Everything was the soul of propriety: "Mrs. Foretich slept with Hilary, as she always did, and Eric had his room, I had my room," Patsy has testified. Patsy, a newcomer to the situation that fall, quickly concluded that Hilary never seemed anxious or frightened with Eric or his parents.

Patsy also supported the Foretiches on another key point: Hilary always called Vincent "Grumpy Gramps," Patsy said, never "Papa." Hilary also used the term "Gramps" during therapy with Mary Froning. Froning said in a 1986 deposition that in a tape-recorded session in which Hilary was identifying dolls with people in her life, the little girl selected "Nanny, Grandpa, Gramp, Daddy, Hilary, and Heather." Not a word on the tape about "Papa," the person who, according to Elizabeth, was one of the abusers.

On Friday, February 14, Eric showed up at Elizabeth's door to pick up Hilary as usual. This time, according to Elizabeth, Hilary clung to her babysitter, Narcisa Ramirez, and asked not to go. Ramirez, at Elizabeth's instructions, did not let Eric take her. "I don't care what court tells me to do it; it is wrong," Elizabeth said at the time. Every two weeks at the scheduled hour, Eric would come back, and each time, Hilary would carry on and refuse to go. The visit that ended February 2 would be Eric's last for more than a year.

Patsy, who was present at three or four unsuccessful attempts, recalls it more as a little game, from Hilary's point of view, than as actual fear: "We would arrive at the door and Hilary would be in her mother's arms and Eric would say, 'Would you please give me my daughter? It's time for visitation.' And Elizabeth would say, 'Hilary, do you want to go?' And she would kind of playfully laugh and say, 'No. No. I don't want to go,' and kind of giggle and put her hand out to slam the door, and then laugh a little more." Vincent, who was there almost every time, said Elizabeth would come to the door with Hilary, who was undressed and barefoot, and say, "You must go with your daddy," but would hold her close to her body. When Eric asked her to put Hilary down so she could walk, Elizabeth refused.

Around the same time that the visits with Hilary stopped, Eric also gave up his visitation rights with Heather as part of an attempt to settle Sharon's case temporarily. To this day, Eric regrets his decision to suspend visitation with his older daughter more than anything else he has done since the lengthy custody litigation began.

At another Fairfax Juvenile Court hearing in November 1985, Heather's therapist Jean Albright testified that Heather had told her about touching Eric's penis. James McMurrer, the psychiatrist in whose office the tiff between Eric and Sharon had occurred that summer, delivered his equivocal conclusion that there had been "touching," but not any form of penetration, and that he could not decide whether the touching was innocent or not. This evidence was quite different from the graphic descriptions of intercourse that Heather had supplied to Daisy Gilstrap the previous spring. But the juvenile court judge ordered, in the interests of caution, that the weekend visits continue but that Joan Beach continue to supervise them.

In January 1986, Eric decided that everyone would benefit if things slowed down a bit. He was already fighting hard to keep his rights to see Hilary, and the strain of battling two ex-wives was beginning to get to him. It was impossible to negotiate with Elizabeth, whose demand, as it had been since 1983, was unconditional surrender. But at that stage Eric thought Sharon's case was still amenable to compromise. He wanted Heather to start counseling anew with a therapist unconnected with the Chesapeake Institute. Eric's lawyer and Sharon's lawyer reached an agreement that Eric and Sharon would both undergo therapy and that Heather would see a neutral psychiatrist. In return, Eric agreed to suspend visitation with Heather for six months. A juvenile court judge, Jane Delbridge, signed this agreement into a court order on January 15, 1986. She said she would revisit the issue in June, and she did, finding that Eric had not abused Heather. But it would soon become clear to Eric and his parents that Eric's absence from Heather's life during the six-month period had jeopardized his relationship with his daughter. The years of good times in Great Falls were over.

CHAPTER 7

March 1986 through August 1986

Three weeks after Elizabeth forbade Eric's visits with Hilary, Steve Mathews, a District of Columbia police detective attached to the sex squad, received new evidence that made him wonder what the truth in the Morgan case really was.

The document was a letter from Kimberly Carr, the Fairfax County social worker who had supervised the Foretich case since Daisy Gilstrap left the previous year. "I recently attempted to gain information from your office regarding the enclosed photographs which have come into my possession," Carr began cautiously. She explained that the photographs had originally come in as part of an investigation into the sexual abuse of Hilary Foretich. "However," the letter continued, "it is the belief of this Department that the taking of the photographs themselves may constitute an abuse of the child." Meredith McEver, Carr's supervisor, countersigned the letter, and Mathews received it on March 7, 1986. Thirteen photos were enclosed. Eleven showed what the police called "a lewd exhibition of Hilary Morgan Foretich's genitals" and nine show Hilary inserting a crayon into her vagina.

In April, Mathews met with Detective Gollhardt of the Fairfax County police, who explained to him that the Fairfax investigation was complete with the criminal case against Eric ruled unfounded. The overall timing was unfortunate for Elizabeth. On February 26, just two days after Carr had written to the police, Eric's attempt to appeal the rulings in the cases of both his daughters was rewarded. In a terse letter that lacked much explanation, DSS Commissioner

William Lukhard had reversed the department's findings based on Gilstrap's investigation. Under Virginia law, that meant the entire social service record of the cases—both the "founded" decision involving Heather and the "reason to suspect" decision involving Hilary—had to be purged, from the central registry of abusers in Richmond and from local files as well. As a result of Lukhard's decision, Eric's name was at last fully clear as far as the Fairfax police were concerned, and they felt free to help the D.C. police investigate Elizabeth. Gollhardt told Mathews he would do what he could to help.

From a legal point of view, Eric was having a good spring. Dixon had reduced his visitation with Hilary but had not found him guilty of abuse. Lukhard's letter improved things even more and, Eric thought, made Gilstrap look like a bumbler. There were also signs that Sharon's case might wind down. Heather, no longer a patient at the Chesapeake Institute, had started seeing her new therapist, Dr. Elizabeth Finch, and was absolutely denying that she had been abused in any way. Eric's relationship with Patsy was going well, so well that the couple was beginning to make wedding plans.

Eric still felt a sense of uneasiness. From what he knew about Chesapeake, he strongly suspected that evaluators there would label Hilary a victim of abuse and give Elizabeth's allegations new fuel. Other factors were affecting his mood: he was not seeing either of his daughters, and important periods of their lives were passing by without him. Eric, who knew nothing of the police investigation of Elizabeth, was concerned that despite all his recent victories, Elizabeth and Sharon would be able to prevent his becoming any sort of father to his daughters. Under the order that Judge Jane Delbridge had signed in Sharon's case in mid-January, Eric had to undergo psychotherapy. He used the sessions with Dr. John Follansbee, his psychiatrist, to help deal with his stress.

At his very first therapy session, Eric denied ever abusing his daughters, but Follansbee did not make (and was not assigned by the court to make) an evaluation of whether Eric was telling the truth. The psychiatrist's key conclusion about Eric's personality structure was that Eric is "often angry before he knows why." This anger, as well as Eric's troubled marital history, could be explained in part, Follansbee said, by Eric's "unacknowledged dependency requirements when it comes to women." When women do not fulfill his emotional needs, Follansbee concluded, Eric tends to become enraged and despondent at the same time. Follansbee tried to help his patient talk through some of that anger and reduce its virulence.

He found no evidence of a severe personality disorder. Later that year, he said he saw no reason that Eric should not have full custody of his daughters.

Before Follansbee ever saw Eric, Sharon had called to warn the psychiatrist that in her view her ex-husband was a pathological liar who could not be trusted. Follansbee did not share that opinion; but just to inform himself, he called Elizabeth Finch, Heather's psychiatrist, to find out about their sessions. On March 18, Finch told him that in her view Heather had never been sexually abused. These excerpts from Finch's therapy notes (included in a later appellate decision in the case) explain why she reached this conclusion:

> She is quite clear that she does not want to be with her father, and also quite clear that her father has not touched her in a bad way. . . . She also says that her father has stolen her mother's car and it's because of him that she and her mother have to live in a one bedroom apartment.
>
> She spontaneously said that her father had hurt her mother a lot, had hit mother, had yelled at her, had stolen mother's car, and had thrown a telephone at mother, and that she never wants to spend time with him again. Father had never touched her in bad places. And I said that her mother thought that perhaps he had. She said that no he had not, that she is telling the truth, that he had not touched her.
>
> Heather is quite clear about not wanting to have any contact with her father for fear that he will not allow her to have contact with her mother and that he will pressure her into spending more time with him. She would like to have some contact with him, but totally on her own terms. . . . At this time I do not believe her father has sexually molested her, however I feel that she feels quite powerless with him and that he has trouble accepting her wants and desires and feelings and would rather impose his own.

Finch was at a loss: it didn't look as if sexual contact had occurred, but Sharon had apparently convinced her five-year-old daughter that her father was violent and dangerous. The only thing Finch could do was to recommend further delay of Eric's visitation. That way, she might be able to work with Heather to repair the damage that had undeniably been done to the relationship. Follansbee took Finch's data as further confirmation that his approach to Eric's problems was correct. He continued to treat Eric as someone who suffered from a stress disorder.

While therapy continued, Eric left the Heather case alone for several months and began to devote more attention to his battle with Elizabeth, who was trying to use the temporary pause in the visits with Heather against him. "Hilary has serious problems," she wrote to Eric. "We agree that she may be the victim of sexual abuse. Should you turn your back on your daughter? I am especially concerned because I understand that you recently decided to no longer see Heather."

Eric grew tired of these ploys and Elizabeth's incessant letters. She would tell him what kind of sun-block lotion to use on Hilary and ask him for advice on what summer camp she should attend. Intermittently, without shifting gears, she would also describe abusive acts he had supposedly committed. But the overall tone of the letters, Eric thought, was not what one would expect of someone who believed her ex-husband was a child molester. (Elizabeth has testified that Hal Witt wanted her to maintain good relations with Eric so as not to appear confrontational and jeopardize her case in Dixon's court. Witt even reviewed most of the letters for her before she sent them out. But like many of Elizabeth's other tactics, the letters would ultimately hurt her a good deal more than they helped.)

Frustrated by what he saw as Elizabeth's erratic behavior and her refusal to permit him to see Hilary, Eric stopped returning her telephone messages and letters. Instead, he asked Lenahan to make a motion before Dixon to try to have Elizabeth held in contempt of court. After all, the visits had been ordered by Dixon the previous fall and by Mencher the fall before, and Elizabeth was not complying. Eric also asked again that he be granted custody of Hilary. Elizabeth countered, moving for a temporary suspension of Eric's visitation rights because of the alleged abuse. Judge Dixon decided to hear both of these requests at the same time as the contempt motion.

When a trial judge finds that a litigant has willfully disobeyed a court order, he or she has the power to find the person in contempt. The judge can then put the disobedient person in jail until he or she relents. Since contempt is supposed to be used to compel obedience to an order, not to punish a person, the procedure does not include the usual trappings of due process such as indictment or trial by jury. The "contemnor," as the person in contempt is called, presumably has already had the chance to bring witnesses and prove his or her case. So, in lieu of a formal hearing, the judge will normally call the contemnor up to the bench, warn him or her about the possibility of being jailed, and listen to an explanation.

For a person who admits that he or she has disobeyed a judge's order, there are very few legally recognized defenses or exceptions.

Elizabeth raised the two that are best known before Dixon in 1986. One is the so-called impossibility defense, in which the contemnor declares him or herself legally or physically incapable of performing the act required by the judge. Another excuse, much less frequently accepted by the courts, is the so-called necessity defense, which declares that imminent harm to a human being takes precedence over a judge's order. From a legal point of view, the problem with the latter defense is that it substitutes a person's perception of morality for the law.

That spring, while the contempt motions were being filed and both sides were preparing for a trial before Judge Dixon, Doris Foretich tried again to cut through the lawyers' language and reach out directly to Elizabeth. She wrote to her on March 26:

> I write this letter to you in profound protest as a grandmother and mother. You know as well as me that no child molestation has occurred to either Heather or Hilary. . . . Heather's mother and other grandparents have arbitrarily taken the law into their own hands and I can assure you this is only temporary. . . . As far as Hilary is concerned, the only abuse that has ever taken place is from you and your mother! The placing of crayons in her genital area and then of all things, taking pictures of this in order to pretend that this had taken place in our home is beyond a sane comprehension. . . . Just how do you think Hilary will feel when she becomes a teenager and sees her picture plastered on the rear of a novel that you wrote? Didn't you as a teenager value your privacy? Calling her "Lucy" and then having her picture taken is lunacy! [Elizabeth's third book, *Custody,* had just been published. Hilary is called Lucy in the book to disguise her identity, but the back cover has a picture of her with Elizabeth.] The mind bending that you are doing to Hilary, in order to justify keeping her from her father, is quite apparent, and we can see that you do not seem to care, just as long as you obtain your desired results.

Elizabeth never responded to this letter. She testified later that Doris's letters angered her so much she broke off contact with her former in-laws.

The case against Eric, prepared by Elizabeth and Witt with some help from Mary Froning, centered on the impossibility defense to the contempt charge. Elizabeth did not deny that Hilary had not gone on the visits. She did try to prove that Eric's abuse had so antagonized Hilary that she had refused on her own to go, and that it was impossible for Elizabeth to send her against her will. Legally, it was an ingenious way to introduce the evidence of abuse. Elizabeth and Witt knew that Dixon had rejected Elizabeth's abuse charges the previous November, and the facts hadn't changed very much. The judge was unlikely to choose to reopen the issue without some sort of new legal angle. The impossibility defense furnished that.

For better or worse, it would still be Judge Dixon that Elizabeth would have to convince. That spring, Chief Judge Fred Ugast of the Superior Court had issued an extraordinary order assigning the case to Dixon for all purposes and specifying that all hearings had to be adjusted to comport with his schedule. The court almost never kept a single judge in charge of a continuing case; the chief judge's order reflected the case's inherent complications and the intensity of the legal battle.

By March 18, after eleven sessions with Hilary, Mary Froning had concluded that the child was a victim of her father's sexual abuse. She believed Hilary's to be one of the clearest cases she had seen in her career of more than one hundred similar cases. Froning believed that the Chesapeake Institute's policy of separating the child from the alleged abuser had worked: "The safety provided by the separation from her father and the things I did to engender her trust in me, explain why she was able to share with me details not previously disclosed to anyone outside of trusted caretakers and makes clear why my predecessors had not diagnosed child sexual abuse with regard to Hilary," she said later. According to Froning, those details, which Hilary demonstrated with anatomically correct dolls, included penetration of her vagina and rectum by Eric's penis and finger. Hilary had a male doll "shit on her chest"; Froning interpreted this to refer to her father ejaculating on her.

Elizabeth continued to bring Hilary to Froning once a week for therapy to deal with the consequences of the abuse.

Eric tried to break through to Froning, complaining, in the stilted, formal style he often adopted, that he was still being excluded from the evaluation and therapy of his daughter. "I find it incredulous [sic] to believe that you would defer to the request of a three-year-old in deference to open communication with both parents," he wrote Froning on April 28. "What possible good can come from this position? Is not Hilary simply parroting the request of her mother? Are you not by participating in this ridiculous request introducing an automatic bias into your assessment?" Eric's effort was fruitless. Froning's mind was irrevocably made up.

In order to bolster his position in both custody cases, Eric submitted to another psychological evaluation. Unlike John Follansbee, the psychiatrist who treated him for stress, and Nancy Fretta, the psychologist who put so much stock in Eric's childhood traumas, Dr. William Zuckerman found in June of 1986 that Eric was suffering from some fairly serious psychological problems that affected his sexuality.

Zuckerman administered the usual tests: the MMPI, the TAT, and the Rorschach. "Dr. Foretich is a depressed and anxious man who suffers some obsessive ideation. He has significant difficulty with issues concerning his identity, and there is difficulty dealing with both sexual and aggressive impulses," he concluded. "His gender identity appears to be appropriate (i.e., male), but there is a great deal of evidence, both in the history and test protocol, for insecurity concerning this identification." Zuckerman thought that Eric had not adequately separated from his mother and that his almost compulsive casual affairs before he married Sharon indicated insecurity about his sexuality.

Zuckerman was struck by the fact that so many of Eric's responses on the Rorschach and TAT tests seemed to deal with sexual themes. In view of the charges against Eric, the most potentially damaging Rorschach response was his idea that an inkblot "included an opening flower in which a bee is able to come and suck the nectar from within the petals." Zuckerman interpreted this comment, which he later restated as that of "a bee sucking honey out of a spring flower in the early stages," as possibly suggesting "sexual ideation with young girls."

This did not mean that Zuckerman had branded Eric a child abuser; no psychologist would draw such a conclusion on the basis of test results alone. T. Richard Saunders, former president of the Maryland Psychological Association, wrote in a recent paper on sexual abuse that "virtually all authorities agree that individual replies to isolated psychological test responses should not be employed as exclusive sources of information." Follansbee, Eric's psychiatrist, gave Zuckerman's report little credence, writing that it "appears to reach too far in its speculations and is inclined to draw conclusions in a form which amounts to innuendo which should not be wrapped in the cloak of scientific validity."

In early June, Lenahan and Witt were ready to proceed to trial on the contempt charges against Elizabeth. By this stage, Elizabeth herself had practically become a full-time member of her legal team. Disheartened by what she saw as the failure of the legal system to protect Hilary, she had applied to and had been accepted by Georgetown University's law school. She hoped to become a legal advocate for abused and neglected children. Elizabeth planned to start school in August, and in June she closed her once successful medical practice and gave her patient files to another plastic surgeon.

In addition to the looming threat of a contempt citation, Elizabeth also learned that she had become the target of a criminal investigation. Detective Mathews called and asked to interview Hilary in connection with the case involving the photographs. Elizabeth said she had to check first with Mary Froning.

In his closed courtroom, away from the gaze of the public and the media, Judge Dixon listened patiently that summer to what must have seemed like endless testimony. Elizabeth's main witnesses were herself, her mother, and Froning. All reported on what Hilary told each of them about the abuse. Doris and Vincent testified for Eric, as well as Patsy, his office manager Theodora Franke, and Darryl Wilson, a live-in caretaker at the Great Falls home.

Early in the trial, Dixon announced quietly that he had been contacted by the D.C. police about an ongoing investigation that had some bearing on the case before him. He gave no further details. Lenahan, however, decided to use the explicit photographs, which Elizabeth had introduced at the trial the previous November, as evidence that Elizabeth had herself abused Hilary. Lenahan brought in a new medical expert, Dr. Edward Weiss, to testify that in his view, Elizabeth had acted with disregard for Hilary's welfare. (Weiss, a child psychiatrist, did not evaluate or treat Hilary but gave his view based on facts before him in the court record.) Froning replied on Elizabeth's behalf that any harm from the photographs was outweighed by the harm done by Eric's abuse of Hilary. Taking the pictures was "inappropriate," Froning said later that year, but Elizabeth was trying to protect her child.

That summer, Judge Dixon also took a look at what was going on simultaneously in Fairfax County in Sharon's case. The six-month cooling-off period had ended there, and on June 30, Judge Delbridge of the juvenile court had recommended continued therapy for Eric, Sharon, and Heather, followed by the gradual resumption of Eric's visitation, at first on a supervised basis. Delbridge ordered Eric and Sharon to enter "conjoint therapy" (therapy in which both divorced parents see a psychiatrist together to eliminate mutual suspicions and make the visitations succeed). On the Fourth of July, Sharon invited Eric to a parade in Fairfax City in which Heather was marching, and for the moment all seemed to be going well. Heather asked her father to lend her some money so she could march in another parade in Williamsburg the next month, and he agreed. Delbridge continued to doubt the truth of Sharon's allegations. Later that year, she said that Eric "has not been found by this Court and to my understanding not by the Circuit Court or any other court in Virginia" to have abused Heather.

All told, Judge Dixon held a total of twelve days of hearings about Hilary, six in June and six in July. Finally, on July 17, he announced from the bench that he had found that Elizabeth had no lawful justification or excuse in refusing to turn over Hilary for the visits. (Again, however, Dixon did not grant Eric a total victory, turning down his motion for a change in custody.) Under the law, he could have held Elizabeth in contempt and jailed her then and there, but he refrained. Instead, he gave her another chance: two days later, on Saturday, July 19, she was to turn over Hilary to Eric for a visit that would last until August 22.

"We got a thunderbolt that day," recalls Alan Alkire, an art restorer who had become Elizabeth's boyfriend that spring. Alkire, a lanky, intense man with a disconcerting stare, was Elizabeth's first serious romantic interest since her marriage to Eric had broken up four years earlier.

Elizabeth should not have seen the ruling as such a surprise. She had already withheld Hilary for seven weekend visits and for the first half of Eric's extended summer visitation period. In all, Eric had missed a total of forty-five days with Hilary.

Just after 1:00 P.M. on Saturday, July 19, Eric, Vincent, and Doris showed up at Elizabeth's door, armed with Dixon's order. Elizabeth had prepared carefully for their appearance. That morning or the night before, she had told Hilary that she was ready to go to jail rather than permit the visit. Jail is something like a motel, she told her daughter, and she would soon come home.

Elizabeth had also visited her father in the old house on Gallows Road. Clutching Hilary in her arms, she had told William he had been right all along about the Foretiches. That year, Elizabeth had slowly let her father back into Hilary's life, and grandfather and granddaughter had seen each other two or three times a week. Now it was time, Elizabeth had said, for William to be there with her at Westover Place to lend whatever support was needed.

William and Antonia's problems had flared again during the preceding year. In June 1985, Antonia had asked William for a divorce on the grounds that they had been living separately for more than a year. William had resisted, arguing that Antonia had treacherously stolen their joint assets for her own use—and that he wanted to be reconciled and live with her. As the crisis over their granddaughter mounted, though, William and Antonia put their differences aside.

William told Elizabeth sternly that it was her obligation to resist Dixon's order at all costs and to accept jail rather than put her daughter in the hands of a "sex molester," his description of Eric. "You have no choice. You can't compromise your conscience," he admonished his daughter.

Eric had told Elizabeth that he and his parents would arrive between noon and 12:30 P.M. At about eleven-fifteen, William walked in. He hid behind a screen, awaiting the Foretiches. Also hiding was Alan Alkire, whom Elizabeth had asked to videotape the event to convince Dixon how terrified Hilary was of her father. Elizabeth and Hilary waited in the small entry foyer. At 1:03 P.M., the doorbell rang. Hilary jumped into Elizabeth's arms and began to cry. But it was only Elizabeth's neighbors asking if Hilary would play with their child. Elizabeth tried to calm Hilary down. A few minutes later, it was Eric and his parents at the door. Elizabeth held Hilary tightly in her arms, all the while telling her that she had to go with Eric. Chaos erupted, with everyone screaming and pointing all at once. The little girl began sobbing, "I don't want to go." William, hearing Hilary's cries, emerged from behind the screen. "This child is having an anxiety attack. This child is having an anxiety attack," he kept repeating. Eric approached Hilary to tease her away from her mother, but Hilary whimpered, "Daddy, please leave me alone. You know why." Eric asked her why, and Hilary replied, "I'm a little sick." After some inconclusive yelling by everyone about calling the police, Eric and his parents left in frustration.

After their departure, Elizabeth was gasping for breath as if she had just gone through a major emotional crisis. But Hilary, not quite four years old, seemed calm and in control. "It's OK, Mommy," she said, apparently trying to comfort her mother. The entire episode lasted at most fifteen minutes.

William Morgan and Alan Alkire have described the confrontation in a rather hyperbolic manner. In a deposition, William said that Hilary "was screaming with fear and anguish. . . . Her cries were primitive cries of helplessness." Hilary, her grandfather testified, was experiencing anguish greater than that suffered by men he had seen on the battlefields of World War II. Hilary "is suffering from an extraordinarily serious anxiety disorder," he wrote two days after the visit in a report to Elizabeth. "If these anxiety panic attacks are permitted to recur, the observer is of the professional opinion that Hilary will have a heart attack, a stroke, or become a completely disorganized personality." (William read his report into the record at his deposition.) Alkire has suggested that Hilary's terror "was greater than if 'mere' sexual abuse was her fear," and that it was actually based on death threats that Eric had communicated to her.

A dispassionate viewing of the tape shows nothing as exotic as all that; it does show a little child crying. The buzzing confusion around her, the conflict being played out between her parents, and the prospect that her mother might go to jail, would be enough to account for the tears. Many children have cried louder when someone took a favorite toy away.

The day after the confrontation, William Morgan wrote to Judge Dixon to warn him that "if Hilary is to be saved, Eric must not be permitted to see her or to touch her or to speak to her." He said that either Vincent or Eric might kill Hilary in order to dispose of the best witness against them.

William accused the Foretiches not only of abusing his granddaughter but of other sexual deviations as well. Hilary, he said, had described Eric having anal intercourse with his father. William told the judge that Hilary was at grave risk of developing AIDS if the Foretiches had other homosexual partners.

On July 28, William hand-delivered a note to Elizabeth, cautioning her that any of the Foretiches could easily drown Hilary in the pond at Great Falls. He added that Eric could, in a fit of rage, strike her and kill her. He urged Elizabeth to have a policeman present in the house whenever Eric was expected to show up.

On August 1, the Foretiches tried yet again to pick up Hilary. This time, the attempted visit occurred on a Friday because Eric and Patsy were getting married the next day in New Jersey. (Eric's psychiatrist, Dr. Follansbee, had expressed a serious concern that Eric tended to be too impulsive and had counseled him not to marry quite so hastily in view of all the stress in his life. But Eric went ahead anyway.)

Patsy arrived at Elizabeth's door with her prospective husband and in-laws, all of whom were hoping that Elizabeth would somehow release Hilary to be a flower girl at the wedding. Instead, Elizabeth, apparently heeding her father, had hired a private investigator, who was waiting with her when the Foretiches arrived. Again, Alkire was videotaping the proceedings. What ensued was a virtual repeat of the July 19 incident, with Hilary carrying on and crying. This time the Foretiches left much more rapidly, again without Hilary. According to Vincent, Elizabeth did have something to give Eric: a wedding gift of four wineglasses wrapped in newspaper, one of which was smashed. The Foretiches thought Elizabeth was trying to tell Eric that she hoped his fourth marriage broke up as quickly as the first three.

The following Tuesday, August 5, three days after Eric's wedding, he was back in court again. Elizabeth had failed to take advantage of the last chance the judge had given her. Obviously, she had not permitted a visit on July 19, or on August 1 either. She was technically in contempt already and had been in contempt for almost six months. The only question was whether Dixon would put her in jail.

Concerned that Dixon did not consider Froning a credible witness, Elizabeth had brought in a new psychologist, Dr. Dennis Harrison, to evaluate and treat Hilary. He was the ninth mental-health professional the little girl had seen in less than four years of life. Elizabeth found Harrison through a referral from a fellow member of her church. On July 23, six days after Dixon's oral ruling against her, Elizabeth signed an agreement to pay Harrison $120 an hour for Hilary's therapy and $1,000 a day for court appearances. Harrison's office was in Columbia, Maryland, halfway between Washington and Baltimore. He terms himself a child advocate and, in disputes between warring parents, almost always sides with the parent who alleges that the child has been abused.

Harrison is as comfortable on talk shows as in the courtroom, but his flair for publicity has helped land him in serious trouble. In September 1990, the Maryland State Board of Examiners of Psychologists ordered his license revoked. Among the counts against him were that he breached a patient's confidentiality in a television appearance, that he failed to complete court-ordered therapy for several patients, and that he discussed details of his sexual-abuse cases with yet another patient and asked her to help conceal an allegedly abused child. Harrison has appealed the revocation of his license. In 1989, Harrison was indicted for his alleged role in hiding a different child in defiance of a court order; the charges were later dropped for lack of evidence.

One of the first things Harrison did for Elizabeth was to suggest that she bring in a lawyer with more experience in trying sexual-abuse cases. He recommended a few names, and from among them Elizabeth and Alkire picked Richard Ducote, a New Orleans attorney. She called Ducote on July 18, the day after Dixon's ruling from the bench and the day before the first unsuccessful visit. Ducote flew to Washington on July 20, and by Monday, July 21, he had already met Hilary and seen Alkire's videotape of the failed visit.

After seven and one-half hours evaluating Hilary during the last week of July, Dennis Harrison reached his conclusion: To a reasonable degree of psychological certainty, Hilary had been sexually abused by Eric, Doris, and Vincent, and it was important to protect her "from any abuse by any possible abuser." Accordingly, he told Elizabeth, "any further contact with her father would be detrimental to Hilary." In addition to Alkire and the private detective, Harrison was also waiting behind the scenes at Elizabeth's house during the second unsuccessful visit August 1. He debriefed Hilary immediately afterward.

At the two-hour hearing on August 5, Elizabeth tried to call Harrison as a new witness. She also attempted to introduce videotapes of Hilary talking to Harrison about the alleged abuse, as well as Harrison's report of his psychological evaluation of Hilary and the videotapes of the two failed visits.

Deciding that the new evidence was only going to be repetitive, Dixon chose not to admit most of it. The only exception was the videotapes of the attempted visits, which he agreed to see. Those videotapes, as it happened, failed to convince the judge of anything: he called them "an unfortunate combination of reality and theatrics, a graphic presentation of the visitation struggle between these parents which has existed virtually since the child's birth." (In a 1989 television interview, Mary Froning conceded that "the videotape is not proof of anything," but was merely "another consistent piece of evidence that this child did not want to visit her dad.")

At the close of the session, Dixon ordered Elizabeth jailed. The once fashionable plastic surgeon was escorted away by United States marshals to be locked up "until such time as she purges herself of her contempt by delivering or having delivered on Plaintiff's behalf the child, Hilary A. Foretich, to the Defendant, Eric A. Foretich." Elizabeth believed that despite the forced separation from her child, she was acting in Hilary's interests by preventing the visits—and the abuse. It was Elizabeth's first taste of jail. Eric and Patsy went off on a delayed five-day honeymoon in Bermuda.

In what has become a legal cliché, a person who is jailed for contempt is said to hold the key to his or her cell. Since the purpose of incarceration for contempt is to coerce, not to punish, its length is unlimited in principle. The "sentence" can last for one minute or for several years; it ends when the contemnor performs the act that the court demanded. Unless Elizabeth permitted a visit, she would probably be in jail for a long time. She was more than aware of the choice.

Elizabeth knew it would be hard to continue her battle from the D.C. Jail, and Hal Witt immediately appealed the contempt citation to the D.C. Court of Appeals, the highest "local" court in the

District. He argued that Dixon was wrong to exclude the videotapes of Hilary and Dennis Harrison's evidence. He also contended that the trial judge was wrong in finding that the sexual abuse probably did not occur and that Dixon should have accepted Elizabeth's "justification" argument because of her duty to protect Hilary. Finally, Witt said, since the case remained sealed, it was unconstitutional to jail Elizabeth in a closed hearing. On August 7, the appeals court, which oversees the decisions of the Superior Court, ordered Elizabeth released from jail until it could hear the lawyers' arguments and decide her appeal.

Instead of keeping Elizabeth imprisoned, the appellate judges ordered her to post a $200,000 bond, which she secured with the market value of her Westover Place townhouse. She would forfeit the bond only if her contempt citation was upheld on appeal and if she failed to show up in Dixon's court. The appeals court also seized Elizabeth's passport to prevent her from fleeing the country with Hilary, and prohibited mother and daughter from traveling more than fifty miles from the District of Columbia without a judge's permission. Elizabeth walked out of jail; she had been incarcerated for two days.

On August 9, William, Antonia, Elizabeth, and Hilary all got together at the home of Elizabeth's brother Robert to celebrate Elizabeth's release. This family reunion was not as tranquil as it might have appeared. Just a few weeks before, Judge Lewis Griffith, the same Fairfax County judge who had urged Eric and Sharon to consider Heather's needs in granting them a divorce back in 1984, had signed a final divorce decree for William and Antonia Morgan. William, acting as his own lawyer, had filed a formal objection to Judge Griffith's decree, trying somehow to keep his marriage alive.

After her release, Elizabeth's next step was to pursue the appeal and get the contempt citation overturned. On August 15, Judge Dixon issued a formal opinion that explained his findings after the twelve days of trial and the August 5 hearing. The key was his flat rejection of Mary Froning's testimony:

> She did not attempt to review records or consult with several of the treating individuals Hilary had seen before. . . . She did not conduct or show any initiative in the type of investigation or inquiry one would have expected under these circumstances. With respect to the so-called "indicators" of sexual abuse that she testified to, the Court finds that it was no more than a recipe approach. She took the indicators and looked for actions of Hilary that might fit them. She

lightly dismissed the indicators that did not fit, including Hilary's early
denial of the allegations. . . . Dr. Froning's opinion of sexual abuse
by the father was a foregone conclusion and a self-fulfilling prophecy.

Dixon also found that Elizabeth's habit in her letters to Eric of
combining casual chitchat and accusations of horrible abuse damaged her credibility. "If she had actually heard such allegations,
then a different type of reaction would be expected rather than the
one which she expressed," Dixon said. (As discussed above, Elizabeth and Witt say many of the letters were redrafted by the lawyer.)

On Eric's side of the ledger, Dixon placed his denials of the abuse;
the testimony of Patsy Foretich and two housekeepers about the
precautions taken to prevent even the suspicion of abuse; Patsy's
testimony about how well Eric and Hilary seemed to get along; and
the absence of any physical evidence of sexual abuse. "On no instance does the Court find that the defendant [Eric] was alone with
the child," Dixon declared.

Dixon maintained that Elizabeth had not gathered a preponderance of the evidence to show that Eric had sexually abused Hilary
in any way. Under the law, the standard of a "preponderance of
the evidence" is the easiest one for a plaintiff to meet. A preponderance, the usual test of a civil case, is far lower than the well
known "beyond a reasonable doubt" in a criminal case. It means
simply that there is more evidence in favor of the plaintiff's position
than there is on the other side. As far as Dixon was concerned,
Elizabeth had not even met that burden.

On Elizabeth's crucial defense to the contempt charges (that Hilary had resisted so much that it was physically impossible for Elizabeth to transfer her to Eric), Dixon found that "on each occasion
[Elizabeth] had the total capability to release Hilary to [Eric] and
that she chose not to do so without justifiable reason or excuse."
Dixon was influenced in this conclusion by a surprising witness.
Elizabeth had asked the Reverend Francis Wade, her minister from
St. Alban's Church, to sit by her during one of the failed visits. Wade
testified that Hilary seemed unhappy and was resisting, but said
nothing about her becoming hysterical or suffering an anxiety attack.

Once Elizabeth got out of jail, she realized that if she really wanted
to stop the visits permanently, she had very few moves left. Eric
hadn't seen Hilary for six months, but how long could that last?
Dixon was assigned to the case permanently, so she couldn't try
again with a new judge. Elizabeth also couldn't hold out much hope
for the appeal. In the American court system, appellate courts al-

most never reverse trial judges merely on the grounds that they disagree with the way in which the trial judge balanced conflicting pieces of evidence. The reason is that the trial judge has seen the witnesses testify in person and can rule on the basis of their "demeanor"—the intangible factor of whether they look and sound credible. So as long as Dixon did not make decisions totally against all evidence, and as long as he did not make any mistakes in the law, Elizabeth had a tough job ahead of her. It would be hard to find a mistake of law, since there are very few inflexible legal principles that govern custody cases. The intentionally vague "best interests of the child" standard is all there is, and it is heavily bound up with the facts of each case. Elizabeth had gotten Froning and Harrison to believe her, but in early August, that was about all she had.

Elizabeth, advised by Alkire and Harrison, decided it was time to change lawyers again. Hal Witt, the William Blackstone of Elizabeth's earlier fantasies, had tried the case long and hard, Elizabeth thought. But he had failed. By the summer of 1986, Elizabeth's social horizons had contracted, and she had surrounded herself with people who believed only the worst about Eric and his family: her parents, Alkire, and Harrison. Just as her brother Jimmy had told her years before to dump Marna Tucker as too ladylike, those closest to her now suggested that she dump Witt. "I don't think Witt ever realized the enormity of the abuse or of Hilary's trauma," Alkire says today. "He was a nice person, but not the right person for Elizabeth." Witt soon withdrew from the case in favor of Richard Ducote, the New Orleans lawyer Harrison had suggested.

Ducote, a former special assistant district attorney for juvenile cases in Louisiana, was only thirty-three and had been in private practice for only two years. He and Dennis Harrison had co-authored articles about how to represent parents of sexually abused children and had worked on cases together in a number of states. Some lawyers who have represented people accused of abuse say, in fact, that Ducote and Harrison are an inseparable team with a standard cookbook approach to such cases: Believe the child and paint the accused person as satanic. Ducote told Elizabeth he had a new strategy that would help her get around the immovable barrier of Judge Dixon.

"If Hilary were hit by a car, she'd file suit against the person who hit her," Ducote says. That was the first prong of his strategy for Elizabeth: he had her take the offensive in mid-August by filing a massive federal lawsuit against Eric and his parents. "Elizabeth's posture hadn't been aggressive enough," Ducote explains. "As Hal Witt testified, she wrote those nice letters to Eric. A lawyer who does a lot of family law wants everyone to talk to each other and stay civil. That doesn't apply to abuse cases. Even though Elizabeth's instincts were to be more aggressive, she really had a vested interest in the system with people like Noshpitz and Hal Witt. Noshpitz was a well-known doctor, but he didn't know anything about sexual abuse."

Ducote immediately decided that Eric, Vincent, and Doris did not merely have to be removed from Hilary's life; they had to be exorcised. "Eric clearly took the photos himself," Ducote insists, referring to the sexually explicit pictures that Elizabeth has acknowledged taking. "He's a psychopathic maniac. There was probably some element of ritualistic religion with satanic overtones to what the Foretiches were doing to Hilary. As Ted Bundy said, 'I was a normal person too, but I raped and murdered women.' " These were the attitudes of the person to whom Elizabeth had entrusted her legal fate. The case was plunging toward darkness and confusion.

Elizabeth, Harrison, Ducote, Alkire, and Witt all met in Witt's downtown office to transfer the reins of power, and on August 18 Witt formally withdrew from Elizabeth's case. The next day, Ducote sued Eric, Vincent, and Doris Foretich for $45 million in federal court in Alexandria, Virginia. The lawsuit was part of a grand plan. "We hoped to get a money judgment against Eric in our case and then go and negotiate with him," Ducote explains. "We planned to tell him, 'You drop your demand for visitation, and you can keep your money.' That's how we could protect Hilary."

The lawsuit specified that "commencing shortly after her birth and continuing in virtually an uninterrupted fashion" until Hilary stopped visiting Eric the previous February, Eric committed acts of "assault and battery, rape, incest, and sexual abuse" upon her. These alleged acts of Eric's—the details of which were taken directly from Elizabeth's accounts of Hilary's statements to her—included fellatio, cunnilingus, anal sodomy, forced vaginal intercourse, forcing Heather to insert objects into Hilary's vagina, masturbating in Hilary's face and hair, and anal intercourse with his own father. Vincent was accused of many of the same acts, and Doris was accused of "various acts of sexual abuse and assault and battery," including putting objects into Hilary's vagina. More than that, all three supposedly threatened to kill Hilary in various gruesome ways if she spoke of the abuse, and they also spanked, tied up, struck,

and choked Hilary. Eric, Vincent, and Doris all responded immediately to the complaint, denying that they had ever abused, injured,
or terrorized Hilary in any way. A few weeks later they filed their
own counterclaim against Elizabeth, alleging that by publicly making
false allegations about them, she had injured their reputations and
caused them emotional distress.

The court in which Ducote chose to file his horrifying charges is
one of the more unusual federal trial courts in the United States.
(The court had jurisdiction because of the law of "diversity jurisdiction," which permits federal courts to hear cases involving citizens
of different states. Elizabeth was a D.C. resident, and all three
Foretiches are Virginia residents.) The Eastern District of Virginia
has long been dubbed the "Rocket Docket" by lawyers because of
the extraordinary speed with which cases proceed to a trial or to
some other conclusion. At the time Ducote filed the case, the median
time from filing of a civil complaint to disposition at trial was only
seven months, compared with an average of twenty months nationwide. The federal court could not directly affect Eric's visitation
rights before Judge Dixon in Washington, who continued to do what
he could to facilitate the visits. But the new case immediately provided Elizabeth with another forum in which to make her charges.
A speedy trial, with a jury verdict that Ducote fully expected to be
favorable, would put immediate pressure on Dixon; and the publicity
it would generate, in Ducote's view, could only help Elizabeth as
well.

As the D.C. Court of Appeals pointed out in a later decision in
the Morgan case, there is no tradition in Anglo-American law that
provides for custody cases to be public proceedings. Historically,
such cases used to be tried in the ecclesiastical courts of Great
Britain, which had a tradition of secrecy, and the practice of keeping
custody matters under wraps has continued. The need to protect
the child's privacy is the usual explanation that judges give today.
The Superior Court case of *Morgan* v. *Foretich* was sealed by Judge
Mencher in 1984 and with minor modifications remains sealed. In
contrast, civil tort cases—those in which one citizen sues another
for damages—are almost always open to the public.

One of the first things Richard Ducote told Elizabeth to do, weeks
before he filed the federal suit, was to bring her cause to the media.
Elizabeth hired a press agent, paying $6,000 for about two weeks'
work. She conducted a press conference from jail, and she was
featured on radio talk shows and television interviews. Elizabeth
knew she had a hot story for the media: the image of a mother

incarcerated to protect her child from alleged abuse was a powerful and dramatic one for the press. The first in-depth newspaper story on the case, entitled "The Public War Over a Child: Ugly Accusations Inflame the Morgan-Foretich Case," appeared on the front page of the Style section of *The Washington Post* on August 26, 1986. The article is written even-handedly, but most readers who had previously known nothing about the case probably sympathized with Elizabeth. Three and one-half years after the original custody petition was filed, the Morgan case had finally burst the bonds of the family court and had splashed onto the public stage. Ducote wanted even more publicity, and the federal trial, he thought, was a good way to get it.

Just as Ducote was preparing to file his federal court suit, Eric took his own step to try to raise the stakes. At the close of business on August 15, a few hours after Judge Dixon handed down his written decision rejecting Elizabeth's evidence, Eric walked into the sex-offense branch of D.C. police headquarters. He wanted to report that he suspected Elizabeth was sexually abusing Hilary by taking explicit photographs of her. The evidence could be found, Eric said, in the form of the 1985 photographs, which were part of the sealed court record. Eric did not know, of course, about Kimberly Carr's letter of referral the previous March. The following Monday, August 18, Detective Mathews and Detective John Burke, as well as Assistant U.S. Attorney Alan Strasser, were given limited access to the sealed files in order to pursue their investigation.

Those sealed files included the videotapes that Elizabeth had tried to offer into evidence before Judge Dixon. On August 21, Robert Sharkey, Jr., a supervisor in the police sex-offense branch, viewed the tapes, while Strasser, an experienced and well-regarded prosecutor, pored through the tangled transcripts of the custody case. After all, the U.S. Attorney's Office was not going to prosecute Elizabeth if it thought Eric was a sexual abuser. But the way Sharkey saw the videotapes, they showed Elizabeth trying very hard, over and over again, to coach Hilary to talk about sexual abuse by Eric— a subject that Hilary didn't seem terribly interested in talking about. In a police report, Sharkey summarized the situation as follows:

What seems real in these tapes is:
(1) that [Hilary] is scared of a confrontation between her mother and father.
(2) she clings to her mother, she wants to be close to her.
(3) Dr. Morgan is impatient with [Hilary] and does not have time for her (unless she wants something from the child).

(4) Dr. Morgan bosses her mother and father, she is running the affair.
(5) Dr. Morgan hates Dr. Foretich.

What seems put on in these tapes is:
(1) Dr. Morgan's concern for [Hilary].
(2) [Hilary's] talk of Dr. Foretich's sexual abuse.

Within a couple of weeks, Mathews, Burke, and Strasser met with Eric, Vincent, Doris, and John Lenahan at police headquarters. The police officers seemed very interested in getting a search warrant for the Westover Place townhouse. But Strasser had a different concern. He politely told the Foretiches that the office wasn't going to prosecute unless it could establish what Elizabeth's intent was in taking the pictures. He strongly implied that there was no case against her if she took them in a well-meaning but misguided attempt to protect Hilary from alleged abuse. Strasser also confirmed something that the Foretiches had suspected—that Robert Morgan, Elizabeth's brother, was a lawyer who worked for the U.S. Attorney's Office. But, he added, he didn't expect that to make any difference in the investigation.

Doris sent impassioned letters to Officers Burke and Mathews, volunteering to take a polygraph test and to do anything needed to push the inquiry along. "We are very concerned as to our granddaughter's safety," she wrote. "We feel that she should be removed from the scene where she was abused with crayons, as she may be undergoing the same abuse even now." But by the time the meeting with the police and the prosecutor had ended, Eric suspected that he would have to look somewhere besides the U.S. Attorney's Office for vindication.

Amidst all the legal maneuvering that summer, Judge Dixon also took a crucial step. At the same time that it issued the order releasing Elizabeth from jail, the appeals court had strongly suggested that the trial judge appoint a separate lawyer to represent Hilary's interests. On August 22, following the higher court's lead, Dixon appointed Linda Holman, a local attorney with a good deal of experience in cases involving young children, as Hilary's guardian *ad litem*. Dixon asked Holman to report back to him by September 22, and scheduled a hearing for September 25 to see how things should proceed from there. Eric and Elizabeth and their lawyers were ordered to cooperate with Holman's requests for information and documents about the case.

The role of a guardian *ad litem* is to serve as a legal representative of the child, authorized by the court to act solely as the child's advocate in the litigation. In recent years, when cases have arisen in which a child's welfare is at stake, juvenile and family courts around the nation have frequently appointed such a guardian to make sure that the child's interests are not lost in the hubbub of the angry parents. Although these appointments were relatively rare in the District of Columbia at the time, family-law experts agree that the Morgan case provided a perfect occasion for a judge to take this tack.

When Holman was named Hilary's guardian, she was only thirty-two years old and only six years out of law school, but she had good credentials. Before leaving the government for a small law firm, she had been a top-flight litigator for the D.C. government in child-neglect and delinquency cases. As is usual for guardians *ad litem* when the parents are people with some money, Holman's fee of $100 per hour was to be shared equally by Eric and Elizabeth. As soon as she was named, Holman immediately went about getting to know Hilary, her new client; interviewing all the key participants; and trying to fathom the complexities of the case, which had already had two full trials and countless motions. No end was in sight. The only certain prospect was that there would be more litigation.

CHAPTER 8

August 1986 through December 1986

On August 15, one of Judge Dixon's key reasons for concluding that Eric had not abused Hilary was the absence of any physical evidence. Elizabeth and her previous lawyers knew that without such evidence, their case was unlikely to get very far. Dennis Harrison, however, thought he knew where Elizabeth could find what she needed.

Harrison had worked in other abuse cases with Dr. Charles Shubin, a Baltimore pediatrician who was frequently consulted by parents who feared that their children had been abused. Harrison suggested that Elizabeth take Hilary to Shubin for an examination of her outer genitalia.

Shubin had specialized for twelve years in the physical effects of sexual abuse on young children. In the mid-1980s, he was one of the first pediatricians to call for the development of a new subspecialty in child abuse—and in 1985, he was part of a team of health professionals who developed the nation's first comprehensive medical school curriculum in child abuse and maltreatment. Shubin's teaching appointment was at the medical school of the University of Maryland, and he had offices at Mercy Hospital in Baltimore.

In the afternoon of August 27, 1986, Elizabeth and Hilary made the hour-long trip. Elizabeth had good reason to think Shubin would take her side. He had a reputation in the legal and medical communities as a physician whose examinations almost always produced evidence of abuse. "He would err on the side of caution, even where the evidence was ambiguous," recalled Bill Grimm, who, as chief of the juvenile division in Baltimore's Legal Aid Bureau, had known Shubin well. "Others would disagree with his evaluation of evidence."

Still, Shubin was a genuine expert, one of the few in the country specializing in the physical diagnosis of sexual abuse, a continually developing and still uncertain area of research.

Elizabeth was not the only mother whom Harrison and Ducote sent to Shubin in the latter half of 1986. In a conversation with Ducote that summer, Sharon Foretich told the lawyer that she "wanted Heather's visitation totally cut out," and Ducote suggested helpfully, "I think one of the advantages of [Shubin's] medical exam is that would nail it shut."

In his office that August day, Shubin told Elizabeth that he was able to diagnose Hilary's condition. After a half-hour examination, only about a minute or so of which involved looking at Hilary's hymen, Shubin concluded that the four-year-old girl had suffered "a penetrating, stretching injury to the hymen and the tissue next to it." The hymen itself he found to be intact, a finding he regarded as "a totally worthless and useless statement." (In this and other cases in which he has testified, Shubin has stated that the hymen, the membrane that partially covers the vaginal opening, often remains present even after penetrating abuse.) Hilary's anal and rectal areas were completely normal.

Shubin made three specific findings. Hilary's hymenal opening was enlarged to 10 millimeters from the width of 4 millimeters or so that he considered typical for her age. Her hymen had a thickening at the "9 o'clock position" (like the clock face, to the examiner's left); and the vaginal wall was thickened at the "5 o'clock position." In short, Shubin's conclusion, based on close observation by the naked eye, was that Hilary's injuries had most likely resulted from partial penetration by an adult penis. Shubin estimated the degree of penetration at about 1 1/2 inches. At the time, Hilary had had no contact with her father for more than six months, but Shubin said that the scar tissue could have easily been formed much earlier. He added that it would not go away with time.

Elizabeth says she cried all the way back to Washington on that warm summer evening. She had believed for a year and a half that Hilary had been horribly abused; now a specialist said she was right. She felt sorry for Hilary, but beyond that, she thought she finally had the evidence necessary to complete her case. Judge Dixon might not matter anymore. Ducote's civil case in federal court would move ahead quickly, and Elizabeth hoped Charles Shubin would be the witness who would clinch the case against Eric.

Elizabeth may not have known it at the time, but Shubin's examination was about to complicate the already complex case even further. The diagnostic techniques pioneered by Shubin and by a few other specialists around the nation were controversial and remain so to this day.

Lawyers representing some alleged abusers had learned that almost all of Shubin's examinations revealed the same thing: hymenal bumps that, according to the doctor, represented healed sexual injuries. A loosely knit group of attorneys around the country had begun to emerge to exchange data on Shubin's findings and to try to challenge their validity. Pediatricians were disagreeing with Shubin's findings and testifying against him.

In a 1988 Pennsylvania case, for example, Dr. Joseph Russo, the director of pediatric gynecology at West Penn Hospital in Pittsburgh, testified that Shubin's findings about an allegedly abused girl, which were similar in nature to those he reported about Hilary, were "not there—and if they were there, I would have seen those findings." Shubin, Russo testified, is "a fraud." And in a 1989 interview, Dr. Mireille Kanda, the specialist in the sex-abuse unit of Washington's Children's Hospital who examined Hilary in 1985, said that although Shubin is well known in the field and she meant no reflection on him, "I prefer to rely on my own exams."

Even now, decades after researchers began to focus attention on sexual abuse, specialists actually know very little about the normal structure of young girls' genital organs. Without understanding normal variations in size, thickness, and the like, it is impossible to verify with any degree of medical certainty that anything abnormal has occurred. "Normative data on nonabused prepubertal girls needs to be gathered," two Duke University researchers concluded in 1987, in an article in the journal *Pediatrics*, "as well as data on hymenal injuries from trauma other than abuse."

Shubin's techniques provided some pediatricians with a new way to approach the vexing question. Shubin studied physics as an undergraduate, and his "scarring theory" of sexual injury is based on applying an engineer's "analysis of forces" to the healing process of human tissue.

Shubin said in a 1988 court deposition that when vaginal injuries heal, the skin contracts. Then, "the tissue is damaged and replaced . . . during the healing process with a scar. That tissue will be shorter, usually thicker." As a result, he continued, "one can certainly see thickenings . . . that indicate that that tissue had to have been stretched and thus injured to lead to the scar or the finding." A doctor conducting a genital examination may not even see the scar, Shubin said, "but rather the effect of the scar on the surrounding tissue. Mechanically, given the vaginal anatomy, this has to be done through penetration."

Shubin later explained that his examination of Hilary revealed "fibrous bands" that constituted evidence of penetration by an object greater than 2 centimeters (4/5 of an inch) in diameter. According to Shubin's analysis, scars of this type are caused by something penetrating the hymen. He says these injuries cannot result from sitting on a bicycle or from similar stresses.

A problem with Shubin's theory, as he readily admits in his court testimony, is that it is impossible to distinguish between an injury caused by the insertion of a penis and an injury caused by the insertion of something else. "I cannot say exactly what the object was, because I wasn't there," Shubin said later on the witness stand in Elizabeth's federal case. In fact, Shubin conceded, two crayons could have caused the injury: "If you add the crayons together to reach the appropriate size, I cannot say what penetrated the child, that is correct."

Another question in Hilary's case is how dozens of acts of intercourse (which Elizabeth alleges) could, on each occasion, achieve only "partial penetration" of an inch and a half. Each act of abuse committed would have to have ended at the precise moment before it left unmistakable tears and lacerations—and Eric would have to have known just when to stop. Even though Elizabeth charged that the abuse began as early as Hilary's second birthday, no such lacerations were ever found in Hilary. (Shubin was asked briefly about this on cross-examination and responded that the penetration was accomplished only "to the point of the child beginning to resist, so that repeated rapes, as you call them, do not cause further severe injury.")

Beyond the basic issue of what caused the thickenings and fibrous bands remains, however, the unresolved question: Do the stretched hymen and the scarring reflect anything unusual? In the most extensive study yet reported in the medical literature, four Harvard University researchers, led by pediatrician S. Jean Emans, studied three groups of girls. One group was composed of girls who had unquestionably been sexually molested; the other two were control groups, one composed of normally healthy girls and one of girls who were being treated for genital complaints not related to sexual abuse. The researchers found that, at least for bumps or thickenings of the hymen, it was virtually impossible to distinguish between the abused girls and the other two populations.

Then the doctors broke things down further, selecting only those girls who had bumps between "3 o'clock" and "9 o'clock" positions, on the theory that sexual abuse is more likely to leave that kind of mark. (Shubin found that Hilary had thickenings between those positions.) The study found that bumps in that area were indeed present much more often in the abused children than in the fully healthy ones. But the non-abused girls with other genital complaints still had the symptom nearly as often as the ones who had been abused.

The Harvard researchers theorized that perhaps some of the "non-abused" girls were actually abused—or that "inflammation and the accompanying rubbing and touching of the area by the child may have led to genital findings similar to what was seen in the molested group." If that is so, the symptoms that Shubin uses to substantiate charges of abuse can actually be caused by unrelated phenomena. Although we do not know whether Hilary suffered from genital complaints, we do know that she placed spoons and other items in her vagina on at least two occasions. Whether or not these actions directly caused any physical trauma, they (and all the encouragement to talk about events involving her genitals) might well have sensitized Hilary to that region of her body and caused her to rub and touch it more than the average three-year-old.

Although Shubin's medical examination was not conclusive, it did give Elizabeth confidence; she believed that she had finally found what she was looking for. She had a new lawyer, Ducote, who had declared all-out war on Eric; she had psychologists Harrison and Froning, who believed what Hilary said; and she had Shubin.

Thus fortified, Elizabeth took the offensive in the fall of 1986 in anticipation of her upcoming battle in federal court. She pursued the battle in other arenas as well. On September 9 she wrote to the social services department in Gloucester, complaining that the Foretiches had abused Hilary at Doris and Vincent's home. In late September she wrote letters to every U.S. senator and representative, saying that she had been jailed for refusing "to turn over my four-year-old, sexually abused daughter to her sexually abusive father." She pleaded with Congress to pass laws to protect sexually abused children. And, since Hilary had once described Eric sexually assaulting a little girl under anesthesia in his dentist's chair, in early October she reported Eric to the Virginia dental board. (She was unable to identify the victim or give other details. Eric explained to the board that as a matter of good medical practice, he never put children under anesthesia in his office, and the complaint was dismissed.)

At Harrison's suggestion, Elizabeth hired a private detective to follow Eric around and dig up whatever dirt he could find. The detective tried to interview a couple of dentists who knew Eric but was unable to find out anything of significance. He contacted Leora Graham, Elizabeth's housekeeper in 1983 and 1984, who said she did not know Eric and recalled only that Elizabeth often "voiced her concern for her daughter's well-being." Finally, the detective, evidently unaware of the still pending police investigation of Elizabeth, interviewed a member of the D.C. sex squad to see if the police had listed Eric in a file containing the names of known "perverts, sex deviates, child molesters, bisexuals, and homosexuals." Eric was not on the roster.

Next, Elizabeth tried to turn the D.C. police against Eric. After Shubin's examination, she and Ducote went to the police with copies of the Baltimore doctor's report. The officer in charge replied politely that he would forward the information to Detectives Mathews and Burke and to Assistant U.S. Attorney Strasser.

With all the lawsuits and complaints, Elizabeth found no time for law school and took a one-year sabbatical leave from Georgetown on October 7 after only six weeks in school. (The first day of classes was August 21, less than a week after Dixon's written decision against her.) Her relationship with Alan Alkire was also a casualty of the stress in Elizabeth's life; the couple had been briefly engaged, but Elizabeth ended the romance in late August. Elizabeth's legal battle against her ex-husband had pretty much taken over her daily routine. On September 16, she started seeing a psychiatrist, Dr. Carol Kleinman, to deal with the pressures.

There was one unexpected source of solace that fall. At a party given by a doctor friend in September 1986, Elizabeth met Paul Michel, then forty-five, a lawyer who as administrative assistant to U.S. Senator Arlen Specter of Pennsylvania at the time. Michel, the father of two daughters, had been separated for three years from his wife (the divorce became final the following year). He was charmed by Elizabeth and "fell in love with her in one-half of one second," he recalls. "Someone said to me, 'That's Elizabeth Morgan, who just got out of jail,' and I reintroduced myself. I had met her five years before, when she performed surgery on one of my daughters." Paul and Elizabeth began dating, and the soft-spoken and well-connected Washington lawyer (he had been an assistant Watergate prosecutor and an associate deputy attorney general) immediately became a de facto member of Elizabeth's legal team.

The next move in the custody case depended on Linda Holman,

the newly appointed guardian *ad litem* for Hilary. On September 19, Holman met with Hilary at Elizabeth's house. She asked the little girl why she didn't want to visit with her father and suggested it might have been because Eric had hurt her. Hilary indicated "yes," and started running around, jumpy and excited. Holman then called Elizabeth in so that Hilary could feel comfortable and explain what she meant. But even with her mother present, Hilary only parroted what Holman had said. She was unable to add anything new. This indicated to Holman that Hilary might be speaking from suggestion rather than actual experience. She decided that Hilary was simply responding to an overly suggestive question and that at least on that occasion, she had nothing relevant to say about any sexual abuse.

Judge Dixon had given Holman thirty days to make a recommendation to him. But, not at all surprisingly, the guardian was still perplexed after the thirty days had run out. On September 25, Dixon convened his hearing, only to hear from Holman that she wasn't ready yet. Dixon reminded her softly that his first order of business was the enforcement of a valid court order with which Elizabeth had not complied. Eric's visits, the judge suggested, still had to proceed while Elizabeth's appeal to the higher court was pending and while Holman was figuring out what was right for Hilary. Dixon didn't specify what kind of visits he wanted Eric to have, though. He gave Eric, Elizabeth, and Holman a couple of weeks to have their say about what should happen next.

Holman seized the opportunity. In early October, she consulted four nationally known sexual-abuse experts from major urban hospitals around the nation. Describing the case without mentioning the names of the parties, she asked them what they would do in her position.

Almost without dissent, all four said the right course was to appoint a multidisciplinary team—composed of a child psychologist, a child psychiatrist, and a social worker—to conduct a full evaluation of Eric, Elizabeth, Hilary, and of the entire context of the abuse charges. Visits should ideally not occur, they specified, until the team's work was finished.

The point that the specialists made to Holman was not that they were convinced that Eric was an abuser or even that they leaned in that or in any direction. Rather, the experts believed that whether the charges were true or not, "no real visitation will occur because the child will be so resistant, either acting out her mother's wishes or her own real or 'conditioned' fears. . . . Unless Dr. Morgan encourages the visits, Hilary will just be unable to withstand being in her father's presence, let alone having any meaningful interaction with him." Basing her view on her talks with the experts, Linda Holman concluded: "There is no doubt in my mind that either consciously or subconsciously, Dr. Morgan's attitude regarding visits will sabotage them."

Holman also spoke with three psychiatrists who had been involved in the case earlier: Edward Beal, whom Elizabeth had picked as her expert witness back in 1983; Joel Ganz, whom Eric had hired at the same time; and Edward Weiss, who had testified for Eric in the summer of 1986 about the photographs of Hilary. None saw evidence of sexual abuse. "Hilary is the victim of a heated domestic relations dispute between her parents," Beal told Holman. Beal and Weiss agreed that Eric's visits should be limited, while Ganz proposed an extensive schedule of visits, a proposal that Holman rejected. Holman consulted Harrison and Froning as well, but both refused to discuss the issue. They said that any discussion of visitation would wrongfully indicate their approval of Eric's visiting privileges.

On October 14, Holman recommended that Judge Dixon appoint the multidisciplinary team described by the outside specialists. Barring that, she urged that Hilary's visits with Eric be limited to one hour a week and that they be supervised by a neutral person such as herself. If they worked out well, they could be increased to twice a week.

A few days later, on October 20, Judge Dixon responded. As he often did, he gave Elizabeth a little and Eric a little. Because Elizabeth's appeal was pending, the judge decided to make no efforts to enforce his August 15 order granting Eric an extended visit. He did not call for the naming of the multidisciplinary team, but he granted the supervised one-hour visit Holman had asked for. It would take place on October 24, at the office of the D.C. Department of Human Services, and Holman would be the supervisor.

"[Elizabeth's] continuing withholding of the child from any meaningful contact with her father is adverse to the best interests of the child, and to provide some meaningful opportunity for the father to visit with his child is in her best interests," Dixon wrote. If Elizabeth did not comply, she would be held in contempt again. After a little more legal maneuvering, Dixon rescheduled the one-hour visit for November 6.

Rather than comply with the latest order, Elizabeth struck back at Dixon with an unusual tactic—a petition to have Dixon recuse, or disqualify, himself from the case on the grounds that he was firmly and irrevocably biased against her. This was a direct challenge to the Superior Court judge. The federal suit, if it succeeded, would constitute an end run around Dixon, but Elizabeth and her attorneys hoped that the recusal petition could quickly get him removed from the case entirely and perhaps replaced by another judge who would view her claims more favorably. Elizabeth filed the petition three days after the October 20 visitation order.

The idea behind a recusal petition is that a judge may have some personal interest in a case, such as a stock investment or a family relationship, that puts his or her impartiality in doubt. But a judge who simply does not believe a litigant's story does not need to disqualify himself or herself. In fact, to recuse in that situation would acknowledge bias that did not actually exist and reduce public confidence in the fairness of the judiciary; it would waste time and money for a new trial; and it would set a precedent encouraging losing parties to obtain new and superfluous appeals simply by requesting recusals. Dixon turned down Elizabeth's motion a couple of months later.

While Holman was in the process of evaluating Hilary for Dixon's case, Eric was bringing an even more controversial evaluator into the federal case in Alexandria, Virginia. Ducote's lawsuit and the Foretiches' countersuit were moving forward rapidly. In October, Thomas Albro of Charlottesville, Virginia, Eric's lawyer in that case, called Dr. Elissa Benedek, a child psychiatrist at the University of Michigan, and asked if she was willing to participate in the case on Eric's behalf. Benedek, one of the leading child psychiatrists in the nation, has written dozens of professional articles, including several on child sexual abuse. She is also an examiner for the national board examinations in both child and adult psychiatry, and at the time Albro spoke to her was secretary of the American Psychiatric Association.

When Albro called, Benedek gave him the answer she gave all attorneys who asked her to testify: She would conduct an impartial evaluation, and if it gave her reason to believe the abuse charge, she would not testify on Eric's behalf. By bringing Benedek in, Eric was taking a significant risk. If she decided he was guilty, he would lose time and money, and Ducote might even be able to subpoena Benedek's notes for Elizabeth's use.

Like her co-author, the psychiatrist Diane Schetky, Benedek frequently substantiates allegations of sexual abuse, even in emotionally charged custody situations. In 1984 Benedek and Schetky wrote in a paper presented to the American Academy of Psychiatry and the Law that children's allegations are "no longer assumed to be fantasy as in Freud's time. Rather, most professionals look upon such charges as valid distress signals worthy of careful investigation. In our experience in dealing with many cases of possible sexual abuse, we have found children to be generally truthful. . . . False allegations of sexual abuse by children and their parents are rare. They do, however, occur particularly in custody cases."

Benedek began an exhaustive review of what was known about *Morgan* v. *Foretich,* poring over Elizabeth's three books, the court records, the diagnostic impressions of the other therapists, and Hilary's medical history. She also reviewed other documents in the case, as well as a good deal of information about Heather's case. As far as Benedek could see, the documents were inconclusive. She couldn't yet tell whether this was an instance of sexual abuse too long ignored or a case of a mother who had used the system for her own purposes. She realized that if she was to reach any conclusions, she would have to spend a lot of time with all the principals.

From the beginning, Elizabeth was anything but friendly to Elissa Benedek. Their first meeting was scheduled to take place in Benedek's hotel room in Washington on Monday evening, November 3. Elizabeth arrived at the lobby at 7:00 P.M., an hour late. She was accompanied by Hilary and Antonia, though Benedek was expecting neither. It was very late for a four-year-old to be just beginning an evening activity, Benedek thought; she was concerned for Hilary's welfare. She planned to spend several hours with Elizabeth, and she couldn't think of anything appropriate for the little girl to do at that hour with her grandmother in the hotel lobby. (Elizabeth later explained that she had brought Hilary along so that the little girl could meet Benedek and not be afraid of her.) When Benedek asked Elizabeth what her plans were for Hilary that evening, Elizabeth became defensive and angry. All Elizabeth would say was that "plans had been made," and that they were none of Benedek's business.

Dr. Benedek suddenly found herself experiencing an inexplicable fear of Elizabeth, one that she had rarely felt in decades as a therapist. Just being in her presence was disturbing. After ten minutes, the psychiatrist was able to pull her feelings together and conduct the interview, but she never forgot her initial reaction. "It's important," she explained later, "as a training psychiatrist to try to understand the feelings that patients whom you evaluate generate in you. You can use that for diagnostic impression; it tells you something. After you have seen hundreds and thousands of people the way I have, the feelings that you have tell you something about the people."

In the interview, Benedek tried to delve into the Morgans' unusual family history: William Morgan's fits of anger, the extraordinarily close relationship between Elizabeth and Antonia, the elder Morgans' lawsuits and their divorce. Elizabeth spoke in broad generalities about her idyllic childhood and denied that her father had ever been physically abusive. (Benedek later heard quite a different story from Antonia, who described conflicts that the psychiatrist regarded as serious indeed. She also saw indications of Elizabeth's tumultuous family life in Elizabeth's own books.) Two hours into the session, according to Benedek, Elizabeth broke it off abruptly and walked out of the room. Elizabeth disagrees, saying it was Benedek who cut the interview short.

Benedek quickly concluded that Elizabeth was not being open and cooperative with her. It seemed to her that Elizabeth was far from willing to share important information with her.

The next day, November 4, Benedek met with Elizabeth and Hilary at the office of Kent Ravenscroft, a Washington psychiatrist who was a friend of hers (and one of the doctors whom Elizabeth had rejected a year before as a therapist for Hilary). Benedek found Elizabeth's mothering style quite odd. She reported that Elizabeth brought Hilary uncombed and unkempt, barefoot, and wearing shorts on an autumn day. Elizabeth apparently did not feel comfortable getting down on the floor to play with her daughter, and when Hilary started crying, Elizabeth picked her up and tried to calm her by reading in sequence the titles of the medical books on the shelves.

Benedek reported that it was almost impossible to get Hilary to separate from her mother, because Elizabeth was, consciously or unconsciously, rewarding Hilary for clinging to her. Elizabeth began the session holding Hilary on her lap, and from time to time, Hilary would cry, "I'm missing school. I have to go back to school." Whenever she did that, Elizabeth picked her up and rocked her in her lap. "You're such a good girl. I'm not leaving you," Elizabeth told her daughter.

When Benedek finally got a chance to play with Hilary alone, she found her "a perfectly delightful child." The four-year-old and the psychiatrist finger-painted together and had a good time. But Elizabeth broke off this session suddenly, telling Benedek that her daughter would never want to see her again because she had poked her in the nipples and in the groin.

Benedek told Elizabeth that she had done nothing of the sort and that she saw no evidence that Hilary distrusted or feared her. In fact, Benedek concluded that Elizabeth had ended the session because she recognized that Hilary was growing comfortable with Benedek and didn't want to leave. Benedek also noted that Elizabeth had unaccountably refused to take off her jacket at either session, even though the hotel room and the doctor's office were both quite warm.

A week later, Benedek had another play session with Hilary. At both interviews she tried to make the child talk about sexual abuse but got no response whatever. "My daddy is a bad man," Hilary said. "He hits me here and here and here and here," pointing to her arm. She was unable to explain what Eric had hit her with, other than his hand, or why. Benedek showed her a set of anatomical dolls, in which Hilary exhibited not the slightest interest. Benedek wrote in a later report:

> There was no indication during any of these interviews of a child who was sexually abused. Hilary did not spontaneously offer any information in regard to sexual abuse when talking about her father or grandparents, nor did she answer any questions that were designed to elicit allegations of sexual abuse. She was only able to say that her father and grandparents did mean things to her and slapped her and her sister, Heather. She was not interested in the anatomical dolls and could not, or would not, demonstrate mean things with the anatomical dolls.

During the second interview, Hilary suddenly reached into Elizabeth's jacket pocket and, to Benedek's surprise, pulled out a microcassette tape recorder. Benedek was astonished; Albro and Ducote had agreed in advance that none of the psychiatric interviews in the case would be recorded. It suddenly occurred to the psychiatrist that Elizabeth had been surreptitiously recording everything that had gone on in all three meetings. That was why she wouldn't take off her jacket. Benedek immediately broke off the interview and called Albro. He called Ducote, who told his client to stop using the recorder. Later, when Benedek and Hilary were alone, Hilary told the therapist spontaneously that her mother had bought the recorder two weeks before because Benedek was "telling lies to the judges," and because Hilary's father was also lying to the judges. Benedek, of course, had not testified before any judge. Two weeks previously she hadn't even met Elizabeth.

This was largely William Morgan's doing. Before Elizabeth ever met with Benedek, her father told her to be careful. This psychiatrist from Michigan was Eric's hired gun, he said, and if Elizabeth didn't watch out, Benedek would deliberately lie to help Eric. The only way to keep her honest was to record the interview. Elizabeth had asked Antonia to call the American Psychiatric Association for an ethics opinion on recording a psychiatric interview; the association's ethics consultant had said taping was all right as long as the person being interviewed knew about it and approved. So Elizabeth went ahead and taped.

After her meetings with Elizabeth and Hilary, Benedek remained undecided about Elizabeth's allegations. She interviewed Eric, Doris, and Vincent, all of whom denied that they had done any of the things Elizabeth had charged. Benedek saw nothing about their mannerisms, family history, or personalities that indicated they were lying.

Benedek had brought in a Michigan psychologist, Dr. Gail Farley, to administer the standard psychological tests to Eric and Elizabeth. Elizabeth's test results were essentially normal. But Farley concluded from what Elizabeth told her at the November 14 interview that she "was relying primarily on her mother and her daughter for support through this very stressful time." To the psychologist, it was unusual that a woman almost forty years old depended so much on support from her mother and four-year-old daughter. "One would hope you'd have a larger network of persons to rely on, friends, significant others," Farley said in a deposition. (At the end of the attempted visit of July 19, Elizabeth had seemed to lean on Hilary for support in an emotional crisis: "It's OK, Mommy," she had chirped when Eric and his parents left the house.)

Farley found Elizabeth excessively angry and overly tearful, in a way that seemed inconsistent with her controlled personality. She also discovered that Elizabeth had an unusual aversion to being alone. Farley associated this with Hilary's separation anxiety; Elizabeth was making her daughter cling to her too closely. In the tests of intellectual ability, Elizabeth did so well that Farley wondered whether she had been exposed to such tests so much from early childhood that her scores were tainted.

Farley viewed Eric as suffering from an "adjustment reaction with a depressed and anxious mood," which she explained was related to the stress in his life. He also had some difficulty dealing with his emotions. People with Eric's test profile, Farley said, often have "basic feelings of distrust, suspiciousness of others, sensitivity to slights." They frequently show difficulties managing their anger—Eric acknowledged that he had problems with his temper—and often resent other people. Like Nancy Fretta, the psychologist in Heather's case, Farley concluded that Eric intellectualized his emotional problems rather than dealing with them. She also said Eric had relatively low self-esteem, a common finding in people who are depressed. But she saw nothing in his profile that suggested anti-social traits.

Before Benedek could use her impressions and Farley's observations to draw conclusions that she could explain to a jury, she needed to see how Eric, Vincent, and Doris interacted with Hilary. This joint interview, involving the alleged perpetrators as well as the alleged victim of abuse, is recommended by the American Academy of Child and Adolescent Psychiatry as an important technique in evaluating allegations of abuse. It is also a controversial technique. Those psychiatrists and psychologists, like Harrison and Froning, who tend to side with parents making abuse allegations, often vehemently oppose such interviews.

Elizabeth fought hard to prevent the joint interview. Froning wrote to Benedek that she feared Hilary would experience "some type of serious break with reality" as a result of seeing Eric and his parents. (Froning declined, however, to use her therapy sessions to prepare Hilary for the trauma. She did not want to imply to Hilary that she had acquiesced to Benedek's participation.) Finally, the federal judge asked a magistrate to look into the issue and make a recommendation. Dennis Harrison testified before U.S. Magistrate Leonie Brinkema on November 12 that Hilary should not see the Foretiches until they "admitted their problem," i.e., confessed that they were sexual abusers. The way Benedek wanted to conduct the interview, "there is no way there cannot be harm," Harrison said.

This was Elizabeth's view as well. In her October 28 deposition in the case she testified as follows:

Q. How would you describe Hilary's feelings now today about her father and grandparents?

A. Sheer unmitigated fear.

Q. If she were to see them, what do you think her reaction would be?

A. I think she would be just unable to cope with her dreadful, dreadful fear . . . they're bringing back all the memories for her of the way they treated her and about the tremendous fear that they would take her away for the weekend. . . . I don't know how she would react. She might just go utterly limp and be unable to move. She might become hysterical. She might become clinging and baby-like. I don't know how she would behave but

I know that she would be absolutely beyond belief terrified, because she had had absolutely beyond belief terrifying things done to her.

Benedek testified at the November 12 hearing that Hilary was definitely suffering from a separation anxiety disorder—the same diagnosis Joseph Noshpitz had made more than a year before. She also testified that she needed the joint interview to decide whether Hilary had been sexually abused. She told the magistrate that she was an objective scientist and that in several other cases she had disagreed with the view of the party who had hired her and concluded that the child in question had been abused. Benedek said the joint interview might be therapeutic for Hilary: it might, in fact, dispel her notion that Eric and his parents wanted to kill her or do terrible things to her. Benedek promised to end the interview immediately if she saw any sign that Hilary was suffering.

Brinkema, who said she was struck by Benedek's "scientific objectivity," recommended that the joint interview proceed, as long as Benedek agreed to terminate it if Hilary became "unduly distressed by the presence of any of the defendants." The judge agreed and ordered the interview.

The meeting, which took place in Kent Ravenscroft's office on December 10, was, in the best sense of the word, a psychiatric experiment. The judge did not permit Elizabeth or Antonia to escort Hilary there, so Elizabeth asked Harrison and Paul Michel to take her instead. Harrison brought his wife, Susan, as a female chaperone—to guard, he said, against charges that he and Michel might have done something inappropriate with Hilary. In the examining room, it took Hilary about ten minutes to separate from Harrison, but once she did, she seemed at ease. Harrison left, took a seat in the waiting room, and listened in. The walls were thin and far from soundproof.

Benedek had asked Doris and Vincent to see Hilary first, an hour before Eric came in. Almost immediately upon seeing her grandparents, Hilary climbed into Vincent's lap and began singing some of the Christmas carols and nursery rhymes he had taught her the year before. Benedek, Doris, Vincent, and Hilary rolled up Ravenscroft's office rug, and Hilary and Doris painted together on the floor. When Eric walked in, Hilary was a little shy at the start, but after he started playing peek-a-boo and hide-and-seek with her, her defenses relaxed. Everyone shared a picnic lunch, and Hilary jumped into her father's arms so he could carry her to the car.

Benedek saw no sign of fear, anger, or suspicion on the little girl's part. The session, which lasted all morning, marked the first time that Eric, Vincent, and Doris had seen Hilary in ten months.

Eavesdropping from the waiting room, Harrison had a different reaction. "She was performing for them. It was two or three people at the same time, singing, drawing, cutting. . . . The whole three hours seemed to be kind of bizarre," he recalled.

Eric believed that Elizabeth had been telling Hilary the worst about him, and he had been concerned before the meeting about what his daughter would say to him. He knew Hilary had watched the television news the day her mother was hauled off to jail. But in the two hours Eric enjoyed with Hilary, he recalls her saying only one troubling thing: "You put my mommy in jail. I saw my mommy on television. You told the judge to put my mommy in jail." And at the end of the three-hour interview, Benedek reported, Hilary said she wanted her grandmother and grandfather to visit her at her house, but she didn't want to see her father, since that would make her mother cry.

Benedek wasn't able to complete the session the way she had planned. After Eric, Vincent, and Doris had left, Benedek was hoping to chat with Hilary privately about her feelings, but Harrison had a different agenda: he whisked her off to a previously scheduled debriefing session with her regular therapist, Mary Froning. Later, Benedek found out that another part of Harrison's agenda was audiotaping the entire day's proceedings, including as much of the meeting with the Foretiches as the psychologist could pick up from his post in the waiting room. The magistrate's order, which had been upheld by the federal judge, had prohibited Elizabeth from interfering with Benedek's examination in any way and had specifically prohibited any tape-recording of the session.

Benedek decided the visit had already been so successful that she did not want to risk a confrontation with Harrison, so she let him take Hilary off to see Froning. "It appeared that once again Hilary had been prepared for this interview and was fearful that she would have to leave with me, with her father, or with her grandparents," Benedek concluded. "She was quite spontaneous, open, playful and friendly. . . . There was no indication of any real fear on Hilary's part. Hilary cried when she first saw me. I've seen that behavior before. It stops when Hilary is left alone with me and there is no observer. There is no indication of any fear on Hilary's part of either of her grandparents. . . . Initially, Hilary was mildly anxious about her father's presence. However, she ultimately sat by his side, climbed on his lap. . . . She was ultimately affectionate, kissing and hugging her father." To Eric, so concerned about how his daughter would relate to him after ten months, the session had succeeded beyond his wildest expectations.

That afternoon, Froning tried to get Hilary to reenact her feelings about the interview that had just ended. Hilary picked out dolls to represent herself, Heather, her father, Vincent, and Doris, and put all the dolls together in one house. At the half-hour session, she told Froning that her grandmother and grandfather had brought her toys and candy and that her daddy had brought her a teddy bear, but she didn't feel like talking much about the experience. Froning concluded (contrary to the observations of Eric, Doris, Vincent, and Benedek, and apparently contrary to Harrison's reaction that Hilary had been "performing") that the session with Benedek had been unpleasant. But Froning also agreed that there had been no evidence of a break with reality. The harm that Elizabeth and her camp had feared had failed to materialize. Harrison had theorized that Eric and his parents had traumatized Hilary so much that their very presence would harm her. On December 10, that theory sprang a serious leak.

Elizabeth continued to believe it, though. Even Linda Holman's cautious step-by-step effort to reintroduce Eric into Hilary's life was not good enough to satisfy her. Froning and Harrison were advising Elizabeth that any type of contact with her father, even one hour at a time at the social services office, would be traumatic for Hilary, and Elizabeth was steeling herself for jail once again. She thought she might soon hear from the D.C. Court of Appeals about Judge Dixon's conduct: on November 18, that court finally heard oral arguments on her appeal of her August jail term. By filing that appeal three months before, Hal Witt had sprung Elizabeth from the D.C. Jail.

Sharon's case in Fairfax was also heating up. Following Richard Ducote's advice, and without the approval of Elizabeth Finch, Heather's therapist, Sharon had taken Heather to Dr. Shubin on November 7. He had found the same type of injury in Heather that he had earlier found in Hilary, and the same type that he has found in a large number of allegedly abused young girls. Because of Heather's resistance, Shubin conducted what he termed a "momentary" examination of Heather's genitals. Shubin found that although her hymen was intact, she had an expanded hymenal opening and a "thickening of the hymenal edge in the four to six o'clock position." This, Shubin testified, represented a healed sexual injury, probably caused by a penis being inserted to a depth of about 1 1/4 inches. Sharon, who had never been quite certain what, if anything, had happened to Heather, finally decided that if the renowned doctor said it, the abuse must have occurred. Sharon immediately told Heather what the doctor had seen.

The next time Heather saw Dr. Finch, she told the psychiatrist that her mother had told her that the doctor had found she had been "hurt" when she was younger and that she had not remembered this until recently. Other than that, Heather told Finch, she did not remember the abuse. Eric believed that Shubin's examination was being used, in effect, to create a memory where none existed.

Jane Delbridge, the juvenile court judge in Fairfax, was still unconvinced that fall that there had been any sexual abuse. The "conjoint therapy" she had ordered the previous summer had never taken place because Eric and Sharon didn't trust each other. So Delbridge tried a new idea. In November, she ordered Eric to meet every other week with Heather and Finch, without Sharon. "If Heather displays any concerns regarding the rebuilding of her relationship with Dr. Foretich," the judge ordered, "those concerns [should] be addressed by Dr. Finch, Dr. Foretich, and Heather through these meetings." Heather's visits with Eric were to resume on a gradual basis, starting with one evening a week and increasing, after six months, to every other weekend.

"Heather still has a right to a relationship with her father, and her father still has a right to a relationship with her," Delbridge said from the bench on November 14. "This Order is final" was the way Delbridge ended the two-page order she issued ten days later, possibly expressing a vain hope that somehow the case would reach a sort of finality. The case, which had been referred by Judge Griffith of the Fairfax County Circuit Court to the juvenile court in March 1985, had spent twenty months in juvenile court.

It immediately bounced right back to the circuit court. Under an unusual Virginia law, even a "final order" from the Juvenile and Domestic Relations Court is appealable on a *de novo* basis to the circuit court. If the losing party has the inclination, and the money, to pursue an appeal, the case is simply tried all over again before a circuit court judge. Unlike appeals to higher courts in almost every other situation—in which the party that appeals is allowed only to argue that the judge has misapplied the law—here the losing side gets a whole new crack at bringing witnesses and proving the facts. Twenty percent of the losing parties take advantage of the opportunity, and Sharon was one of them.

Sharon had picked up two new lawyers—Valerie Szabo, a Washington domestic relations attorney, and Richard Ducote, who offered his services and those of Dennis Harrison to Szabo late that fall. Szabo, an aggressive lawyer with a rapid-fire delivery, was just learning the complicated facts of the case, and she welcomed Ducote and Harrison's help. The first thing the new team did was to appeal to the circuit court, and Judge Delbridge's whole complicated visitation schedule was held in abeyance until a new trial could take place. The court set a very rapid trial date for early January.

The first session Eric had with six-year-old Heather in Finch's office took place on December 2. Before Eric came in, Heather told her she had something to tell her—that her father had "hurt her" and had put his "man thing in her girl part." Finch asked her why she suddenly decided this had happened; Heather answered that she "had just learned what the doctor in Baltimore had found." When the psychiatrist followed up by asking whether this was a real memory or a memory of what the doctor had found, Heather said it was a memory of what the doctor had found. When Finch asked her if her father had hurt her from what she could remember, she did not answer. Then Eric came in, and Heather told him she did not want to see him anymore. He told her he loved her and would love her no matter what. Heather told Eric the same thing she had told Finch: that "my mommy told me the doctor said you hurt me in my private parts." Just as Finch had a few minutes before, Eric asked Heather if she actually remembered that event. Heather said no.

Not very convincing evidence, one would suppose. But Shubin's testimony had had its effect. Even though the Fairfax County judges were unimpressed with Shubin's findings, and even though the findings were soon to be flatly contradicted by another specialist, the nature of the case had changed irrevocably. Heather now apparently believed that there had been a time earlier in her life when she had been sexually abused by her father; Sharon now apparently believed it as well; and even more important, Finch also believed it. Finch decided that Heather was "sealed over" with respect to the abuse. In other words, she believed that Heather had suppressed her memory of the abuse because she wanted to go on with her life. Eric finally realized what a mistake it had been the previous year to give up visitation and to put Heather's case on the back burner, but now it was too late.

Chapter 9

December 1986 through
February 19, 1987

As 1986 ended, both tracks of Elizabeth and Eric's case—the
D.C. Superior Court litigation over Eric's visiting rights and the
federal suit in Alexandria, Virginia—were building toward their
denouements. In Judge Dixon's court in the District, the questions
were whether (and under what circumstances) visits would resume
and whether (and for how long) Elizabeth would go to jail. Linda
Holman had assumed the role of mediator, trying to ensure that
Hilary would not be harmed by her father's visits—and also that
Elizabeth would agree to enough visits to avoid further incarceration, a prospect she feared would hurt Hilary. In the federal case,
however, there was clearly no room for compromise. A trial would
be scheduled quickly, everyone knew, and a jury would decide the
issues framed by Richard Ducote's suit on behalf of Elizabeth and
Thomas Albro's counterclaim on behalf of Eric. Did Eric, Doris,
and Vincent put Hilary through gruesome sexual, emotional, and
physical abuse—repeatedly sodomizing her, choking her, tying her
up, and threatening to shoot her and chop off her head—or did
Elizabeth defame the Foretiches by publicly accusing them of acts
they did not commit?

In the District, Judge Dixon had long since realized that Elizabeth
was not about to comply with his visitation order. She simply refused
to allow Eric the weekly supervised visit. If it would take another
trip to jail to force her to agree, jail it would have to be. A three-
day hearing in early December produced only a new order that
Dixon signed on December 19, an order that directed the U.S.

marshal to take Elizabeth into custody. She would also be fined $50 a day until she purged her contempt by allowing Eric to spend one hour a week with Hilary under Holman's watchful eye. The new decree also scheduled three brief visits, to take place at the D.C. Department of Human Services on December 30, 1986, and January 8 and 15, 1987.

Elizabeth immediately filed an appeal at the D.C. Court of Appeals. That court, which was still considering her appeal of the two-day contempt term she had served the previous August, stayed Dixon's latest order, temporarily preventing it from taking effect. Again, Elizabeth had bought herself some time. But unless the court of appeals saved her by handing down a decision condemning Dixon's handling of the case, she knew she could not hold out forever. And even Elizabeth's supporters did not expect such a dramatic reversal.

In the Virginia federal court, the "Rocket Docket" was living up to its name. On December 18, a federal judge in Alexandria set the trial date for Tuesday, February 17, 1987. Albro, Ducote, and teams of other lawyers on each side raced through a whirlwind of depositions, cramming lengthy trial preparations into a few weeks. This process, known as "pretrial discovery," is where trials are usually won or lost as attorneys try to identify the strengths and weaknesses of the opponent's case and bolster their own case with newly uncovered facts. In an ordinary commercial dispute, discovery normally means going through thousands of pages of corporate records. But in most child-abuse cases, the documents are few, and the most important part of discovery is deposing (questioning under oath) the potential witnesses for the other side.

Both Elizabeth and Eric cast their discovery nets wide in the Alexandria litigation. Ducote went so far as to have boxes of Hilary's clothes shipped off to a forensic laboratory in California to check for traces of semen; the results were negative. The people who were named, by one side or the other, as possible witnesses in the case, and whose depositions were taken or sought, included key figures (Eric and Elizabeth themselves; Vincent and Doris Foretich; William and Antonia Morgan; Daisy Gilstrap; Elissa Benedek; Dennis Harrison) as well as more peripheral ones (housekeepers Sheryl Smith and Leora Graham; Nancy Fretta, the psychologist in the Heather case). Others included Sue Arrington, Eric's first wife; Norman Coleman, the dentist who was with Eric in Switzerland when Eric was told Hilary was crying about the crayons; and Voja Russo, Hilary's first pediatrician, named by Eric as a witness who could cast doubt on the abuse claims. (Sue Arrington's lawyer managed to get his client, who had moved to the Atlanta area, excused on the grounds that she had never observed Eric's behavior with children and knew nothing relevant. Coleman testified in a brief deposition but was not called as a trial witness; Russo told Eric she did not want to be involved and did not testify.)

No-holds-barred litigation is expensive. Albro eventually billed Eric and his parents for about $135,000 in fees, and Eric estimates that with court costs, expenses, and expert-witness fees thrown in, the federal case cost him $175,000. Ducote signed on with Elizabeth for a contingent fee of 40 percent of whatever money she got from the litigation; using his usual hourly rate, he pegs the value of his time in the case at $100,000.

In early December, Albro attempted a surprising gambit by trying to compel six-year-old Heather to submit to a deposition. For a variety of reasons, including the stress of subjecting young children to formal court procedures, neither Heather nor Hilary had ever testified under oath in any of the cases. (In his August 1986 opinion, Judge Dixon said he had considered interviewing Hilary but rejected that course as unnecessary.) Eric, concerned that Ducote would try to use Shubin's medical testimony against him, told Albro he wanted the deposition as a preemptive strike. He felt confident that as long as Sharon was not in the room, Heather would say nothing that incriminated him. To make sure that Sharon did not intervene, Eric asked the magistrate to bar her from the session.

Sharon's new lawyer, Valerie Szabo, immediately fired back with a motion for a "protective order" to prohibit Heather from testifying under oath. A deposition, Szabo claimed, could result in irreparable damage to Heather. If Sharon were not present, she argued, the risks would be increased. Dr. Finch, appalled that her patient was being drawn into Hilary's case, wrote an affidavit to support Szabo's objections. It said that Heather had told Finch that Eric had "stuck his man thing in my girl thing" and that Heather had said he had "hurt me down there." The psychiatrist did not, however, mention Heather's explanation that she made the allegation after "she learned what the doctor in Baltimore had found."

"Under no circumstances should this child be subjected to questioning by anyone other than me," Finch said in the affidavit. The magistrate turned down Eric's request. There would be no deposition.

As the case heated up, one of Elizabeth's supporters tried using a back channel to get some information from Eric. Late in the fall, Eric received a telephone call from Elizabeth's former boyfriend

Alan Alkire, a man he had heard about but had never met. (During the attempted visit of July 19, Alkire had stayed out of view while operating the video camera.) Alkire, it seemed, wanted a private meeting with Eric. Eric and Albro were suspicious but decided to hear him out. Cautiously, Eric set up the meeting for a few evenings later. At a McDonald's in McLean and then for about forty-five minutes in the waiting room of Eric's dental office, Alkire met with Eric, Albro, and Patsy. Eric and Alkire both had cassette tape recorders running, and the air was tense with mutual suspicion as the four adults debated the emotional state of one small child.

Alkire tried to draw Eric out. He wanted to know just how Eric planned to present his case in federal court. He tried a ploy that he thought was sure to anger Eric. From what he could tell, Alkire said, Elizabeth would be able to put on a strong case in Alexandria, much stronger than she had put before Dixon. That was because Hilary had recently started to talk about the abuse, Alkire said. This immediately caught Albro's attention. He shot back, "She was not talking when you first started dating Elizabeth? This was something she started to do since that time?" Albro knew that February, when Alkire and Elizabeth had their first dates, was also the time when the visits with Eric were freshest in Hilary's mind. Eric refused to take Alkire's bait. Following his lawyer's advice, Eric listened quite a bit more than he spoke, controlling his temper.

Alkire also tried to uncover contradictions in the testimony that Eric and Patsy had given before Dixon the previous summer—but it was Patsy who turned his arguments aside and said there was no contradiction. "I'm impressed, but I'm not convinced," Alkire responded.

"I want to meet you again," Eric recalls Alkire saying as the meeting ended inconclusively. "Just don't have your attorney with you next time." Alkire explained later that he continued to take Elizabeth's side and believed Eric guilty of the abuse. He said he asked for the meeting, without consulting Elizabeth, because he wanted "to see how horrible a person Eric was." Alkire was not disappointed, he later recalled; he had concluded afterwards that Eric was "a pompous, pretentious sociopath, and an obnoxious nerd who was lying through his teeth."

The feeling was somewhat mutual: Eric found Alkire "a bizarre-looking guy who gives you the quivers." Alkire's disdain for Eric did not prevent him from calling him at least twice afterwards to ask for further face-to-face meetings; Eric, feeling uneasy and perplexed about Alkire's motives, turned him down.

One of the more notable depositions that December was Mary

Froning's, taken at the Chesapeake Institute on December 17. Melvin Guyer, a psychologist and attorney from Ann Arbor, Michigan, who had just joined Eric's team, took the lead in questioning Hilary's therapist.

A professor at the University of Michigan's medical school and in the university's psychology department, Guyer's specialty is the link between psychology and the law. A media-savvy advocate like Dennis Harrison, Guyer generally ends up opposite Harrison in psychologists' debates—and sometimes in court. If Harrison tends to believe parents who claim sexual abuse, Guyer tends to discount the charges. Against Froning that day, Guyer's skepticism proved effective:

Q. What in your opinion was the act of sexual abuse that took place between, in your opinion, Dr. Eric Foretich and his daughter Hilary?

A. I feel confident that he used his penis to hit her on various parts of her body, that he put his penis in her vagina.

Q. He spanked her with his penis?

A. Yes.

Q. What parts of her body did he hit with his penis?

A. She showed it on an anatomically correct drawing, her head, her chest, her vaginal area, her legs and toes, her rear end, the back of her head.

Q. Do you suppose he did those things?

A. I believe the child.

Q. You believe Dr. Eric Foretich struck his child about the head, face, body with his penis?

A. Yes.

Q. Have you ever seen Dr. Foretich's penis?

A. No, sir.

Q. Have you ever had it described to you?

A. No, sir.

Q. Did you ever inquire of Dr. Elizabeth Morgan as to how long Dr. Eric Foretich's penis may be?

A. No, sir.

Q. Suppose it was a very small penis. Can you still imagine him striking the child about the head and body with his penis? I assume the penis was still attached to his body, as he supposedly strikes and these blows are being delivered, these spankings with the penis.

A. I think the minimum size is about six inches for a fully erect penis.

Q. He was striking her with an erect penis, is your understanding?

A. It would be difficult to do with a limp one.

Q. It might be difficult to do if it weren't, depending on what we understand took place. This is what Hilary reported and that is what you believe occurred?

A. Yes.

Q. Dr. Foretich, with a six-inch erect penis, struck Hilary about the head and body, spanked her with his erection?

A. Yes.

Guyer was able to get Froning to admit that she believed every medical and psychological finding "consistent" with sexual abuse: a happy child, a depressed child, a child who makes consistent statements about the abuse, a child who makes inconsistent statements about the abuse. And it made no difference, Froning said, whether there was physical evidence or not. Froning denied that day that she had diagnosed Hilary in light of her preconceived notions. But Albro and Guyer knew that if Elizabeth called her as a trial witness, her deposition could be used to show she had done precisely that. Eric and his lawyers were confident that Guyer had neutralized Froning, Hilary's longtime therapist, as a witness in federal court. By the time she was finished, it was easy to understand why Elizabeth had brought in Harrison, the experienced expert witness, and why she preferred that her case stand or fall with him. Mary Froning did not testify at the federal trial.

Continuing his winter offensive, Albro arranged in January 1987 for all three of his clients to take polygraph tests. They all passed—Eric for the third time, and Doris and Vincent, who had not come under suspicion in 1985, for the first. Eric's parents told the examiner they never abused Hilary. Doris said she knew of no one in her family who had ever had sexual contact with Hilary, and Vincent denied ever having anal intercourse with Eric while Hilary watched. The examiner found no evidence indicating deception. It is possible, experienced polygraph operators say, for a single liar to beat the test, but it is extremely unlikely that three co-conspirators can all fool the machine.

Knowing that Charles Shubin, the Baltimore pediatrician who had made findings suggestive of abuse, was likely to be a convincing trial witness for Elizabeth, Albro also suggested to Eric that he have Shubin's results checked out with another specialist. Through his contacts around the country, Albro came up with the name of Dr. Catherine DeAngelis, deputy chief of the pediatrics department at the Johns Hopkins School of Medicine in Baltimore. DeAngelis agreed to participate—but only if Hilary was brought by her custodial parent. DeAngelis also stipulated that she would work only as Hilary's advocate, not as an advocate for either parent. DeAngelis easily qualified as an expert: as a specialist in pediatric gynecology, she had seen thousands of children with vaginal complaints. On January 15, 1987, Elizabeth took Hilary to Baltimore to be examined for a second time.

DeAngelis found that Hilary's hymen was not intact. She noticed a fibrous band of scar tissue near the "12 o'clock" area and learned that Hilary's hymenal opening had been stretched to about 10 millimeters in diameter, about twice normal. A rule of thumb in pediatric gynecology says that 1 millimeter for one year of age is normal, so for Hilary, then four and a half, an opening of between 4 and 5 millimeters could have been expected. DeAngelis found the increased width to be the only unusual finding. The scarring in the upper portion of the hymenal area she considered normal. It could have been caused by riding a bicycle or straddling the seat of a chair. She saw no abnormality whatever in the lower portion nearer the anus, the area where Shubin had found the thickenings and where he believes most abuse-related injuries occur.

To explain the increased diameter of the hymen, DeAngelis suggested that an object at least 10 millimeters wide (less than half an inch) had been inserted a short distance. Like Shubin, DeAngelis acknowledged that no specific object leaves a medically distinguishable "signature mark" when it is inserted. DeAngelis could not say with any certainty what the object was; but a month later, when shown the 1985 pictures of Hilary inserting crayons in her vagina, DeAngelis said that could easily have been the cause of the damage she saw. Had she known about the pictures, she said, she would have looked no further.

Regardless of which pediatrician was correct—and neither could say definitively what caused Hilary's injuries—there remains a difficulty that neither team of lawyers fully explained in the Alexandria litigation. In January 1985, and again in August and September of that year, Dr. Mireille Kanda and her sex-abuse team at Children's Hospital found no abnormality whatever in Hilary's genital area. Kanda saw no unusual scars and measured the vaginal opening at "pinpoint to two or three millimeters," well within the normal range. (In February 1985, Hilary's regular pediatrician Voja Russo also found nothing abnormal.)

Elizabeth's advocates need to contend with the fact that all three of Kanda's negative examinations occurred after the abuse had allegedly been going on for years. Her charges against Eric, first leveled in January 1985, dated the abusive acts to the visits that occurred throughout 1984. And Eric's advocates, who blame Hilary's injuries on her acting out for the photo sessions at Elizabeth's house, need to explain why Kanda's negative results persisted after the pictures were taken in February, March, and April 1985.

Did Kanda, one of the most experienced sexual-abuse specialists in the nation, miss something three times? Unlikely. "We look for labial adhesions, what one might call scars, in all our routine examinations," says Dr. Annette Ficker of Children's Hospital, a pediatrician who founded the sexual-abuse group there nearly two decades ago and who has worked closely with Kanda.

If Kanda's results are credible, it is possible to speculate that the widened vaginal opening—one finding about which Shubin and DeAngelis agree—was caused by some still unidentified cause, other than abuse by Eric and Hilary's behavior during the picture sessions. This event or series of events would have occurred in the year between Kanda's last examination in September 1985 and the visit to Shubin. In July 1986, for example, Hilary complained to Elizabeth that Heather had manipulated her by inserting her fingers in her genital area. The incident was upsetting enough to Hilary that Elizabeth told Froning about it. Perhaps there was abuse by some other as yet unidentified person. As is often the case in sexual-abuse cases, the findings of three well-known pediatricians left only uncertainty in their wake.

To one expert, however, the situation was becoming much clearer. Elissa Benedek testified at a January 6 deposition in Ann Arbor that she had finally reached some conclusions of which she could be

confident. She had found no convincing psychological evidence that
Hilary had been sexually abused. Hilary's statements about abuse,
she said, could be attributed to the fact that Elizabeth "misinterpreted and misperceived what Hilary said and reinforced statements
which she believed Hilary was making about daddy and his
fucker. . . . Hilary over time has been conditioned to make those
statements and rewarded for that kind of behavior." Elizabeth sin-
cerely believed that the abuse was going on, Benedek concluded,
but "had no understanding that any of Hilary's current disturbance
may be related to the parental separation and divorce, separation
from her father and grandparents, loyalty conflicts, her [Elizabeth's]
overprotectiveness, and her rewarding, consciously and unconsciously, Hilary for making accusations."

Elizabeth's persistence about the charges, Benedek went on,
could be explained at least in part by the fact that Elizabeth herself
was suffering from a mixed personality disorder. This illness com-
bines some of the features of three recognized disorders from the
psychiatrists' *Diagnostic and Statistical Manual*: the histrionic, borderline, and narcissistic disorders. The diagnosis meant that in Benedek's eyes, Elizabeth was suffering from a good deal more than
the normal consequences of a stressful life. People with "borderline"
disorders are considered to have a propensity to engage in psychotic
behavior on an occasional basis.

To psychiatrists, a personality disorder is a habitual way of per-
ceiving and relating to reality that interferes with a person's occu-
pational and social functioning. Benedek said, for example, that
Elizabeth had "enduring patterns of social maladaptation and oc-
cupational maladaptation." Key pieces of evidence were Elizabeth's
decision to close her medical practice at least twice, her perceived
indifference to the feelings and needs of others, including Hilary
(Benedek recalled the disturbing evening encounter in the hotel
lobby), and her sense that she was someone special to whom the
usual rules of the world did not apply. Benedek was also struck by
the quality of Elizabeth's anger: "She is overcontrolled with her
anger, but underlying that is a very intense rage that is discernible
when one interviews her." In contrast, Benedek said at her deposition that Eric, Doris, and Vincent were suffering from "adult adjustment reactions," which are basically normal reactions to stressful
events.

Elizabeth too had found a psychiatrist who took her side. In the
fall of 1986 she had been referred to David Corwin, a San Francisco–
area psychiatrist who had, the year before, taken on Benedek in a

debate in the medical literature over whether the profession should recognize a "sexually abused child syndrome" as a separate diagnostic entity. (Corwin supported the proposal; Benedek opposed it as lacking scientific rigor.) Elizabeth asked Corwin to evaluate the entire custody case, and at Elizabeth's expense, he spent about two hundred hours on the case, including ten hours at three meetings with Hilary. At his January 1987 deposition, none of which was introduced in court, Corwin called the Morgan case "a very complex, tragic situation, excruciating to all involved . . . the single hypothesis that seems the most strongly supported is that Hilary is an abused child; a sexually abused child." Hilary, Corwin continued, was "most likely caught in a terrible struggle which it appears most likely is precipitated by the belief that she has been sexually abused."

Corwin said that Eric had probably sexually abused Hilary in some ways and that he suffered from a mixed personality disorder, with narcissistic, histrionic, and borderline features. He was much more cautious than Froning, however, in identifying the sexual acts that Eric had allegedly committed. The only one he was willing to specify with any certainty was "dry," non-penetrating intercourse, which he called "mock intercourse." Corwin thought oral-genital contact to be a possibility but a less likely one. (He based his conclusions on how consistently Hilary mentioned each sexual act in statements to him and in statements described to him by Elizabeth.) Noting that Heather, two years older, had never implicated Vincent, Corwin placed the probability that Vincent had abused Hilary only "in the 50–50 range, and maybe a little bit less."

Corwin's conclusions leave open some questions about which he was not pressed during the deposition. Based on her interpretation of things Hilary had said, Elizabeth had accused Eric of having intercourse with his father while Hilary watched; yet Corwin did not address that charge. If so, was there reason to doubt the credibility of Hilary's other descriptions of assorted "fuckers" and "heinies"? If Vincent was not an abuser and Eric was, why didn't Hilary ever tell her grandfather about the horrible things that were happening to her practically before his eyes? Is Shubin's physical evidence consistent with non-penetrating mock intercourse and oral-genital contact?

Corwin also believed that Elizabeth had potentially serious psychological problems. She had told Corwin that she had had "a difficult relationship with her father," a relationship she termed "emotionally abusive." (Elizabeth's description, to a basically sympathetic psychiatrist, of her relationship with her father clashes notably with the picture she presented to Benedek and later interviewers.) Elizabeth suffered, according to Corwin, from "some degree of heightened narcissism" that was less severe than a full-fledged disorder.

Corwin did not rule out the possibility that Benedek was right about the origin of Hilary's sexually charged statements. He noted that the fact that Hilary tended to talk about the abuse mostly to Elizabeth could "create the dynamic" for Elizabeth to unconsciously reinforce Hilary's statements. "In an ideal world or situation, such things would be adequately evaluated without leaving it to parents to be the primary interviewers and evaluators of their own children," Corwin added.

Two weeks later it was Dennis Harrison's turn to set forth his psychological theories. At his January 20 deposition in Washington, Harrison explained that based on his tests and interviews, all the Foretiches suffered from personality disorders. Doris was a hysterical, overly emotional person. Vincent was very compulsive and tended to intellectualize his feelings. Harrison said that Vincent's sexual and emotional problems stemmed from his early childhood sixty years before. When Vincent was ten years old, he told Harrison, his father had prostate trouble and had to use catheters to excrete his urine. "Watching his father have to urinate through tubes, into a jug . . . that takes a heavy toll on a kid. . . . Children who have been through things like that, terrible experiences, they usually grow up being very controlled, and very tuned to the body processes." Harrison did not explain why the disorder made Vincent a child molester in his later years. But he did say that both Doris's and Vincent's cases were severe enough to amount to mixed personality disorders.

Harrison said that Eric suffered from a mixed personality disorder of a much more dangerous kind than his parents'. Eric's disorder included borderline aspects, paranoid aspects, and antisocial aspects. He did not control his impulses well, had an excessively strong need for emotional excitement and arousal, and projected blame onto others. Harrison also thought Eric had problems relating to women. "That is just a dynamite combination to put in a hopper and shake up," Harrison added.

Harrison testified that during their day-long interview, Eric had made a telephone call to Christine Thompson, an associate of Albro's, about something connected with the litigation. Harrison said he heard Eric yelling at Thompson and concluded this was just another example of Eric's difficulties with women. "Any attempt by a female to control him, gets an immediately intense, hostile reaction," Harrison said. Eric recalls that he called Thompson to ask whether he had to sit through the whole day of evaluation and that she told him to stay, even if it meant rescheduling his dental patients for the day. He says he never raised his voice at her. Thompson confirms his account. "Eric was very upset with Dennis Harrison that day, but he was always very pleasant with me. He couldn't have been nicer, throughout the litigation," she says.

Harrison found no disorder in Elizabeth. She had been seriously depressed the previous fall because of the stress of the case, but suffered from no more than an "adjustment reaction," not a personality disorder.

Harrison's deposition marked the last of the key pretrial evaluations in the federal case, which looked as if it would come down to a battle of the experts: the self-confident Benedek versus the equally poised Harrison; Shubin, the abuse specialist with the controversial scarring theory, versus DeAngelis, the pediatric gynecologist.

For a few days that crucial winter, the spotlight shifted to the District, where Judge Dixon convened yet another contempt hearing on January 29. Elizabeth had not permitted the three one-hour visits Dixon had scheduled, and the judge again ordered her jailed. "There is a danger with one judge being assigned to a case," Dixon said, calm but obviously exasperated. "The danger is that the judge will hear the testimony of the parties over several occasions and will note the differences. The danger is that the court comes to know the parties. The danger is that the court becomes very familiar with the case and in this instance, very confident of its ruling."

During the hearing, William Morgan, unable to contain himself, shouted from the gallery, "This is not a court of law. This is like Stalin's Russia." Elizabeth's brother Jim chimed in sardonically, "Give the child to the sex abuser." In a matter of moments, an emergency call went out for a dozen U.S. marshals, who pushed both men out of the courtroom. Dixon was not going to tolerate disruptions in his court.

The D.C. Court of Appeals immediately issued yet another stay of Dixon's order, and on February 6 that court finally announced its ruling on Elizabeth's appeal from the previous November. The decision, written by Judge John Steadman, was the first decision handed down by an appeals court in the Morgan-Foretich case. It was curiously inconclusive.

The court postponed addressing most of the issues Elizabeth had raised about Dixon's conduct of the trial the previous summer and the contempt citation he had issued in August. Instead, it focused on Elizabeth's argument that Dixon had violated her rights to a public trial by closing the August 5 hearing at which she was incarcerated. Under the Fifth Amendment, the appeals judges said, a contemnor has a constitutional right to an open contempt hearing under certain circumstances. Dixon should have explained why that right did not apply to Elizabeth.

"The trial judge should have recognized [Elizabeth's] limited right to have an open hearing and weighed that right against the interests of the child and [Eric] . . . and made explicit findings supporting his ruling," the appellate court said. It sent the case back to Dixon to explain why he had decided that Elizabeth's right to an open trial did not outweigh Hilary's privacy rights and Eric's interest in protecting his reputation against unproved charges. Only after hearing further from the trial judge would the appeals court render a full decision. The court specified, however, that it implied no criticism of Dixon, who had "handled a difficult case with skill and impartiality."

Six days later, Dixon provided his explanation. The "alleged acts, abuses, and occurrences" in the case would, if revealed, be embarrassing and damaging to Hilary and would compromise her right to freedom from "notorious public scrutiny," he wrote.

The next day, Friday, February 13, the appeals court took a step that had a more immediate effect on the case, ruling not to extend the stay of Dixon's then-current order of incarceration. Appellate courts are not required to issue such stays of trial court rulings. They grant them only as acts of grace and discretion—generally only if they see enough merit in the appeal to justify putting the trial judge's order into effect while the appeal is pending. The D.C. Court of Appeals did not explain why it lifted the stay. It is possible to infer, however, that the judges had learned enough about the case from their review of Elizabeth's fall appeal to decide it was unlikely that they would ultimately side with her and reverse Dixon. That day, the trial judge's order to the U.S. marshals to seize Elizabeth finally went into full effect.

Time had run out for Elizabeth again, at the worst possible juncture for her. The federal case upon which she had pinned her hopes was going to trial the following Tuesday. Federal Judge Richard Williams, a gruff, no-nonsense type, was going to try it before a six-member jury, and he certainly was not going to put off the start of the trial just because the plaintiff happened to be in jail.

February 16 was Washington's Birthday, a federal holiday. The marshals seized Elizabeth on February 17, just as her trial was beginning in Virginia. That afternoon, facing the prospect of jail again, Elizabeth told Judge Dixon she would permit Eric his one-hour visit the next day at 3:30 P.M. Dixon decided to incarcerate her anyway: Elizabeth's own lawsuit for damages made Eric unavailable to see Hilary in the social services office in downtown Washington. So the jail doors clanged shut that day upon Elizabeth for a second time.

"This is a fairly narrow, simple case," Judge Williams told the lawyers in his stuffy, overheated courtroom in Alexandria as the trial began on the morning of February 17. But despite the judge's attempt to keep the case within bounds, it really was no ordinary trial. (Later, the judge announced that he thought the case the most difficult in his district in a decade.) The press, whose interest had been piqued by Elizabeth's jailing the previous August but which had been relatively silent since then, was back in force. *The Washington Post* sent a reporter to the trial every day, and local television reporters jammed the courthouse steps during lunch recesses, begging Eric, Doris, Vincent, Elizabeth, and their lawyers for scraps of comment.

Elizabeth's brother Rob, the assistant U.S. attorney in the District, took time off from work to watch. Paul Michel, the congressional aide who was Elizabeth's boyfriend, sat through part of the trial as well; and immediately behind Eric's seat at the counsel table, in the first row of spectators, sat a tall gaunt man with an expressionless face. The man kept his trench coat tightly buttoned in the stifling, antiquated courtroom. When Eric's lawyer Melvin Guyer asked him who he was, the man replied, "I'm a friend of Hilary." This is an odd bird, reflected Guyer, the trained psychologist. Eric told Guyer that the man was Alan Alkire, Elizabeth's boyfriend from the year before. Alkire sat through every day of trial, and Vincent and Doris saw him having lunch with Rob Morgan on two of the trial days in a Roy Rogers restaurant.

The district court in Alexandria dispenses justice speedily, and, the judges believe, effectively. Williams was determined to keep the case short and straightforward. To this end, he signaled Elizabeth's chief lawyers—Ducote and James Sharp, a well-regarded Washington trial attorney—that he was unlikely to admit evidence that did not bear directly on the major issue: Did Eric sexually abuse Hilary or not?

In their case-in-chief (their main case before their opportunity to rebut Eric's case), Elizabeth's lawyers put only four witnesses on the stand. Charles Shubin was the first. He led the jury through his

findings briefly and succinctly. "These findings are essentially diagnostic of this child having had a penetrating, stretching injury to
the hymen and the tissue next to it that is molestation," he concluded. Shubin conceded on cross-examination, however, that he
could not specify exactly what had caused Hilary's injuries and said
two crayons, pushed together, could have done so.

Dennis Harrison, the next witness, testified that he was convinced
that Eric, Vincent, and Doris had all abused Hilary. However, he
added that the abuse, at its root, had nothing to do with sex.

"This is an issue of power and domination with a real hatred of
females, hatred of women involved. It's not a sex act. It's not a
turn-on. It's a way of using this child to punish Elizabeth Morgan.
The child becomes a pawn," Harrison testified. He supported this
conclusion by referring to Eric's anger at his own lawyer, Christine
Thompson, and at Elizabeth. "This man has an anger towards
women," he said.

Harrison said that as a result of the abuse, Hilary had been severely damaged psychologically and was beginning to develop a
multiple personality syndrome. This syndrome, in which the patient
literally splits himself or herself among perhaps dozens of separate
personalities, is quite distinct from the "mixed personality disorders" that were at issue in Elizabeth and Eric's evaluations. Multiple
personality is a rare condition that appears almost exclusively among
people who have been subjected to truly horrifying abuse as children. Not every abuse victim develops the syndrome, and very few
people do who were not abuse victims. Psychiatrists theorize that
the condition results from the mind's efforts to dissociate itself from
the effects of torture. "That is a defense mechanism. They become
somebody else in order to live," Harrison explained in his testimony
about Hilary.

Harrison's implication was that this was a case where the abuse
went beyond sexual acts. To develop the multiple personality syndrome before her fifth birthday, Hilary would have had to have been
brutally victimized over and over again. Harrison was the first evaluator in the case who saw evidence of multiple personalities; Benedek, for example, did notice that Hilary behaved differently when
in the presence of different people. But she attributed this to stress,
emphatically denying that there was even a hint of dissociation into
multiple personalities. Corwin, who found that Hilary had been
abused emotionally and probably sexually, did not even mention
multiple personality in his January 1987 deposition.

While Harrison was testifying for Elizabeth in Judge Williams's federal courtroom, Heather's custody case in Fairfax County remained muddled. Judge Delbridge had rendered the most recent decision the previous fall in Eric's favor. The juvenile court judge continued to hope that therapy would bring about a normal father-daughter relationship between Eric and Heather. Sharon's hopes of a rapid January appeal to circuit court had fizzled. Eric's lawyer had told the judge he was not prepared to try the case if Harrison was to come in as Sharon's expert witness; he had not had the opportunity to take the deposition of this new authority. The trial was postponed until May.

So nothing had ever been proved about the abuse of Heather. Still, Ducote made it clear from the start of the Alexandria trial that his strategy was to bring up Heather's case at every opportunity. He relied on articles in the psychological literature indicating that a person who had abused one of his children was likely to have abused a sister or brother as well. After Shubin and Harrison had testified, Ducote had them explain on the witness stand, in the jury's absence, their views of how Heather's problems illuminated Hilary's case. Shubin discussed his brief physical examination of Heather. Harrison, who was disadvantaged by the fact that he had never conducted a psychological evaluation of Heather, described what Elizabeth Finch had told him about Heather's statements to her.

Judge Williams was not impressed. "I will not try that second case . . . it may have some probative significance, but its prejudice is so great . . . because the symptoms of these things are so really questionable and they lend themselves to a lot of different diagnoses, in fairness to the defendants without having the full-scale trial, I wouldn't feel right in letting a jury hear it," he told the lawyers outside the hearing of the jury the first morning of the trial.

Deprived of the chance to use evidence about Heather, Elizabeth's lawyers put on Elizabeth as their third and last key witness. She was spending her nights in jail and, by special order of Judge Dixon, attending her trial during the day. She was allowed to wear street clothes rather than prison garb, but she remained in chains, under the watchful eye of a marshal.

Under gentle questioning by her lawyer James Sharp, Elizabeth began her testimony with her usual earnest intensity. "[Hilary] had been really a bouncy happy baby, a little colic in the beginning, but otherwise she was just a delight," Elizabeth said. "And then I had been told by psychiatrists I had asked for advice that children up to the age of two years if they go away overnight they have trouble, and she seemed to have a lot of trouble. She couldn't sleep anymore without me there, she cried a lot. She just wasn't happy."

But Elizabeth soon broke down while describing the way Hilary was behaving in 1985. She fell to her knees from the witness stand, crying out. "My baby, I can't stand it. I cannot stand it. I—my God." Just as she had done two years earlier in the custody hearing before Judge Mencher, Elizabeth broke down on the stand. Sharp had to ask the judge for a five-minute recess, and the judge warned him that if the lawyer didn't control his client better, he would declare a mistrial then and there. Ducote felt that Elizabeth was a pitiable figure, falling apart because she had been so abused by the legal system. Eric just thought she was putting on an act to gain the jury's sympathy.

Elizabeth finished uneventfully. On cross-examination, Albro tried to show that the abuse charges were rooted in Elizabeth's personality and in her strongly held beliefs about what was good for Hilary. He repeatedly asked her about things she had written in her book *Custody*:

Q. Now, you also felt generally that so far as rearing children were concerned, men weren't suited for that, correct?

A. It's—I think it's a traditional woman's role. . . . I think that's obvious.

Q. All right. And in fact what you really feared for Hilary was that Eric Foretich would be like your father; isn't that true?

A. No.

Q. It is not true?

A. He is not like my father, no.

Q. Isn't it true that you said that in your book?

A. I don't remember. You will have to read me the passage. It was written a long time ago.

Q. All right. Page 4. "It had taken me thirty years to untangle my feelings toward my own father. I had to protect Lucy," which was the name you used for Hilary?

A. Yes.

Q. "I had to protect Lucy from what I had suffered."

A. When I left Eric, I thought he was like my father; but I know he is not like my father.

Ducote then called his fourth and last witness, Hal Witt. The crackerjack divorce lawyer played an unusual bit part, confirming that he had indeed reviewed most of Elizabeth's letters to Eric in 1985. He said he had thought it important for Elizabeth to seem rational and to keep lines of communication open with her ex-husband. Elizabeth's lawyers then introduced some of the deposition of Daisy Gilstrap, the former Fairfax social worker. Gilstrap was living at the time in the Chicago area, and the parties had agreed that since she did not want to testify in person, they would use her sworn deposition in lieu of testimony.

Mary Froning, Hilary's regular therapist, did not testify in the federal case. Neither did any of Hilary's pediatricians. Also silent were Antonia and William Morgan, who had given depositions, and Elizabeth's various housekeepers, who had done so as well. To Ducote, Elizabeth's case was very simple: Believe the child, at least the mother's reports of what the child said, and believe the renowned sexual-abuse experts.

Thomas Albro, Eric's lawyer, also omitted calling some witnesses who might have helped him: child psychiatrist Edward Beal, Children's Hospital's Mireille Kanda, Elizabeth's friend Voja Russo, the pediatrician. Eric, Vincent, and Doris all took the stand to deny that they had ever done any of the things they were accused of. "I would not live with a man that would sexually abuse a child. And I would disown a son who would sexually abuse a child," Doris said.

Albro also called Daniel Gollhardt of the Fairfax County police, Dr. Noshpitz of Children's Hospital, Eric's housekeeper Evie Dimageba, and Donna McClure, Hilary's nursery school teacher at Metropolitan Methodist. (McClure said she was shocked to hear about the accusations of abuse because she had always found Hilary to be a "very loving, very well-adjusted child.")

For connoisseurs of courtroom drama, the most dramatic moments came in the confrontation between Elissa Benedek and Richard Ducote during cross-examination. The brash lawyer from New Orleans tried to make the practiced expert lose her cool, but he couldn't shake her:

Q. Do you consider Dr. Noshpitz one of your colleagues?

A. Yes, sir; I do.

Q. He is a good friend of yours, is he not?

A. He is not a good friend.

Q. Isn't it true you greeted him with a kiss during the recess?

A. That is true.

Q. Isn't it true that you place a great deal of weight upon the fact that Dr. Noshpitz did not conclude that there was sexual abuse?

A. Dr. Noshpitz saw Hilary from January through September of 1985. He was aware of the allegations of sexual abuse. . . . I thought that Dr. Noshpitz was an important person who had a long opportunity to evaluate Hilary and saw no signs of sexual abuse; therefore, I did consider what he said very important.

Q. Didn't [Hilary] tell you she didn't want to see her father and she didn't want to visit him?

A. Hilary told me that she wanted her grandparents to come visit her; that she didn't want her father to come visit her, because he wasn't on the list for the birthday party.

Q. Does that have any significance?

A. It certainly does have significance. It only substantiates what I believe to be true, that this poor child has had a great deal of coercion to deny feelings that she has about her father. It's clear that the most important person in her life, her mother, is very angry at her father and that anger has been communicated.

Q. Do you believe Dr. Foretich has a history of good relationships with women?

A. Dr. Foretich has, as you know, had problems in his relationships with women. He has used, I think, extraordinarily poor judgment in his marital relationships. I think Dr. Foretich himself recognizes that as a result of his therapy and some of the incidents that have occurred.

Q. Would trying to choke his second wife, Sharon, be one of the things that you consider poor judgment?

This last question was quite improper, since up to that point there had been no evidence of Eric's alleged violence toward Sharon. Guyer immediately objected, and the judge asked the jury to disregard the question. Ducote moved on to something else, and Benedek did not have to answer it. But the jury had, of course, heard the objectionable question, and as the lawyer's phrase has it, it is impossible to unring a bell once it has been rung.

An hour or so later, a hushed courtroom heard Catherine DeAngelis, the doctor from Johns Hopkins, testify for Eric. The previous month, when Elizabeth had taken Hilary to DeAngelis, she had not shown the pediatrician the explicit pictures she had taken of Hilary. DeAngelis had never seen or known of them until Christine Thompson, Albro's associate, showed them to her on the witness stand. DeAngelis was the first witness Thompson had ever examined in a trial, and she had not given a deposition in the case. DeAngelis looked at the pictures, then paused for a full thirty seconds.

Q. Doctor, do you need a better light to look at those?

A. No, I can see. First of all, I can tell you if indeed two crayons— if these are the normal-size crayons, if you put two—one is normally 4 to 5 millimeters, so two would be 8 to 10 millimeters . . . If she put it in and sat on it, that can cause a widening. . . . So I would say that what I am seeing here could well account for what I saw when I saw her in January. If these were taken—if these pictures—if this activity was taken before I had seen the child.

Q. What if the child had in fact walked around the room for some 10 or 15 minutes with a crayon in her vagina, would that make your opinion any stronger?

A. Yes. Why would the child walk around the room? Excuse me, I'm sorry.

Thompson had the answer she wanted, and Eric felt vindicated. For two full years, Elizabeth had been relentlessly accusing him of abusing Hilary; yet a well-known pediatrician had just concluded that all the signs of abuse could have been caused by something for which Elizabeth acknowledged responsibility.

Eric's testimony the next day was brief. He described his affection for Hilary. He "would blow his brains out," he said, rather than commit the acts of which he was accused. Ducote, who at the time represented Sharon as well as Elizabeth, tried to question Eric about the incident five years before when he had supposedly pulled out the intravenous tube Sharon was using. Ducote wanted to use it to illustrate Eric's anger toward women, but the judge rejected the line of questioning as collateral to the main issues.

If Ducote had painted for the jury the picture of a woman whose desperate cries for help had gone unheeded, Albro had effectively depicted three relatively normal human beings who were being falsely accused. But considering that the Foretiches had filed a counterclaim against Elizabeth for millions of dollars, Albro's presentation came across as surprisingly defensive. The notion that

Elizabeth had damaged the Foretiches' reputation by making the charges hardly emerged.

Ducote put on a short rebuttal case. Sharon testified that her marriage to Eric was stormy and troubled; the judge refused to let her say that Eric was "abusive." Elizabeth then briefly returned to the stand to explain the sequence of events related to Benedek's December interviews of Hilary and of her. She recalled the four-year-old writing a note to Benedek, "Hi, Pig." The final witness in the trial was David Corwin, the California psychiatrist.

Corwin's job was to neutralize Benedek's damaging testimony. He said it was outrageous for the Michigan psychiatrist to have asked Hilary about the abuse allegations in the presence of the alleged abusers. Moreover, he added, Benedek's evaluation was flawed since she relied so heavily on Noshpitz's findings from 1985. "If you don't want to ever uncover child sexual abuse, then don't ask direct specific questions and you won't uncover it," Corwin said. "The procedure that's been taught to psychotherapists and psychiatrists for years that has not uncovered the sexual abuse of children is to use non-directive play therapy techniques such as Dr. Benedek apparently did and Dr. Noshpitz did. It's not powerful enough to penetrate the defenses of compartmentalization and splitting that sexually abused children use to survive."

Since rebuttal witnesses are limited to explaining away matters that were part of the other side's case, Corwin did not tell the jury what his own ideas were about the abuse or how the details differed from Harrison's account. Nor did the jury hear Elizabeth's own expert say that Elizabeth had had an unhealthy relationship with her father.

The four men and two women on the jury had heard all the evidence they were going to hear. It was time for closing arguments, and both lawyers hit as many emotional high points as they could manage.

"Little children are at the mercy of their parents for love, for food, for clothing, for shelter," Ducote began his summation to the jury on February 19, the third day of the trial. "They are also at the mercy of their parents when their parents and others choose to subject them to their perversion. . . . Dr. Foretich and his parents lied to you. They want you to be deceived as they have been able to deceive other people in the last couple of years. Mr. Foretich tells you if you charge one of us, you might as well charge all of us. And I agree. They were there at every visit. They were always together. They all take up for each other. They are all covering up. . . . I wish the world were such that grandparents could be what grandparents are supposed to be and dote on their children. I wish the world were such that fathers, particularly doctors, were such that they weren't molesting little children. But that's not how the world is." Finally, taking up a theme of the child-advocacy movement whose views he so eloquently expressed that day, Ducote implored the jurors, "Please tell these people that you heard all the evidence, that you believe this little girl. You believe Hilary, and you are going to save her."

Albro countered that the case was just "a domestic relations case that went bad. And it is the end of the line . . . because this evidence has been rehashed and rehashed everywhere else, and has not been found persuasive. . . . Why is this the end of the line? Because now all that's left is to sue these people for all the money they have. . . . When she [Elizabeth] lost in Dixon's court, she brought a suit for a staggering sum of money, this lawsuit, and because those two kind people could explain their son's whereabouts over the years, she decided she would bring them in, too, for the first time and sue them for everything they had. Mr. Ducote agrees with me on one thing. It is an all or nothing case. . . . She has indicted the integrity of, the goodness of an entire family. . . . You have gotten to know them. Use your instincts. . . . Are they the sadistic psychopaths that she makes them out to be? No. They are a good, close, religious family. . . . How do you give back people time they have lost? She has been out of their lives for 25 percent of her life. She is only four. As Doris said on the stand, 'It was like losing my little girl who died in infancy all over again.' "

The case went to the jury around 3:00 P.M. that afternoon. A little more than four hours later the foreman passed a note to the judge: they needed more time to decide. The judge let them break and come back the next morning. During their deliberations, the jurors first took up Elizabeth's claim, and only after finishing with that did they reach the Foretiches' counterclaim. Just after lunch on Friday, after eight hours of deliberation spread over two days, they announced that they had reached a verdict. It was a defendant's verdict—for all the defendants, on both sides. Elizabeth had lost her case, and the Foretiches had lost their counterclaim. No one was awarded a cent in damages. The case of *Morgan* v. *Foretich* had gone to a jury trial, something that had happened in precious few divorce cases in American history; yet the jury had been unable to render a decisive ruling.

The split decision was more of a loss for Elizabeth, who had brought the case to begin with, than it was for Eric. From Elizabeth's point of view, Ducote's riverboat gamble had failed miserably. He had hoped to gain leverage over Eric with a judgment against him from the federal court, but six months of furious litigation had gotten him nothing. True, Elizabeth's media blitz had turned public opinion her way, but she had been unable to convince six ordinary citizens, even by the civil standard of "a preponderance of the evidence," that Eric and his parents had abused Hilary.

Ducote told reporters outside the courtroom that he was very disappointed in the verdict, and Albro called the decision "a complete exoneration and vindication for the Foretiches." Eric was relieved but not elated. Albro had fallen short of the big win the Foretiches had hoped for. It wasn't the money that Eric wanted but the vindication. By rejecting Eric's counterclaim, the jury had said it wasn't convinced that the majority of the evidence went his way. Doris said later that she felt the jury might have awarded damages if not for Elizabeth's "hysterics" on the witness stand. "They had sympathy for her because she acted so crazy," she said.

Whatever the jury's motivations—and its members have never discussed their verdict—the public spectacle was over for the time being. The histrionics before the jury were done, and Ducote and Albro, the trial lawyers, slowly receded into the background. The newspaper reporters went on to other assignments; the television cameras averted their gaze. James Sharp immediately filed an appeal on behalf of Elizabeth, primarily on the grounds that Judge Williams should have let the jury hear what Shubin and Harrison had to say about Heather. For better or for worse, the case was back where it had started, as a visitation dispute in the D.C. Superior Court.

Even while the lawyers were making their oral arguments in Alexandria on the 19th, Elizabeth extended an offer that Eric and Dixon could accept. Just a few days over a year after that February morning when she began to follow Froning's advice and keep Hilary home, she would let the visits resume. Ducote violently opposed this decision. You don't make concessions to a child abuser, he told his client. From that moment on, he felt that Elizabeth had lost confidence in him and was following Sharp's advice. After three days, the jail doors again swung open, and Elizabeth walked out. Dixon set the first visit for the following Tuesday, February 24, at the offices of the D.C. Department of Human Services in downtown Washington.

Chapter 10

February 1987 through
May 27, 1987

Linda Holman, Hilary's guardian *ad litem* in Dixon's court, knew Hilary was going to have a hard time adjusting to the visits with her father. No matter who was right or wrong about the charges of abuse, Holman realized that it was going to be difficult for Hilary to rebuild a trusting relationship with a father whom she had learned to fear. So, in early 1987 Holman decided to make it her duty to reduce the trauma for the four-year-old, at least as much as she could.

Holman was taking on an additional role, one that is unusual but not unheard of for guardians *ad litem* in difficult custody cases. Besides being Hilary's advocate in court, she was also trying to shield her against psychological damage from her parents' bitter dispute. Holman realized that as a neutral observer she could function as the de facto eyes and ears of the judge. Dixon could not attend every visitation, but he could read Holman's detailed reports.

One step Holman took to protect Hilary was to set forth a very strict ground rule for Eric's brief visits at the Human Services Department: he was not to initiate physical contact of any sort with Hilary. Hilary would touch him if she felt like it.

The first visit at Human Services, on February 24, went well from Eric's point of view. Even though Hilary had not seen him for more than a year, she greeted him cheerfully, "Hi, Daddy." In a drab playroom in the Human Services Building, no more than 6 feet by 9 feet, father and daughter got down on the floor together and played with clay. Hilary, though far from effusive, seemed at ease. There were no hysterics. Holman was encouraged, hoping that the second visit, scheduled for March 3, would be even more successful.

Half an hour before the second visit was to begin, Holman met Hilary in the reception area of the downtown Washington office of G. Allen Dale, a hard-driving litigator with a Tom Selleck mustache and a flair for the media. Elizabeth had brought Dale in that winter to help in the custody case. (Elizabeth felt that Richard Ducote had failed her, and he was on his way out of the case. James Sharp and his partners were still pursuing Elizabeth's appeal of the Alexandria case in the U.S. Court of Appeals for the Fourth Circuit in Richmond.) Also in Dale's office that afternoon was William Morgan, who had driven Hilary over.

Linda Holman had brought along a drawing game she hoped Hilary could play with during the visit with Eric. But Hilary was a little shy about going, and William launched into one of his tirades, this time about what a terrible job Holman was doing as Hilary's advocate. Holman was only bringing toys in order to "lure" Hilary away from the Morgans, William declared. Hilary started crying, and Holman told William that it was inappropriate for him to speak that way in front of the little girl. William asked Dale to get a court order permitting him to be present at the visits. Dale had to calm William down before Hilary and Holman could leave.

The visit itself was relatively uneventful. At the start, Hilary was much more subdued than at the first visit, but she soon loosened up. She climbed all over Eric in a playful manner, although she did not hug or kiss him. The two played with Holman's drawing game. When it came time for the visit to end, Hilary did not want to break it off, and she did not ask to see her grandfather Morgan. To Holman, she seemed happy and in no distress.

Hilary had brought a toy gun and a plastic sword to the visit, rather unusual toys for a four-year-old girl. But she hardly touched them in Eric's presence. When Eric had left, Holman asked her why she had brought them, and she answered, "To kill my daddy." Holman then asked her if she was angry at Eric. Hilary responded incredulously, "No! I like my daddy." Hilary was playing out her ambivalence again—or she had been programmed. On her way out, she nearly forgot to take the sword home with her.

Holman drove Hilary back to Dale's office. As they drove up, they saw Elizabeth and her father standing outside. Elizabeth rushed to the car and tried to open the door even before Holman could unlock it. Elizabeth tried frantically to extricate Hilary from the car, not even permitting Holman time to disengage her from her seat belt.

Not surprisingly, Hilary became more and more anxious as Elizabeth swept her up. From the car, Holman waved goodbye, saying, "See you later, alligator." The words had become something of a happy catch phrase between Holman and Hilary. William Morgan confronted Holman and yelled at her: "Never call Hilary an alligator again." That was the last time William would be involved in delivering Hilary for the visits.

A week later, before the next scheduled visit, it was Elizabeth who drove Hilary to Dale's office. Upon arrival, Hilary started to cry, but she calmed down during the short drive to the Human Services office. To Eric, she seemed a bit more distant this time, but she chatted and played normally and showed no obvious distress. Holman wrote a positive report to Dixon about the visits.

Three days later, around 8:00 A.M. on Friday morning, March 13, Eric got out of his car to begin what looked like a routine day at his McLean office. As he turned to take a bag of trash out of his back seat to throw in a parking-lot dumpster, he remembers seeing a man running toward him. "Hey, Eric. I want to ask you a few questions," the tall man in the trench coat shouted. Eric thought he recognized the man, but for the moment he couldn't place him. "OK. Let's talk while I walk to my office," Eric said. Quickly, according to Eric, the man gave him a slight shove and pulled something out of his coat pocket. A gun, Eric thought. Eric tried to fight, but his assailant was too strong. The man pushed him to the ground, and they scuffled for two or three minutes. Eric realized there was no gun. The man was beating him repeatedly on the head with something that looked like a lead pipe, about 18 inches long. Blood began to flow from gashes in his forehead and scalp. Eric has always maintained that he did not bring the pipe with him in his car and that he had never seen it before.

From the second floor of the medical building, an office worker saw the two men struggling and ran to the parking lot, where she saw the larger man, about 6 feet 2 inches tall, on the ground on top of Eric, striking him with the pipe. She knew Eric, but she had never seen the other man. She yelled at the man to stop and dialed 911 for the police. Eric, although bleeding profusely from his head wounds, was able to run away. He was more than a bit dazed but was able to identify his assailant. It was Alan Alkire, he realized. He had seen him a month before in federal court.

Eric was given first aid and was taken to Arlington Hospital with severe cuts and bruises on his head and face and a sprained wrist. The police arrived on the scene, and Alkire surrendered without a struggle. "I'm the other combatant," he told the officer. "And there's the pipe over there." Alkire—who has always maintained that he drove to the parking lot that morning to speak with Eric, not to attack him, and that he brought no weapon with him—was arrested and charged with assault and battery.

Eric, who had not lost consciousness, remained in the hospital overnight. "That man was trying to kill me," he told his cousins, Robert and Linda Kelly, in his hospital room that evening.

The custody case had turned violent. Eric did not know why Alkire had chosen that particular time and place to confront him, or who, if anyone, had encouraged the attack. He did not understand why it had happened at that juncture in the litigation. In any case, he thought, it was thoroughly unlike Elizabeth to try to physically injure him. She would use the courts, the experts, and her own devious means, but he did not believe that she would support strong-arm intimidation—or murder. And she certainly would not bring back a former boyfriend, with whom she had broken up seven months before, to do the job. There has never been any credible evidence linking Elizabeth with what happened that morning in McLean. Still, Eric was shaken, emotionally as well as physically.

Eric's parents were more suspicious than their son. A few days later, Doris and Vincent wrote to Commonwealth's Attorney Robert Horan of Fairfax County, urging the prosecutor to give personal attention to the case: an "attempted murder," they called it. The Morgans, they said, were "violent, hostile and bizarre people." As one example, they cited the plastic gun and sword Hilary had brought to the visitation and her statement that she was going to kill her daddy. They also pointed out to the prosecutor that they had seen Alkire having lunch with Rob Morgan at the Roy Rogers near the Virginia courthouse. According to Vincent Foretich, the Virginia police told Eric it might be prudent for him to purchase a gun, and Eric did.

Eric, however, was not going to let the incident stand in the way of his continuing efforts to reestablish a relationship with Hilary. The next one-hour visit was the following Tuesday, March 17, and Eric showed up at the Human Services office twenty minutes late. Still recovering from his wounds, he was unable to drive himself. So Vincent, a much slower driver than his son, had taken the wheel.

Hilary waited for her father anxiously in the Human Services playroom. "I want to see my dad, I want to play with him," she said. At one point, chatting with Holman, she lapsed into baby talk, but Holman snapped her out of it.

When Eric finally arrived, Hilary was fascinated with his injury and kept asking him about the stitches on his forehead. Holman was relieved that Hilary assumed Eric was hurt by a "robber," and that she had not been told about Alkire, whom she had gotten to know the year before. Hilary and Eric played and shared a snack. On the way out, Hilary asked her father to promise that they would see each other soon for a longer time. "Let's not make promises," Eric replied. "Promises are good," was Hilary's response. "If you can keep them," said Eric.

At the next visit, Hilary asked Eric out of the blue why he had sent her mother to jail. Eric said he did not do that, but Hilary replied, "For real, I saw her on TV at jail, two times." She said her mommy had wanted her to watch.

By the end of March, there had been six successful one-hour visits at Human Services. But when Hilary was with Elizabeth at Westover Place, she seemed troubled. Bernadette Bropleth, a frequent weekend babysitter, noticed that Hilary—always an unusually happy, loving, and intelligent child—was becoming frightened and confused. From time to time Hilary would start to cry, and when Bropleth asked her what was wrong, she would say someone was going to take her away and she "would never see her mother again." The fear of separation was not surprising. Elizabeth and Hilary remained unusually close. The sitter reported that except for the time she and Hilary spent on outings, 95 percent of Hilary's home playtime was spent in the basement near her mother's office.

Paul Michel, whom Elizabeth was still dating, also noticed Hilary's emotional deterioration after the visits began. Hilary made ugly, contorted faces at him, she talked baby talk, she started spitting food and hitting people. She would stare into space and not respond when spoken to. Michel, who used to visit Elizabeth at her house almost every day, said in a court affidavit that Hilary's unusual behavior, in his view, was "clearly linked to the visits with her father."

At that juncture, Holman had not seen any of Hilary's negative reactions to the visits. In fact, without any prompting by Holman, Hilary was telling her guardian how much she was enjoying her time with Eric. At the end of March, Holman wrote in a formal report to Judge Dixon:

> All in all, the supervised visits themselves have gone very well. Hilary and her father have seemed to get very comfortable with one another very quickly. . . . The reports that I have received from [Elizabeth]

and Hilary's therapist, Mary Froning, regarding the ill aftereffects Hilary suffers as a result of the visits trouble me very much. There may be any number or combination of a number of reasons why Hilary has post-visit ill effects. For whatever the reason, I believe at this stage, Hilary has conflicting feelings about the visits and about her father. As the visits become more regular and more natural, I hope that Hilary's adjustment to them will be less and less stressful. Hilary most certainly seems to enjoy the visits as they take place; hopefully the ill effects she seems to experience as a result of the visit will end soon.

On April 1, on the basis of Holman's positive reports, Dixon expanded the visits to unsupervised four-hour Sunday occasions at Eric's Great Falls home. Elizabeth was supposed to take Hilary to Holman's office first, and Holman would drive Hilary to and from the visit itself. Although nothing in the judge's order obligated them to include Holman in their plans, the Foretiches invited the guardian to attend every visit.

A few days later, Dixon opened a new round of hearings in the case. After the three-day trial in November 1985 and the twelve days of hearings in the summer of 1986, this round marked the judge's third detailed inquiry into Hilary's well-being. It was touched off by Eric's renewed motion for a change of custody and for termination of Elizabeth's parental rights. That spring, Dixon had decided to ask Phyllis Savage, a Superior Court probation officer assigned to the social services division of the court's family branch, to conduct a full investigation of Eric and Elizabeth to determine which parent, if either, was suited to have custody of Hilary. Savage immediately set about interviewing everyone involved, including Hilary, whom she found at her initial interview on April 17 to be "gregarious, manipulative, and at times rude."

The expanded Sunday visits continued as Savage's investigation began and quickly proved just as successful as the ones at the Human Services office. On April 12, Hilary was greeted at Great Falls by Eric, Patsy, her Foretich grandparents, Eric's cousins Robert and Linda Kelly, and their son Robert, Jr., a year younger than Hilary. "Make sure Linda Holman keeps Hilary in her sight at all times," Robert told Eric before the visit. "That can only help your cause."

As soon as Hilary arrived on April 12, Eric drove to the video store in Great Falls and took out a Strawberry Shortcake movie and a Care Bears film, both of which Hilary enjoyed immensely. At one point, Doris brought Hilary a sweater because she seemed cold, and later she helped Hilary change into a dress that the child particularly liked. As Holman ambled around the grounds with her legal pad, dutifully recording every detail, Hilary ate dinner with the family. She seemed well behaved and happy.

Holman needed to understand how Hilary interacted with her mother as well as with her father. Back at Westover Place, she had a brief visit with Hilary and Elizabeth. The two women had coffee and Hilary sipped juice. She was affectionate toward her mother and showed her some ballet steps. Then she insisted that Holman join in, and the three danced together, eventually reaching what Holman recalled as "almost a feverish pitch." Later, Hilary told Holman she had a stomachache and was feeling ill. She pulled on her shirt and lifted it up several times. On one occasion, she seemed to be touching her crotch, although Holman wasn't certain that she was masturbating.

The next visit was Easter Sunday, April 19. This time the Foretiches filled their house and yard with friends and family. The Kellys were there again, as were Eric's dentist friend Kenneth Ison, his wife Bobbi, and their five-year-old daughter Molly. Two families from the Great Falls neighborhood were also guests for an old-fashioned Easter egg hunt organized by Patsy. "The children could not have had a better time," Holman reported. Hilary blew kisses at everyone when she and Holman had to leave. The scene at Elizabeth's house upon their return was similar to the previous Sunday. Hilary greeted her mother happily and performed an imaginary concert on Elizabeth's piano. At another point in the evening, though, she took a candy bar she was eating and placed it between her legs. Again, Holman wasn't quite sure what Hilary was doing.

"Hilary is becoming more and more relaxed about the visits as somewhat evidenced by the lack of crying when she separates from her mother now," Holman reported to Dixon. "Dr. Morgan is also much more relaxed acting about the visits and I believe that contributes greatly to Hilary's emotional state. I hope that this trend will continue for Hilary's sake. Of interest is a report that I received from Dr. Froning; Hilary had reported that she was forced to change her clothes at the April 12, 1987 visit. It is interesting that the things she chooses are the things she reports she is forced to do." Holman was present when Hilary was "forced" by Doris to change clothes that afternoon, and she saw nothing suspicious—only a normal, placid scene between grandmother and granddaughter.

On April 21, during the continuing hearings on Eric's motion to change custody, Dixon again decided to change the nature of the visits. The next visit, that coming weekend, would be an unsupervised one that would begin that Friday afternoon, April 24, and last until Saturday evening, April 25, and there would be another similar visit the weekend of May 1–3.

In granting these unsupervised visits, Dixon was, of course, only trying to restore the status quo of more than a year before. The visit would be similar to, actually shorter than, the ones that Eric had been granted under Dixon's November 1985 order. Those visits had also been technically unsupervised except for the presence of Doris and Vincent as friendly "watchdogs," and the 1987 visits would be the same. Dixon had decided in 1985 and again in 1986 that Elizabeth's allegations of abuse were unsubstantiated. Certainly Eric had had no opportunity to abuse Hilary since February 1986; he had never been alone with her for even a minute.

Beyond the abuse allegations, Dixon also had to be concerned about the problems in reestablishing a father-daughter relationship. Here Holman's reports satisfied the judge that the situation was becoming more stable. But as events were to prove, Dixon may well have overestimated how well Hilary could handle being forced to leave her mother overnight.

Elizabeth was terrified of the overnight visit, and she made it clear to Mary Froning—and by means of the therapist, indirectly to Hilary—that she feared something bad might happen to her daughter on the visit. She filed a motion at the D.C. Court of Appeals for an emergency stay of Dixon's order. Holman, concerned that Dixon was moving too rapidly, joined in the motion and again urged the courts to proceed with caution.

For better or worse, however, one of the features of the American family court system is the power of the trial judge to make day-to-day decisions as he or she sees fit. Appellate judges have relatively little leeway to disturb trial court decisions on an emergency basis. The appeals court still had the key issues in *Morgan* v. *Foretich* before it in the form of Elizabeth's appeal of Dixon's 1986 order, and—unless Dixon was acting in a manner that was directly contrary to law—the appellate judges were unlikely to interfere with a specific visit until they decided the earlier appeal.

But on April 24, it looked as if the appeals court was going to keep the suspense alive for a while. The day came without a decision on the motions to stay Dixon's order. When Holman arrived at Westover Place that spring afternoon to pick up Hilary, she realized that the little girl knew that the adults around her expected some sort of harm to befall her at her father's house. (Hilary had been at Froning's office earlier in the day for a therapy session, and

Froning had told her that if Eric did something she did not like, she should talk to Vincent.)

When Holman told Hilary that she would be seeing her father for a "sleepover visit," Hilary began sobbing and crying, but she could not explain why. She told Holman she would tell Elizabeth first and whispered to her mother that Eric had "poked her in the heinie," something that could not possibly have happened in the previous fourteen months. Elizabeth repeated those words to Holman. But when Elizabeth asked Hilary to tell Holman directly what Eric had done, Hilary would say nothing. She was articulate enough, however, to tell Holman that same afternoon that she was tired of visiting her father and that she did not want to leave her mother.

A few minutes later Hilary got into her bed, asked her mother to sit next to her, and, according to Holman's report, placed her mother's hand on her upper thighs. It was hard for Elizabeth to get Hilary to stop. "You're embarrassing me," she told her daughter. Hilary was clearly not herself; but this disturbing behavior occurred before anything improper could have happened to her on that day's visit, or on any in the 1987 series.

Linda Holman's description of the day's events, our most objective and unbiased source, is entitled, significantly, "Guardian *ad litem*'s report of her observations regarding Hilary A. Foretich before and after her overnight visit with defendant on April 24, 1987." According to Holman's observations, all the fright, the terror, and the overly sexualized behavior occurred *before* the visit. There had been nothing comparable before the visits with Eric at the Human Services office, when Hilary might have been expected to be the most fearful; after all, they were her first meetings with her father in a year. There would be nothing comparable after the visit.

While still at Westover Place, Holman received word that the appeals court had ruled that the visit would go on as scheduled. Suddenly, Holman reported, Hilary's mood changed from apprehension about seeing her father to pleasant anticipation. She began running around the house trying to decide what clothes to pack, finally rejecting the bag that had been prepared by her nanny Narcisa Ramirez. "I have lots of clothes at my daddy's house, many more than at home," she told Holman. She had to make sure, she said, to give back the pink undershirt and the yellow sweater that belonged to her father. Elizabeth carried her to the car, and Hilary happily waved goodbye, honking the horn as Holman drove off. On the way to Holman's office, the designated meeting place, Hilary told her guardian that she had been sick but that she felt better.

When she saw Eric and Doris in the street, she bubbled over with enthusiasm. She jumped into her father's arms and giggled.

Eric headed out of the city on the George Washington Parkway along the Potomac River. On the winding country road that leads to Great Falls, the first stop was the local video store for a couple of children's movies for Hilary; she would watch one Friday night and the other Saturday morning, then go right back to the first one and see it again.

On Saturday evening Eric, Patsy, Doris, and Vincent all met Holman at an ice-cream parlor near Westover Place to drop Hilary off. Hilary told Holman she had had a good time in Great Falls and that she had slept with her grandmother that night. She gave Doris a big hug and hugged Eric as well. Doris said Hilary had been "a real joy" the entire time.

Once back at Elizabeth's house, Hilary lapsed into her erratic behavior. She talked baby talk, sucked her thumb, and insisted that she was a baby. She sat on her mother's lap and put her hand between her thighs, again appearing to masturbate. She began licking Holman's shoe and making a game out of it. Elizabeth and Holman had to tell her to stop.

According to Elizabeth, the next day Hilary said her father had licked her face, arms, upper body, and nose, but said nothing about actual abuse. She told Antonia that Eric had told her to talk into a tape recorder and that if she didn't say what he told her to say, "he would put my mommy in jail." She said her father had told her to say into the recorder, "My daddy didn't poke me in the heinie. My mommy poked me in the heinie." On this visit, however, she said her father had not "poked her in the heinie"; that happened only when she was three, she said. Elizabeth called Holman, who made an appointment to talk with Antonia the next day, Monday, April 27.

Monday also meant a scheduled visit from Phyllis Savage. When Savage arrived that afternoon, Hilary was hiding under the kitchen table and was acting "extremely angry, hyper, and aggressive," according to a report Savage compiled later that year. Hilary grabbed Savage's pen and began to jab it into the sofa. She went upstairs and began playing with her gerbils in a rough manner. When she finally calmed down, she told Savage she was happy with her mother but unhappy with her father. Savage asked her why she was unhappy with her father, and Hilary said, "Because. I'll never tell you." Savage took Hilary to a nearby playground. On their way back they ran into Holman, on her way to interview Antonia. As Holman got closer to the front door, Hilary started throwing her shoe and banging on the door, telling Holman to go away. For some time, Hilary would not let Holman in to keep her appointment with her grandmother.

Holman was deeply troubled by the behavior of her young charge that Monday. In court papers, she argued to Dixon that "the overnight visit and/or its prospect had a very detrimental effect on her," and urged Dixon to cancel or modify his plans the next visit he had ordered for the weekend of May 1–3. Holman was, however, not concerned about possible sexual abuse so much as about Hilary's having been thrust once more into the ugly battle between her parents. As the child's guardian, Holman had been granted the power by the judge to stop the visits at any time if Hilary found them unpleasant. This arrangement was not good enough for Holman: "If [Eric] did take Hilary's statement [i.e., by forcing her to say bad things about Elizabeth into a tape recorder], the Court should reconsider the appropriateness of his unsupervised contact with her now. If [Eric] did not . . . it is quite disturbing to think that [Antonia] would manufacture such a story," she told the judge.

> Hilary is only 4 and a half years old. She is caught in the middle of a very, very difficult situation. Unquestionably, she is very confused and has very conflicting feelings about spending time with her father. She is just too young to adequately and maturely integrate these feelings, especially when the visits are progressing so rapidly. Before she becomes adjusted to one form of visitation, the visits change character. We beg the Court to be a bit more empathetic in Hilary's favor.

In a therapy session on Tuesday, April 28, Hilary refused to talk to Froning about her visit with Eric during the previous weekend. Instead, according to Froning, Hilary undressed two anatomically correct dolls and enacted a scene in which the daddy doll put his penis between the legs of the little girl doll. If this meant she had been abused, she apparently did not tell her mother or grandmother anything about it. It seems that Hilary gave three, and possibly four, accounts of what happened that weekend, depending on who was doing the asking. Elizabeth, Antonia, Holman, and Froning all drew different conclusions from Hilary's statements and actions.

Elizabeth and Holman, each for reasons of her own, asked both Dixon and the appeals court to postpone the May 1 visit, but without success. When the day for the visit arrived, Holman had further doubts. She feared that if she picked Hilary up, the child's negative associations with the visits could interfere with her efforts to develop a trusting relationship with her. She asked Savage to make the pickup that Friday afternoon. On arrival, Savage found that Elizabeth had set up an audio recorder and a video recorder and camera to tape the exchange. Savage was horrified, viewing the taping as "manipulative and unwarranted." Elizabeth told her that Holman had already agreed to it, a statement that Holman has denied. Hilary came downstairs in her mother's arms, crying and sobbing according to Savage, although not hysterical. Savage asked her why she did not want to go with her father; Hilary gave no reason but kept protesting. But as soon as Elizabeth said she would accompany her to Savage's office, Hilary snapped out of it. Savage was amazed that Hilary's mood had changed just because Elizabeth would be with her for another half hour. The tapes of the few minutes in which Hilary was crying were later shown on news programs across the nation.

After the Foretiches picked up Hilary, this time in Savage's office, she again warmed up to them rather quickly. The five of them— Eric, Vincent, Doris, Hilary, and Holman, who had arrived later at Savage's office—had dinner at a restaurant on the Washington waterfront. After a few minutes in which she kept her distance, Hilary relaxed and seemed to have a very enjoyable time. During dinner she played happily, especially with her grandfather. Holman said goodbye after dinner but made plans with the Foretiches to come by the next day. She came as scheduled at six-thirty in the evening and found Doris upstairs in the kitchen preparing dinner and Vincent watching a cartoon video with Hilary. Eric was out jogging, and Patsy was at the store. Hilary shared a secret with Doris and Holman: she was wearing a "beautiful" slip underneath her shorts, and no one knew but the three of them. There was a pleasant family dinner, with pie and ice cream for dessert, and Holman went home just before nine o'clock. (Vincent and Doris later told Holman that any coolness on Hilary's part that day was because Hilary thought Holman's arrival meant it was time to go home, and she didn't want to go home.)

Savage came by the next day and saw what she described as "a nice family day in a beautiful physical setting." She chatted with Vincent Foretich, who told her that Hilary had slept in the same room with Doris the night before and that she had come into his room and playfully jumped on the bed in the morning. During the day, Savage observed Hilary playing with her younger cousin Robert Kelly, Jr., with Eric, and with Patsy. "Hilary was very much at ease, comfortable and engaged in fun times at her father's house," Savage concluded. "Her interpersonal relationship with her father was appropriate and he, the father, reciprocated appropriately. The child's play with Robert was very good as was her interaction with all other persons in the home."

That afternoon, on the way home from the visit, Linda Holman took the opportunity to ask about the alleged tape-recording incident, which continued to trouble her. Holman said she had heard something about Hilary's father having her speak into a tape recorder. Hilary replied in a flat tone that her father had made her speak into a tape recorder. She did not remember what he had made her say. Hilary also told Holman she did not know why she cried before the visits. Hilary showed no distress when Holman dropped her off. "Hilary does exhibit signs of distress right before the visits begin," Holman concluded in a report dated May 6.

> I am not sure what can be done to alleviate this problem, short of having the visits stopped or supervised. I do believe, however, that Hilary needs to be weaned into these visits. . . . It is in Hilary's best interests to have the transfers go smoothly, insofar as the visits must take place. I am hopeful that if [Elizabeth] cannot bring herself to deliver Hilary to a neutral person . . . she will designate someone to do so on her behalf.

Holman said she would do anything appropriate to make Hilary more comfortable. Holman noted in her report, incidentally, that Hilary reported to Elizabeth that she was not abused during the May 1–3 visit.

At the same time, during the first half of May 1987, the Heather case resumed with a week-long trial before Judge Bruce Bach of the Fairfax County Circuit Court. This was the much-postponed trial resulting from Sharon's appeal of the decision in Eric's favor by Judge Jane Delbridge in the juvenile court. The cameo appearances on Heather's behalf by Dennis Harrison and Richard Ducote were over; both had left Hilary's and Heather's cases soon after Elizabeth had lost her federal trial in February. This time, Eric (now represented by Bob Machen, his friend from the William and Mary Alumni Association) came up with a new piece of evidence that directly contradicted Dr. Shubin, Sharon's key witness.

Machen had asked Catherine DeAngelis at Johns Hopkins to examine Heather for signs of sexual abuse. DeAngelis agreed, stipulating as usual that she would be acting only as the child's advocate. She asked that Sharon bring Heather to the appointment in Baltimore. On May 8, as Sharon looked on carefully, DeAngelis conducted the examination. In contrast with what Shubin later termed his "momentary but adequate" examination, DeAngelis asked Sharon to hold a small light so that she could see clearly. Using a magnifying glass and measuring tape, DeAngelis measured Heather's vaginal opening at 4 millimeters, well within normal limits for a girl almost seven years old. DeAngelis saw no evidence of any scarring, stretching, or lacerations. She concluded that "there is no physical evidence for penetration of the vaginal and hymenal areas." The pediatrician added the usual, and proper, caution, stressing the impossibility of detecting non-penetrating molestation.

On May 19, after a week-long trial, Judge Bach announced from the bench that Sharon had not proved by the standard of a "preponderance of the evidence" that Eric had abused Heather. But in a brief written decision issued on June 8, Judge Bach found (as Judge Delbridge had found the year before) that it would take time and patience before Eric could resume anything like a normal relationship with his older daughter. Then Bach sent the case back to Delbridge—for the second time.

Bach ordered Dr. Follansbee, Eric's psychiatrist, and Nancy Fretta, the psychologist who had evaluated Eric and Sharon, to select a new mental-health professional to counsel Heather "with the goal of effecting a reconciliation between Heather Foretich and Dr. Eric Foretich so that as soon as it is in her best interest she will be able to have frequent visitation with him." After that, Judge Delbridge was supposed to set up a visitation schedule. Valerie Szabo, Sharon's lawyer, immediately appealed Bach's order to the Virginia Court of Appeals. Bach refused to grant a stay pending appeal.

Back in Hilary's case, the visits continued. Linda Holman was on vacation for the next regular visit on the weekend of May 15–17, so Phyllis Savage agreed to pick up Hilary again. This time Elizabeth and her lawyer brought Hilary to the downtown Department of Human Services office. As Savage reached for the little girl, she clung tightly to her mother once more, crying and sobbing. Elizabeth told her daughter to touch her necklace, which had a small crucifix, to make the sign of the cross twice, and to pray. According to her report that spring, the social worker felt that injecting religious symbols into the situation would only cause "a reinforcement of a negative image of the father."

This time Hilary took a good deal longer than usual to calm down, and Savage was disappointed with what she saw of Eric's response.

"Dr. Foretich did not make any normal gestures to allay the child's anxiety level," she wrote. "He did not empathize with her plight, did not reassure her that there was no need to be afraid or anxious or even to ask her what was wrong. [I] did not observe any signs of comforting on Dr. Foretich's part." (The fact that Eric was not supposed to initiate physical contact with Hilary may have played a role in Savage's observations.)

Patsy and Eric drove Hilary back from Great Falls the following Sunday, and Savage was there to meet them. Eric tried to explain to Savage the difficulties they had had on Friday. It had taken Hilary longer than usual to adjust that time, he conceded, but as soon as they had reached the Chain Bridge, about fifteen minutes from Elizabeth's house, Hilary had been fine. Savage noticed that after the weekend Hilary clung to Eric the same way she usually clung to Elizabeth. On the way back to Elizabeth's house, Savage asked Hilary why she cried before the visits, but Hilary did not answer. The court officer asked the girl whether part of her wanted to be with her mother and part of her wanted to be with her father, and she nodded her head yes.

According to Savage's report, Hilary told her mother that she had not been abused on this visit. But in late May, Hilary's therapist found that her patient's problems had reached a new and alarming level. At two therapy sessions with Froning, Hilary had expressed suicidal thoughts for the first time, suggesting that she might want to kill herself by darting into the path of an oncoming car, by taking medicine, by "sawing herself" with a knife, or by drowning herself. Dr. Froning wrote to Eric on May 27:

> It is my opinion that Hilary is currently suicidal because she believes she is worthless. This feeling of worthlessness is based on the fact that although she has told many people that she was sexually abused by her father and that she doesn't want to have visits with her father, she has been continually forced into visits which she considers frightening situations. As you are aware she handles this by dissociating— pushing her memories of the abuse down and concentrating on the positive around her. Thus, she can appear to be happy during the visits with you. However, her defenses are still fragile. Should these defenses collapse under stress, Hilary may act impulsively to harm herself. That is why I am encouraging you and those who take care of her in your absence, to be watchful.

Eric had never seen any evidence that Hilary wanted to kill herself, and he disregarded Froning's letter as just another example of the manipulation of his daughter. Eric does recall that Hilary seemed troubled at the beginning of the visits that spring, but he says the problem was separation anxiety, not sexual abuse. "Elizabeth did nothing to smooth the transition. . . . Her only message to Hilary was that my folks and I were bad. All this abruptness left Hilary with unresolved feelings that she just couldn't handle at her age," Eric explains.

On May 27, the same day that Froning wrote her letter to Eric, Dixon set another weekend visitation for the week of May 29–31. Elizabeth sought a stay, as did Holman, who was concerned about why Hilary should be talking about killing herself. Dixon and the appeals court again refused to block the visit.

Under the best of circumstances, overnight visitation is not easy for young children. With all the mutual suspicion around her, the circumstances must have been particularly difficult for Hilary, a bright and perceptive girl who had a good idea of what was going on. Her mother had gone off to jail twice, her mother had sued her father, her father had sued her mother, and all she could figure out was that the two people she wanted to love more than anyone else seemed to hate each other. At her nursery school, director Barbara Rollinson said that Hilary, who had always been one of the happiest children she had ever known, had suddenly become a little aggressive. She had started hitting other children for no apparent reason. It wasn't that Hilary was becoming a problem child, but she had started to behave out of character, Rollinson said.

Even assuming that Hilary did express suicidal feelings to Froning, they cannot be securely linked with sexual abuse. The sessions with Froning in which she spoke of suicide immediately followed two weekend visits with Eric where Hilary reported that she had *not* been abused. Indeed, if we rely on Hilary's statements that spring to Eric, Elizabeth, and Holman, and discount Hilary's play with the anatomical dolls in late April, we can conclude that Hilary had not been sexually abused even once in 1987 when she started talking about killing herself. In her report that spring to Dixon, Savage concluded only that the suicidal thoughts were "a major concern" that had to be addressed in Hilary's best interests. She did not tie them to abuse, and they can be explained without resorting to the theory that Hilary was abused. The stress was just too much for the girl, not yet five years old, to bear.

Chapter 11

May 29, 1987, through
August 28, 1987

On May 29, Elizabeth decided to drive Hilary to Great Falls herself rather than to use Savage or Holman as an intermediary. This seemed, at least for the moment, to be the best solution to Hilary's problems with the transition from parent to parent. Both Eric and Elizabeth agreed that Hilary seemed more relaxed that day. She was able to rely on her mother's comfort until the time the visit actually began, and having Elizabeth take her seemed more natural and less contrived. Eric did think it odd that day that Elizabeth kept making the sign of the cross over her daughter. "It's as if Hilary was going to her executioner," he told his parents.

Hilary did not mention abuse to anyone after this visit and Froning briefly noticed that she seemed to be thinking less and less about suicide. As June began and tempers seemed to cool a bit, Eric tried again to reestablish a relationship with Heather. Encouraged by Judge Bach's favorable decision in May in the Fairfax County court, Eric arranged in early June to attend Heather's seventh birthday party at her elementary school in McLean. It was the first time he had seen her since the December visit in Dr. Finch's office and, by all accounts, it was uncomfortable. Eric had already missed too many months of Heather's life, and she had learned to fear and distrust her father.

Judge Dixon was still determined to maintain Eric's relationship with Hilary that June. His convictions must have been strengthened on June 17 when he received a detailed 28-page home-study report from Phyllis Savage, the court social services specialist. Savage had

had access to the entire court record during the time she prepared
the report and had interviewed all the principals, including Hilary.
In fact, Savage had herself become a player in the case when Holman
asked her to drive Hilary on May 1. Savage's report, complete now
after almost three months of study, described a divisive battle between Hilary's parents, not a horrible instance of child abuse. "The
parents have had their individual agenda," she wrote. "The mother
[wants] to vindicate her views that the sexual abuse did take
place. . . . Dr. Foretich's position has been to adamantly deny the
allegations of sexual abuse, to restore his name and position to
respectability and to pursue his legal right to relate to the child.
Hilary is the victim in this scenario." Savage recommended that
Dixon appoint yet another evaluator, a neutral therapist to review
the data and examine Hilary again.

Hilary was "bonded to her mother, physically and emotionally,"
Savage said. She had "tremendous difficulty separating from her
mother for even brief periods." Hilary did not project a positive
image of Eric when Savage spoke about him, but during his visits
she "appropriately enjoys herself and engages in a rewarding relationship with him."

Savage also agreed with Elissa Benedek, the psychiatrist, that
Elizabeth may have, consciously or not, rewarded Hilary for thinking and saying bad things about Eric:

> Though the child does not verbalize in parrot-like fashion, suggesting
> overt brainwashing on her mother's part, [I] tend to think that she
> does respond, to some degree, to her mother's non-verbal mes-
> sages. . . . She may feel guilty about having a good time at her fa-
> ther's house and thus reports some negative images of her father.
> There is also the suggestion that there is some role reversal in that
> the child finds the need to protect the mother.

Savage said that both Eric and Elizabeth needed "intervention"
by a mental-health professional: Eric had to learn to react more
appropriately to Hilary's obvious distress at the outset of the visits
instead of focusing on his own needs, and Elizabeth had to adjust
to the fact that the visits were going on. Savage was particularly
concerned about Elizabeth's invocation of religious symbols.

"Overall the mother is viewed as the most suitable parent and
only in reaction to visits does she become imbalanced," Savage
concluded. "Sending the child for visits with crosses and prayers is
symbolic of protection in an unsafe environment. Also, how much

should this four and a half year old child be expected to process if there are extreme overtones to religion?" After the "intervention," the "relentless battle between the parents" might dissipate. In any case, Savage wrote in her report to Dixon, Elizabeth should keep custody despite her abnormally close relationship with Hilary—as long as the neutral therapist did not find that Elizabeth suffered from serious psychiatric problems.

In light of this evalution and Linda Holman's reports (which continued to show Hilary as happy during visitation despite feeling psychologically torn between her parents), it is easy to see why Dixon did not endorse Elizabeth's repeated motions in June and July to suspend the visits.

On June 10, Judge Dixon scheduled additional weekend visits for June 12–14, June 19–21, July 2–5, and July 17–19. In the order, the judge specifically granted Linda Holman the right to "monitor the child's well-being as she deems appropriate."

The June 12 visit was uneventful, but three days after the June 19–21 visit ended, Elizabeth reported in an affidavit that Hilary told her and Antonia that she had been abused on that visit. On Wednesday morning, June 24, according to the affidavit, Hilary said that while Doris and Vincent were grocery shopping, Eric locked her in the bathroom and wouldn't let her out. Later, he "had gotten in bed with her and touched her between her legs with his hand." Elizabeth immediately called Allen Dale, her attorney in the custody case, and Linda Holman. She also made an appointment for Hilary to be seen that afternoon at Georgetown University Medical Center for a sex-abuse evaluation, and she called Charles Shubin in Baltimore to see if he could examine Hilary again. At Georgetown, Hilary's regular pediatrician, Ann Richmond, was off, so one of her colleagues, Dr. Francis Palumbo, performed the exam. Palumbo observed what he describes as "a very scant vaginal discharge" and found that Hilary's vaginal area was red; his other findings were all normal.

Vaginal discharges can be a sign of sexual abuse, Palumbo knew; he also knew that they can result from a bubble bath, sitting in a sandbox too long, a hot-tub bath, or masturbation. (Elizabeth told him Hilary had not had any of these experiences recently; but they could, of course, have occurred on a visit with Eric, or, in the case of masturbation, at any time without anyone's knowledge.) As the law requires, Palumbo reported the suspicions of abuse to the D.C. police.

Around six o'clock that evening, Detective Samuel Williams of the police sex squad arrived at the hospital. With Hilary sitting on Elizabeth's lap, Williams asked her questions about the alleged abuse. She never addressed him directly but just indicated yes or no to his suggestions by shaking her head. In this manner, Hilary communicated to the police officer that Eric had her say bad things into a tape recorder, that Eric had hit her on the neck, and that Eric had touched her genitals while she was in bed. Williams decided the case was worth investigating. But he realized that he would have to interview Hilary again before he could reach a conclusion.

Elizabeth now had some physical evidence, however equivocal, that the abuse had resumed, and she had Hilary's description of one alleged abusive act. She again asked Judge Dixon to suspend the visitations, and Linda Holman again joined her, for somewhat different reasons. On June 30, Holman asked that the visits be suspended until a multidisciplinary team could be appointed, or at least until Dixon could name an unbiased mental-health professional to evaluate the situation. Alternatively, she said, the visits should be supervised. (At the continuing hearings that summer, responding to a hint from the D.C. Court of Appeals on May 29, Dixon had suggested that naming such a professional might be the best way to resolve the issues, and that had been Savage's recommendation as well.) "If not her physical health, most assuredly Hilary's mental and emotional health are now in jeopardy," Holman wrote in her court papers. "If the allegations of abuse are true, the issues become fairly easy to resolve. If the allegations are untrue, the issues are so very complicated." In response to these emergency motions, the judge scheduled two days of hearings on July 1 and 2, postponing the scheduled start of the next visit by one day in order to hear Elizabeth's new evidence.

Also on June 30, the D.C. Court of Appeals finally issued its ruling on Elizabeth's appeal of her original contempt citation from the previous summer. It was the first full consideration of Elizabeth's case by an appellate court, and it was a smashing victory for Eric.

The appeals court accepted Dixon's February findings that it had been necessary to close the trial to protect Hilary from undue publicity. Tackling Elizabeth's other grounds of appeal, the court held that Dixon had acted within the bounds of a trial judge's discretion when he refused to admit the videotapes of Hilary with Dennis Harrison. The appellate judges also endorsed Dixon's rejection of her "impossibility defense" to the contempt charge, in which she had contended that it had been impossible for her to send Hilary on the visit. They found ample basis in the trial record for Dixon's finding that Elizabeth could have released Hilary to Eric had she wanted to do so.

The reviewing court was struck by Dixon's patience with Elizabeth: "Even after ruling against Morgan on the abuse issue on July 17 and finding sufficient basis for contempt, the trial court exercised considerable restraint by affording Morgan the opportunity to avoid judgment and incarceration by allowing her two additional opportunities to permit visitation." Finally, the court did not disagree with Dixon's handling of the underlying issue of sexual abuse, saying that it had seriously considered the evidence on both sides and could not find that Dixon was erroneous in concluding that the abuse had not occurred.

So, by the beginning of July, it had become clear to Elizabeth that her arguments were failing not only in Dixon's court but in the appeals court as well. While she hoped that James Sharp and his partners could get a reversal of the federal jury verdict against her and give her a new shot at a trial in Alexandria, she also saw the possibility of a third contempt citation in Superior Court if she stopped sending Hilary on visitation again. And she knew that if she took the drastic action she was considering, the ramifications would be more than just another three-day jail term.

Again, Elizabeth needed another lawyer. Although Richard Ducote was long gone from the case, Elizabeth still had Allen Dale, an experienced D.C. trial advocate, as her custody lawyer; she had Sharp and his firm pursuing the federal appeal in the Fourth Circuit; and she had retained a team from Covington & Burling, the District's most prestigious large firm, to help with the appellate work in the D.C. Court of Appeals. But if Elizabeth was going back to jail— she and Paul Michel decided—she needed someone else as well. She needed a lawyer who knew the world of politics and publicity as well as he knew the courtroom.

Michel thought he had just the man: Stephen Sachs. Sachs, Maryland's liberal former attorney general, had just become a partner at the well-known D.C. firm of Wilmer, Cutler & Pickering (after losing a hotly contested 1986 Democratic gubernatorial primary). Sachs is not an experienced domestic relations lawyer, but Elizabeth wanted something else. A quick-witted and engaging man, Sachs looked a good ten years younger than his actual age of fifty-three and had a fine reputation as a litigator. His roots were in Baltimore, where he had practiced before he was elected attorney general and where he first met former U.S. Attorney General Benjamin Civiletti, a partner in a major firm there.

Michel also had a Civiletti connection. Before becoming a U.S. Senate aide, he had been a Department of Justice official under Civiletti. That connection drew Michel (and thus Elizabeth) together with Sachs. In July 1987, Michel called Sachs and introduced himself as an old comrade-in-arms of Civiletti. It was a personal matter, he told Sachs. His woman friend had a serious problem concerning a daughter from a previous marriage. Could Sachs help? As it happened, Sachs soon became aware of another link with Elizabeth: Carol Kleinman, Elizabeth's psychiatrist, was married to Sachs's wife's brother. Sachs, who (despite the newspaper publicity) had never heard of Elizabeth Morgan, was intrigued.

Elizabeth paid Sachs a retainer of $25,000 and told him to try to minimize her time in jail. Sachs immediately saw a touchy ethical issue that he felt obligated to talk over with some of his partners at Wilmer, Cutler. Members of the Bar are required to uphold the rule of law, and a lawyer is therefore not supposed to advise a client to disobey a lawful court order. Could Sachs take Elizabeth's case?

Sachs decided that as long as Dixon was ordering the visitations with Eric, he would not be allowed to tell Elizabeth to stop sending Hilary. But he felt that he could still plead her cause before Dixon. He began to plan his strategy. As a civil libertarian and a media-savvy litigator, Sachs saw three issues he could push in the courtroom if the case came to a contempt hearing again. They were the closed nature of Dixon's proceedings, the necessity of defense against the contempt citation (i.e., the importance of protecting Hilary in the name of a higher good), and the "summary" nature of contempt proceedings (judges can enforce their orders without juries and without the usual trappings of due process).

Sachs felt that even if these arguments didn't work before Dixon, they might well succeed before an appellate court, since, as he believed, the underlying evidence of sexual abuse was more convincing than it had been the year before. If not there, then he could take his case to the U.S. Supreme Court, or to the court of public opinion. Perhaps the Superior Court judge would relent in the face of public pressure. Sachs didn't think much of Ducote's venture into federal court to end-run Dixon, but he thought he had his own ways of getting around a judge who seemed so obstinately opposed to his client's position.

First, Elizabeth had her two-day hearing before Dixon on July 1 and 2. Elizabeth testified about Hilary's most recent statements, as did Antonia. Other witnesses for Elizabeth included Mary Froning; David Corwin, the California psychiatrist; Dr. Francis Palumbo of

Georgetown; and Hilary's babysitters Narcisa Ramirez and Bernadette Bropleth. Dixon did not permit Detective Williams to testify; an attorney for the D.C. Police Department had intervened with the judge and urged that the testimony not be allowed. Williams's sex squad was still conducting its child-pornography investigation of Elizabeth, and the department feared that its position would be compromised if Williams testified for Elizabeth. Instead, Elizabeth, who had been present during Williams's interview, was allowed to testify about what Hilary had said to Williams.

On Eric's side, Eric, Patsy, and Doris were the chief witnesses. They told Dixon that the alleged abuse could not possibly have occurred: while Hilary was awake, she was never alone with Eric; at night she slept in the same room with Patsy or Doris, never with her father. Generally, Patsy would crawl into bed with Hilary, wait until she was sound asleep, then sneak out to rejoin the adults. When Patsy wanted to go to sleep herself, she went right back to Hilary's bed.

Eric's witnesses also told Dixon how happy Hilary was when she was with them. They supported Linda Holman's contention in one of her reports that Eric's visits included "a full schedule of events for Hilary that includes swimming, visiting families with children near Hilary's age, going on outings, shopping, etc." Following Froning's psychological theories, Elizabeth discounted the evidence of Hilary's happiness. Elizabeth explained in later testimony that "these were the signs and symptoms compatible with a split personality and predicted by experts in sexual abuse as a protective mechanism of an abused child, a superficial happiness put on by the child who has no escape from a life of terror."

Again, Judge Dixon, heavily influenced by Holman's reports and other consistent testimony from Great Falls, was not persuaded that the Foretiches were abusing Hilary. "The child is not in danger of abuse in the ensuing weekends . . . and it is in the best interest of the child that the visits occur," he concluded in a later order that explained his July 2 decision. "If the visits do not occur, then the child will lose the beneficial effect of the continuation of the visits and will thereby be adversely affected by the conflict [between her parents]." Elizabeth's and Holman's motions were denied.

Matters were again approaching a crisis point. Mary Froning wrote to Elizabeth on July 1 that she strongly recommended that Elizabeth not "compel" Hilary to go on the visit. A year and a half before, when Froning had given similar advice, Elizabeth had prevented the visits for a full year but had eventually had to resume them. This time, Elizabeth thought, she needed to find a permanent solution to Hilary's problems. Since the spring, she had been talking to Hilary about whether and how she should hide her. That summer, the plans became more concrete. "There was never any doubt in Hilary's mind at all that she wanted to be hidden," Elizabeth testified the following year. She said Hilary's desire to be concealed from her father became clear as soon as the supervised visitation at Human Services began in February. At that time, of course, there had been no "reabuse." The freshest memories in Hilary's mind at the time were of her parents' conflict and how her mother had gone to jail to keep her from seeing her father.

Judge Dixon's written order, issued in the middle of August, explained his rationale for denying the July 1 emergency motions. (Because all the parties needed an immediate decision about the visits, the judge would sometimes take this course of ruling from the bench first, then writing a decision later to give his reasoning.) It was in this decision, which was issued on August 18, that Dixon first used the word "equipoise"—a word that would resonate for years in public and private discussions of the Morgan case.

More than anything else Dixon did, the choice of the term "equipoise," which means that evidence is evenly balanced in two directions, would convince Elizabeth's advocates that he was insensitive to the trauma of child abuse. Elizabeth interpreted Dixon as saying that he approved the visit even though there was a 50–50 chance that Hilary would be abused. "How would you like equipoise for your daughter?" a Morgan supporter asked at a public protest in 1989. "Let's say she brings a note home from Girl Scouts. Dear Mommy, can I go on a campout with the Girl Scouts? It will be supervised by people who may rape us. But they may not rape us. The chances are about 50–50. Would you send your daughter on that camping trip with the equipoise?"

The opinion itself, read in context, shows that Dixon may have chosen an unfortunate turn of phrase—but that he did not have the cavalier attitude toward sexual abuse that Elizabeth and her supporters have attributed to him. He did say in his opinion that he found the evidence to be "in equipoise," meaning that he was "unwilling to find as more probable or not that the alleged abuse occurred or did not occur."

Although that is what Dixon said, the opinion makes it clear that he gave the evidence against Elizabeth's allegations much more credence than the evidence in their favor—and that he did not believe Hilary was in any danger of abuse. The passages immediately after the "equipoise" paragraph read as follows:

The Court has taken into account the history of this case, including the history of the relationship between the parties, prior orders of the Court, the long history of allegations of abuse dating back to January 1985, and the absence of any finding of abuse by any public agency as well as the absence of any criminal charge arising out of the allegations of abuse.

The Court has also taken into account the reports of the guardian *ad litem* and the defendant's evidence that once the visitations take place the child is both happy and healthy throughout the visitations.

The Court is satisfied that if the visitation take place over the ensuing weekends of July 2–July 5 and July 17–July 19, 1987, that the conflict between the parties will continue. Nonetheless, if the visits do not occur, then the child will lose the beneficial effect of the continuation of the visits and will thereby be adversely affected by the conflict.

The Court finds that the conflict between the parties will not worsen or lessen if the visits take place.

The Court further finds that the child is not in danger of abuse in the ensuing weekends of July 2–July 5 and July 17–July 19, 1987, and that it is in the best interest of the child that the visits occur, based on all of the evidence which the Court has heard thus far.

Dixon's later orders made it clear that he was relying on the presence of Patsy, Doris, and Vincent to forestall any possibility of abuse. Also among his considerations were Holman's right to monitor the visits as she saw fit; the judge's own availability for emergency hearings; and Elizabeth's right to call Hilary on the phone during the visits. He said earlier in the same opinion that if Elizabeth's charges were true, Eric was "a psychologically deranged sex abuser." Whatever Dixon was, he was not a fool. Like anyone entrusted with the welfare of a child, he would not turn a child over to someone he really believed was a "psychologically deranged sex abuser" with free rein to do what he wanted.

As a purely technical legal matter, Dixon was correct in permitting the visits even if the evidence of abuse was evenly balanced. The parties making the motion to stop the visits—here Elizabeth and Holman—have the burden of showing that there is more evidence on their side than against it (the "preponderance of the evidence"). A situation of "equipoise," an absolutely even balance of evidence, would mean that they had failed to meet that burden. Strictly as a legal matter, a judge could then consider the abuse as not having occurred.

This approach may be acceptable for a dispute over real estate or a traffic accident. But when the emotional and physical health of a child are at stake, no judge should put a child at risk on the basis of such a legal technicality. Whenever there remains some uncertainty—even considerably less than a 50 percent chance—in a case of alleged abuse, almost all family lawyers agree that the best alternative is supervised visitation, to guard against the possibility of abuse. Dixon evidently believed that, in view of all the safeguards he set forth in his opinion, the visits were the equivalent of supervised visits.

On the last day of June, just as Holman was preparing papers requesting a suspension of the visits, the court action shifted briefly back to Fairfax County, where Alan Alkire was being tried on assault charges before Judge Lewis Griffith and a jury. Alkire's defense in the one-day trial was self-defense. He said that although he had confronted Eric verbally in the parking lot on March 13, Eric had started the fight.

"The supervised visits had just begun, and I thought Eric wanted to arrange Hilary's accidental death," Alkire said in a later interview. "I went to talk to Eric, to tell him that I and others were aware of his death threats. Then, out came the pipe. He had the pipe behind his back." Alkire's trial testimony was not quite so specific about why he wanted to see Eric that morning, but he insisted to the jury that he did not take the lead pipe with him to the parking lot.

Alkire's lawyer, Stanley Klein of Fairfax, challenged the jury to find that the prosecution had proved its case beyond a reasonable doubt. "Did Eric Foretich have reason to be scared in view of everything that was going on with all the publicity he was getting, the allegations and everything else? Maybe he did. Maybe when he saw Alan Alkire out in the parking lot, he took a lead pipe out of his car because he was scared. And then he lost his cool," he argued.

The judge had told the jurors to disregard in their deliberations the bitter and well-publicized Morgan-Foretich case, which, obviously and inescapably, formed the larger context of the criminal case before them. That, however, proved to be impossible. In a case of self-defense, evidence of the victim's history of violence is admissible. To bolster his theory, Klein asked several witnesses about alleged violent behavior by Eric. Sharon Foretich retold the old stories about the strife during their marriage including, once again, the episode with the IV tube. Cornelius Sullivan, Sharon's father, described a heated confrontation he had with Eric concerning child support in the lobby of the Regency apartment building in 1984. And Allen Dale, Elizabeth's attorney in the custody case before Dixon, described an incident that had occurred that April in the hallway near Dixon's courtroom.

That episode began after Dale had finished a tough cross-examination of Patsy Foretich, who had emerged from the D.C. courtroom in tears. Eric took offense, and (as Dale's testimony goes) approached Dale. Standing only four or five inches away from him, he yelled: "I almost strangled you in the courtroom. I'm going to strangle you now." Eric's lawyer, John Lenahan, pulled Eric away in seconds. Even Dale conceded, though, that Eric never touched him. (Lenahan agrees that he pulled Eric away but says his client was angry and upset, not violent. "He has never assaulted anyone in or out of my presence, as far as I know," Lenahan said in an interview.) Part of Eric's testimony at Alkire's trial was his explanation of what happened with Dale and his version of the long-ago events with Sharon and with her father.

The prosecuting attorney put on the stand the office workers who had seen Alkire repeatedly beating Eric on the head with the pipe. Eric also testified about what he considered a brutal, intentional attack. It probably hurt the prosecutor's cause, though, that he presented no theory about Alkire's motive—except that it "probably had something to do with the child-abuse case." As merely an ex-boyfriend of Elizabeth's, Alkire's presence at the parking lot that day seemed inexplicable; there was no evidence that he had acted at anyone's direction or had conspired with anyone. The jury returned a not-guilty verdict in less than an hour of deliberation. Now it was the Foretiches' turn to fume over a decision that they thought was a miscarriage of justice.

The Foretiches, at least, continued to see Hilary. As the visits at Great Falls went on through July, Elizabeth, Antonia, and Froning continued to chronicle the child's strange behavior. But they were not the only ones disturbed about things the little girl was saying. On Tuesday, July 7, immediately after the July 3–5 visit, Doris called Holman, according to Holman's later report to the court, and told her that during that visit, Hilary had described details of her ongoing therapy with Froning in a very disconcerting manner. It seemed, Doris told Holman, that Hilary and her therapist used to play "Big Bad Wolf." The wolf was Eric, and she was supposed to shoot him and make him die. As for the "bad things" she was saying about her father, they were just "jokes" she was playing on him. And Hilary, who according to Holman's reports had become quite close to Patsy, once asked Patsy wistfully, "Why does my mommy make me say nasty things about my father?" On another occasion, according to Eric, she told Patsy, "What's wrong with my mommy? I wish you were my mommy."

Holman was now deeply troubled by what she was hearing from

both sides about Hilary. She quickly scheduled two visits to Elizabeth's house so she could talk with Hilary directly in a situation where the girl would presumably be comfortable and in a mood to unburden herself.

On July 10, across a table at a Roy Rogers in Elizabeth's neighborhood, Holman asked Hilary whom she slept with in Great Falls, and she said she slept with Doris and Patsy. "Does your father ever sleep with you?" Holman inquired. Hilary, very incredulous, answered no. The next time the two got together, on July 23, they went to a McDonald's. This time Hilary, lowering her voice to a confidential whisper, told Holman that she had lied to Detective Williams of the D.C. police the month before and that her father had never touched her between her legs. An excerpt from Linda Holman's report of that same conversation reveals the incredible pressure Hilary was feeling:

> I also told Hilary that her Nanny [Doris Foretich] said that when she goes to her father's home for visits she acts sad and cries but then smiles and waves at her Nanny when no one is looking. Surprisingly, she agreed with me, admitting that she did just as Doris Foretich described. I asked Hilary why she acted that way and she told me because of her mother. When I told her that her mother wants her to be happy, she told me no. I reminded her that her mother loved her very much and always wanted her to be happy. She insisted that her mother did not want her to be happy about the visits.
>
> I asked Hilary whether she acted sad and then happy when she waved and smiled at her Nanny because she thought that her mother wanted her to act sad and Hilary told me yes.
>
> I asked Hilary if she really wanted to visit with her father and she told me no. When I asked her why not, she told me that she did not know. I asked her if her father hurt her and she said no, that he was nice. When the subject came up again, she said her father had hurt her. Hilary did, however, deny that her father touched her in her private parts between her legs.

At the end of July, Holman could only remark, in a report to Judge Dixon, "how incredibly complicated this matter is and how Hilary feels emotionally torn between her mother and father and how much in conflict her feelings are in reference to both of them." She pointed out that "at no time has Hilary complained of any mistreatment or unhappiness with her father and his family," noting however that "I would not have expected her to do so, even if she were unhappy."

Elizabeth did not report any abuse in July, but her expression of concern about her daughter escalated that month. Echoing William Morgan's letter to Dixon of the previous summer (the letter describing a potential drowning in the pond at Great Falls), and echoing the concern that Alkire expressed, Elizabeth told Holman on July 15 that she was terrified that Eric might soon kill Hilary. The supposed motive? Hilary had just talked to Detective Williams about the alleged abuse, and it was important for Eric to shut her up to keep his guilty secret from coming out. Elizabeth handed Holman transcripts of Sharon and Cornelius Sullivan's testimony in Alkire's trial, describing Eric's past violent behavior, as well as a copy of a letter she had written to Patsy in which she asked Patsy to serve as a twenty-four-hour guardian over Hilary, for her own sake and Hilary's sake.

According to one of Holman's reports, Patsy, who had seen no evidence of any violent tendencies on Eric's part, was quite disturbed that Elizabeth would write such a strange letter. (This was not the first time that Elizabeth had utterly perplexed Patsy. A few days before, Elizabeth had quoted Hilary as saying Patsy had threatened to leave Eric unless he stopped abusing the child. Elizabeth wrote this in a letter to Holman, who immediately checked with Patsy. Patsy denied that she had ever even thought such a thing and told Holman that nothing she had ever said could possibly be misinterpreted in that way.) In any case, Patsy never wrote back to Elizabeth and did not behave any differently in Hilary's presence than she had before. Those who were present at the visits—including Linda and Bob Kelly, Doris Foretich, and Linda Holman—continued to describe innocent good times: hayrides, barbecues, and Fourth of July fireworks with the neighborhood children. Eric even had a ten-year-old girl from the neighborhood testify about the good time she had playing with Hilary and staying overnight in Eric's home.

On July 9, Elizabeth took Hilary back to Baltimore to see Charles Shubin, who by this time had decided to limit the terms of his participation in the case. He would do so only through Linda Holman. Before he permitted Elizabeth to schedule the appointment, Shubin told Holman he would not examine Hilary again unless the guardian approved. After consulting a psychologist for advice on how traumatic further physical examinations would be for Hilary, Holman finally agreed. Shubin again found a "fibrous band" in the hymen and a larger-than-normal opening, findings that he said were consistent with sexual abuse. The findings were, however, essentially the same as those of the year before; the hymenal measurements had changed only by 1 millimeter, a difference that Shubin said was within his margin of error.

Since Shubin had decided to give no further testimony for either party and to appear as a witness only at Holman's request, Holman had to decide whether to call him. Although she had seen and heard nothing from Hilary indicating abuse, Holman still decided to call Shubin in August "so that the court should have before it as full and complete a record as possible."

In addition to Shubin's pediatric expertise, Eric and Elizabeth both called in nationally renowned psychiatrists to bolster their positions that summer. When Mary Froning began to fear that Hilary was developing a multiple personality disorder, she consulted Dr. Frank Putnam of the National Institute of Mental Health in Bethesda, Maryland. Putnam is the author of a textbook on multiple personality and perhaps the nation's leading expert on the subject. He has a loose association with the Chesapeake Institute as the principal investigator in a study of sexually abused girls.

Putnam never met Hilary. Instead, Froning sent him videotapes of Hilary just before and just after visits with Eric. In an affidavit, Putnam concluded that Hilary's behavior was disturbed and was "most consistent with continuing sexual abuse." Elizabeth seized upon this conclusion as confirming Froning's diagnosis.

Multiple personality disorder, like most other serious psychiatric ailments, is virtually impossible to diagnose without direct contact with the patient, and in an October 1989 interview, Putnam stated emphatically, "I never made a diagnosis in this case." He said that what Hilary needed was "a formal psychiatric evaluation in an inpatient setting." In other words, the only way anyone could understand what was really wrong with Hilary would be "to get the child away from everyone, to see what the child looked like in a structured setting." That process, Putnam explained, normally requires about two weeks in a psychiatric ward of a children's hospital. When Linda Holman asked Elizabeth about Putnam's recommendation in open court in 1988, Elizabeth responded, "Dr. Putnam has never met Hilary. He does not know all that she has been through and I as her mother can tell you that I think that it is very probable that her confinement in a hospital separated from everyone she trusts would probably make her feel suicidal again. I would not agree to that." Again, Elizabeth, "as her mother," knew what was right for Hilary. She relied on experts only when they agreed with her.

Eric's nationally known expert was Dr. Arthur Green, a Columbia University-affiliated child psychiatrist. Like Putnam, Green never met or evaluated Hilary; he gave his opinion based on his reading of the court record. That summer, Eric had asked Dixon for permission to take Hilary to yet another psychiatrist for evaluation, but the judge turned him down, firmly believing that Hilary had already been through too much testing. Elissa Benedek, who had already completed her evaluation the previous fall in the federal case, had withdrawn by then; according to two sources familiar with her thinking, she had had enough of the Morgans, whom she regards as among the most frightening and disturbing people she has ever met. (Benedek has indicated that she has in no way retracted her view that Eric is not an abuser and that Hilary's problems were in part caused by her mother.)

Judge Dixon let Eric bring Green in for a limited purpose—not to testify about Hilary directly but about Hilary's therapy with Froning. Like Benedek, Green strongly dissents from the methods of diagnosing sexual abuse that are espoused by Mary Froning and by David Corwin. "I got the impression that anyone who is seen at the Chesapeake Institute is considered to have been victimized. Their approach seems to introduce a bias, a preconceived notion," Green says. Although he did not interview Hilary, he did interview Eric, and he concluded that there was no good argument against unsupervised visitation. "The guardian didn't feel the child was at risk, and the child had done well during visits," Green says. Green also relied heavily on the opinions of Noshpitz and Benedek, both of whom he knows and respects.

The psychiatrist was quite concerned about Elizabeth's photographic sessions with Hilary. "The so-called indicators of sexual abuse are not specific," he points out, meaning that they can be caused by other experiences as well. "If a mother puts stuff in a girl's vagina and questions her incessantly about abuse, that child can be sexually preoccupied. Sometimes you have to look at an alternative scenario." But the fact that Green did not evaluate Hilary makes his opinion less persuasive than it otherwise might have been.

As July went on, the Foretiches saw Elizabeth's behavior deteriorate before their eyes as her anger and frustration started to well up again. Whatever improvement there may have been seemed to have disappeared. Elizabeth again began clutching Hilary tightly for half an hour or more before turning her over to Eric. At the end of the visit of July 17–19, the Foretiches called Holman to tell her that Elizabeth seemed to be acting deranged. She had seemed so enraged when picking up Hilary, they said, that some of their friends were afraid she would smash up her car driving Hilary back to Westover Place.

Elizabeth's darkening mood may have resulted from a July 16 letter she received from Froning, telling her that her efforts to obey the court orders might themselves harm Hilary's emotional state. Although Froning said she was aware of the legal problems involved in not sending Hilary, she urged that Hilary "should not be continually placed in the jeopardy that these visits place her." Hilary's emotional health was deteriorating, Froning said, "particularly since her disclosure to Detective Williams of recent abuse."

The next visits, the ninth and tenth overnight visits of 1987, were ordered for August 1–2 and August 15–17. Elizabeth found it too emotionally wrenching to drive Hilary to the August 1 visit, so she asked Michel to do so. With a dutiful air, the lawyer followed Elizabeth's instructions and the visit itself went uneventfully. But when Hilary returned from that visit, Elizabeth reported, she started playing a strange and disturbing game involving cooking and eating her baby doll, and she hit and scratched her mother. Elizabeth also noted that Hilary said her father "always says 'prisoner' when he wants to poke" her and that Eric had "poked" her. (In a 1990 interview, Eric, continuing to deny that he had ever abused Hilary, seemed thoroughly unfamiliar with the word "prisoner" in connection with the alleged abuse, and the word apparently never came up before in any of Elizabeth's allegations.)

Judge Dixon was almost done with the custody trial he had begun in April, lasting through seventeen full days of hearings. On August 13, he announced from the bench that he intended to order a two-week unsupervised visit. Michel drove Hilary to the August 15 visit, which was apparently without incident, except for a couple of things that the Foretiches claim Hilary said. Eric and Doris recall Hilary saying as she left Michel's car, "I love my mommy, but there's something wrong with her. Please don't send me home." And a few hours earlier, after Doris had just reprimanded Hilary for something, Hilary said, quietly and wistfully, "But you don't understand, Nanny. You may not see me for a long, long, long time."

On Wednesday, August 19, Dixon entered his order calling for the visit to begin that Saturday, August 22, and to extend through Saturday, September 5:

> The summer of 1987 is nearly over. The court is informed that the child is scheduled to resume school on September 8, 1987. Whatever the court's ultimate ruling may be on the pending motions, to further delay the defendant-father's entitlement to summer visitation with his child until that ultimate ruling results in a denial of said summer visitation by default.

In other words, by stretching out the litigation as she had, Elizabeth was denying Eric the right to see his daughter. Again, Dixon said, any prospect of harm to Hilary "beyond that already caused by this litigation" would be neutralized by the same safeguards that Dixon had set forth after the July 1–2 hearing, including Linda Holman's ability to "monitor the child's well-being as she deems appropriate." The order also set forth a schedule of seven regular weekend visits for the fall of 1987.

Elizabeth and Holman both asked the D.C. Court of Appeals to stay Dixon's order, but the court denied the stay on August 21. On the same day, Dixon finally closed the seventeen-day custody trial and asked the parties to submit their final briefs by September 11. By this time, however, it was too late. Elizabeth had long since put her plan into motion. Hilary was not going to go on the visit that Saturday, or on any other visit with Eric. She really would be away for a "long, long, long time."

On Tuesday afternoon, August 18, 1987, Elizabeth had driven Hilary to a farmhouse near Warrenton, Virginia, more than an hour away from Washington in the foothills of the Blue Ridge Mountains. William Morgan was waiting there. After seven years of on-and-off legal bickering with Antonia, he had finally made his peace with his former wife. That very day, William had signed a formal settlement agreement dismissing yet another case he had brought against Antonia in which he had tried to obtain a larger share of the couple's joint property. As recently as May 22, William had said in a court hearing that Antonia "stole him blind," and that she had left his home in the middle of the night in 1980 after "just about completely looting me." Now, though, Elizabeth's parents were reunited to help their granddaughter elude the forces of the law.

At four o'clock on the afternoon of the 22nd, the Foretiches waited in the kitchen of Eric's home with balloons, streamers, toy horns, presents, and a cake for Hilary's fifth birthday. Linda Holman was there too with a cake of her own. A few minutes before four, Elizabeth called. "I just wanted to tell you that Hilary's not going to be coming today," she told Eric on the upstairs phone. She said nothing more. Doris slumped down in an antique kitchen chair and cried.

The following Monday, August 24, Linda Holman went to court to tell Dixon that the visit had not taken place. The judge scheduled a contempt hearing for Wednesday, August 26. Holman had done more than go to the judge. As soon as she found out that Elizabeth had not sent Hilary on the visit, it immediately occurred to Holman that her ward was probably being removed, forcibly or otherwise, from the Washington area. She would never see Hilary again, she feared. Holman asked Elizabeth to arrange for her to meet with Hilary. Elizabeth, in turn, asked Michel to lead Holman in his car to a diner in Warrenton, Virginia, about an hour from Washington. There, on the morning of Tuesday, August 25, six people rendez-voused: Holman and Michel, who had come, in separate cars, from their offices in Washington; Elizabeth, Hilary, William Morgan, and Hilary's babysitter Narcisa Ramirez, who had presumably driven from the farmhouse that was Hilary's hiding place.

Holman and Michel had to wait about an hour for the others. Holman brought the birthday cake with her, and when Hilary finally showed up, she ate some of the cake—then chopped up the rest into little pieces. In a corner booth of the diner, Holman chatted with Hilary for more than an hour. Hilary told her she was staying somewhere in Virginia and was not living at home; Elizabeth, how-ever, would not tell Holman exactly where Hilary was living. In the parking lot of the diner, Elizabeth and Hilary said a tearful goodbye. Holman and Michel returned to Washington, and Elizabeth, who had resumed her surgical practice in June, drove quietly to Fairfax Hospital to make her scheduled rounds. William Morgan and Ra-mirez went on together, taking Hilary back to the farmhouse and then to the next step of her circuitous route away from her father and from the reach of Judge Dixon's visitation orders. Elizabeth said in a later interview that at the time she arranged the meeting with Holman, she figured she had twenty-four hours to get Hilary away safely from the police.

That same day, with their future and Hilary's so uncertain, Eliz-abeth and Michel became formally engaged. "It was like a wartime romance," Michel said in a *Washington Post* interview two years later. "There were bombs and blood all over the place, so it was an unusual circumstance in which to carry out a courtship." Both knew they were likely to be separated for a long time.

The next day, August 26, Judge Dixon convened what began as a public hearing on whether he should hold Elizabeth in contempt for not taking Hilary to Great Falls the previous Saturday. The first thing Dixon did was to deny Stephen Sachs's motion to participate in the proceeding on the grounds that Sachs was not admitted to practice in the District of Columbia. Juanita Crowley, another law-yer from Wilmer, Cutler, took Sachs's place. Almost at the outset, Dixon decided to close the hearing after Elizabeth, contrary to his instructions, insisted on describing the details of the abusive acts Eric had allegedly committed. Both the protection of Hilary from undue publicity and "the reputational interest of [Eric Foretich]," he said, justified closing the courtroom. The hearing was reopened to the public just in time for Linda Holman to declare, the day after the Warrenton meeting, "I have seen [Hilary] and anticipate no problems in making contact with her in one way or another in the next several weeks. So I have no reason to believe that I would not be able to see her or make contact with her by phone." As Elizabeth well knew, Holman's statement would immediately prove untrue.

At the hearing, Dixon asked Elizabeth and her lawyer where Hilary was. The lawyer, Juanita Crowley, said she did not know; Elizabeth said, with more than a touch of superciliousness, that she knew but would not say. "I'm *not* going to tell you," she said. Dixon again rejected Elizabeth's "necessity" defense. He held Elizabeth in contempt and ordered that she be incarcerated—for the third time in a little over a year—until she delivered Hilary to Eric for the extended summer visit. On the 27th, Dixon wrote a formal order mandating that Elizabeth go back to jail and that "any duly authorized law enforcement officer" must find Hilary, take her into custody, and return her to the jurisdiction of the Superior Court.

Elizabeth immediately filed an appeal in the D.C. Court of Appeals. The next day, Friday, August 28, Judge Dixon gave Elizabeth one last chance to change her mind and purge herself of the contempt. Appearing calm and impassive, Elizabeth spoke only once. When Dixon asked her to say where Hilary was, she said only, "I'm not going to answer that." Then the marshals hauled her off to the D.C. Jail.

At that point, after seventy-five witnesses and four thousand pages of trial transcript, the custody case before Judge Dixon was essentially over. As soon as Elizabeth went to jail, her incarceration, not Hilary's psychological and physical condition, became the focus of the court hearings and of public attention. Sachs began a legal campaign on many fronts to secure Elizabeth's release, while Eric, fearing for the safety of his daughter, asked his lawyers to try to uphold Dixon's authority and keep Elizabeth in jail. It was the only leverage he had over the Morgans and their extralegal acts, he figured. Linda Holman, the one person whose job it was to look out solely for Hilary's interests, was thoroughly frustrated. The Morgans had snatched her client away practically from under her eyes. Between Dixon's refusal to slow down the visitation process and appoint the multidisciplinary evaluation team, and Elizabeth's decision to bypass her and conceal Hilary, Holman felt that her long hours of working on Hilary's behalf had gone for naught.

Holman stated the essence of the dilemma in a legal brief she wrote during this period:

The facts and circumstances surrounding this case are tragic for a child of Hilary's tender age: her whereabouts are unknown; her mother is incarcerated; her father and grandparents have been accused of the most heinous acts against her; eminent child specialists disagree as to her diagnosis; she is emotionally distressed. Hilary, an innocent child, is in reality, the only victim in this case. The intervention of this court and the lower court can only do but so much to protect Hilary; her parents have the ultimate responsibility.

CHAPTER 12

August 28, 1987, through
December 15, 1988

Elizabeth was not the only American woman in her situation in 1987. By the middle of the decade, many women in various parts of the country had decided to hide or run away with their small children after adverse court rulings on their charges of sexual abuse. By the fall of 1987, a well-publicized "underground railroad" had sprung up, with a nationwide network of telephone contacts and safe houses to keep children a step or two ahead of their pursuers. Activists—borrowing techniques from the federal government's Witness Protection Program—used aliases, disguises, and false IDs to conceal the identity of the runaways, and a few committed mental-health specialists helped behind the scenes. According to a June 13, 1988, article in *U.S. News & World Report,* some researchers put the number of fugitives in the thousands. At the beginning of 1989, Faye Yager of Atlanta, the best-known organizer of the under-ground, said she had helped hide more than 120 mothers and their children.

The Morgans, though, went their own way, falling back on their own resources rather than link up with Yager. While Elizabeth spent her first few days in jail, her parents continued to put into effect their plan for hiding Hilary from whatever forces Eric and the D.C. police could muster.

As William later explained, he took Hilary and Narcisa Ramirez, the babysitter, back to his home on Gallows Road. Then, using a ruse reminiscent of his CIA days, he instructed Ramirez to "escape" from the house with a bundle of clothes and luggage. Fearful that he was being watched, William wanted to make it look as if she had run away with Hilary. The trick worked, throwing attention away from William and Antonia, who quickly left the United States for Nassau in the Bahamas with five-year-old Hilary in tow.

As it happened, the surveillance that William feared never materialized. Although Eric went directly to the D.C. police with his story once Hilary had disappeared, he found the department "utterly ineffectual" in its efforts to locate the child and her aging grandparents. With the District's skyrocketing crime rate, the police evidently decided they had more important things to do than look for a child who, by all accounts, was in the care of members of her family. "In custody cases, the authorities won't put much effort into locating a missing person," says Nicholas Beltrante, a retired D.C. police detective who is now the dean of private investigators in the Washington area. The public sympathy for Elizabeth further dampened the enthusiasm of the police. "Everyone was trying to do the best they could," says one police source, "but this case was a political football from the very beginning."

Within a short time after their escape, William and Antonia were forced to return to the United States. In view of the laxness of the authorities, it is not surprising that they were able to do so with impunity. After six weeks in Nassau, Antonia became ill with a rheumatic condition and briefly returned to Washington for medical treatment. Later, William flew to Miami to renew his passport. Then they moved on to Toronto, where Antonia had more medical treatment, then to Vancouver and to Glasgow, Scotland. Wherever the odd threesome ventured, they remained in surprisingly plain view. "At that time, the controls for people leaving or entering the United States were about zero," explains Beltrante, who was not involved in the case. "It was quite easy to remove a child from the country."

The Morgans used their own names on airline tickets and other papers, though there was one significant change. Somewhere along the way, as Antonia explained it, Hilary decided to call herself "Ellen Morgan." Apparently the name "Hilary Foretich" had too many bad associations.

Glasgow was "too cold and depressing" for Antonia, so after two days, the three fugitives moved to England, where they rented a home in a suburb of Plymouth. There Hilary enrolled at Beechfield College, a local private school, and granddaughter and grandparents finally settled down.

Back in Virginia, it became clear to Eric that he had lost control of the situation. A top-notch investigator like Beltrante, who has located missing children as far away as Colombia, Austria, and Jordan, can cost as much as $1,000 a day. Cash-poor because of his legal fees, Eric felt he couldn't afford to hire a detective and didn't have much confidence in the breed. He spent a few thousand dollars on investigators, then dropped the idea. Eric gave repeated interviews to the police but found the pace of the investigation maddeningly slow. He went on radio talk shows to offer a $25,000 reward. He began to rely on a newly rediscovered religious faith, affiliating with a Lutheran church in Great Falls where he prayed for Hilary's safe return.

Eric spoke frequently with Linda Holman, tossing around ideas about where Hilary was. Whatever differences the two had had during the hearings surrounding the visits that summer, they now shared one mutual interest—bringing Hilary back. Holman feared for the safety of the little girl about whose whereabouts she knew nothing—only that she was on the run, away from both parents. Eric, who knew that William and Antonia had disappeared at the same time as Hilary, told Holman that he was concerned about William's potential for violence. He fretted that Hilary might be dead, a supposition that the police did little to discourage. Soon after Hilary was hidden, a police detective told Eric he thought the girl might have been "offed."

More important to Eric than the police investigation or the talk shows, though, was the leverage he believed he had over his ex-wife: with each day that Elizabeth remained in jail, he thought, it became more likely that she would relent. Judge Dixon, too, although he declined to be interviewed for this book, apparently was relying on the coercive power of the contempt citation to bring Hilary back.

There had been another flurry of publicity when Elizabeth went off defiantly to jail, but in the first few weeks and months afterwards, the case hardly registered in the news media or the public consciousness. All that was known was that Hilary had disappeared—and that her grandparents had vanished at around the same time. It was widely assumed that they were somewhere together. Most people speculated that they might be in England since Antonia was of English birth.

Other members of the Morgan family seem to have known much more. According to a newsletter circulated by the Friends of Elizabeth Morgan, Jim Morgan flew to various hiding places, carrying money that his parents needed to continue their odyssey; in all, William Morgan estimated later, the family's travels cost about

$200,000. Although he has denied acting as a liaison between Elizabeth and her parents, brother Rob, still an assistant U.S. attorney in the District, visited her once a week in jail. He made sure to sign in jail as Elizabeth's attorney; jail regulations permit attorneys, but not ordinary visitors, to confer with inmates in glassed-in booths that afford some privacy. Paul Michel also continued to visit regularly, signing in as an attorney as well. But, he has testified, he never discussed Hilary's whereabouts with his fiancée. "When I was working in the Justice Department and later in the Senate," he said at a December 1988 hearing, "I learned . . . that the only way to maintain secrecy was . . . not to discuss some things at all ever."

Elizabeth made other choices out of fear that Hilary would be found. She explained in later testimony that unlike many other women in her situation, she chose not to flee with her daughter, even though Hilary "would have preferred" that she come along. Elizabeth gave two reasons: First, she had become a recognizable public figure before she went to jail and might have been identified more easily by police or private investigators. Second, she thought that Hilary was "entitled to protection under the laws of this country and she is . . . entitled to hold her head out and to live in the country freely, and I felt if I ran with her, that is something she would lose."

As Elizabeth's days in jail stretched into weeks and months, her friends and supporters slowly began to pass the word on the outside that a miscarriage of justice had occurred. A selfless woman had gone to jail, putting her life and career on hold, to protect her child from abuse. Less sympathetic observers, such as Melvin Guyer, the Michigan psychologist who was acting as Eric's attorney, speculated publicly that Elizabeth's desire for publicity would be more easily fulfilled in jail than in hiding. "She is a mother who doesn't have to take care of her child, a doctor who doesn't have to practice medicine, a fiancée who doesn't have to see her fiancé," Guyer said. "She loves it in jail. Everyone comes to her to hear her story."

In those first days and months after Elizabeth was jailed, Stephen Sachs and Juanita Crowley continued their legal maneuvers in an attempt to free their client. The D.C. Court of Appeals turned down their emergency pleas to stay Dixon's last visitation order while their appeal could be heard, or at least to order the appointment of the multidisciplinary team that Linda Holman was urging. So they went to the U.S. Supreme Court, which also refused to take the case. On September 6, the scheduled dates for the two-week visit expired; two days later, Elizabeth filed a statement with Judge Dixon, reminding him that his order had therefore lost its original force. Did that mean she was out of jail, she asked the judge.

On September 11, Dixon held another hearing to clarify his point, and the marshals brought Elizabeth back to court to hear it. She was still in contempt, Dixon said; she could leave jail only if she turned Hilary over to the social services division of the court or to the D.C. Department of Human Services, or if she brought her to Eric for an unspecified period of time. Elizabeth again refused to do any of these things and was returned to jail. This time, it was clear that the impasse would continue and that Elizabeth's term would run far more than the few days of her two previous incarcerations. Elizabeth was not going to compromise and the appeals court was no longer interested in granting any stays. She settled into the daily routine of the institution, vowing that she would stay in jail until the year 2000, when Hilary would turn eighteen and be permanently beyond the jurisdiction of Dixon's family court.

Despite Melvin Guyer's suppositions, Elizabeth appeared to visitors in 1988 as a woman who was genuinely suffering in jail. As an inmate who had not been convicted of a crime, she wore an orange prison jumpsuit (convicted criminals wear blue) and shared her life with accused prostitutes, drug dealers, and petty criminals. She and another inmate occupied a room the size of a very small bathroom. There was no door, and Elizabeth would occasionally have to dress or relieve herself as others, including prison guards, watched. Rock music blared sixteen hours a day, making it impossible for her to sleep regular hours. Elizabeth awoke at 4:30 A.M. for breakfast, then tried to catch some more sleep later in the morning.

Elizabeth spent whatever quiet time she had reading world literature, keeping up with plastic-surgery developments, and studying current research on child sexual abuse. And she whiled away many long hours keeping her diary going and composing short stories for Hilary to read when they were finally reunited.

The articulate, Harvard-educated doctor was not a typical resident of a gritty, noisy urban jail. Gradually, the media became attracted to the story of Elizabeth's indefinite jailing. After a few months, reporters (who had given the sealed case little coverage after the February 1987 federal jury verdict) began lining up in the jail's dingy visiting area to hear Elizabeth tell her horrifying tale of brutal rape ignored by legal and social service professionals. In June 1988, Elizabeth was asked by an editor of *U.S. News & World Report* to write a one-page account of her plight. It was her first appearance in a popular periodical since her *Cosmopolitan* days. "The present situation . . . is exactly comparable to that of a judge ordering a burned child back into a flaming house ignited by a disturbed parent," Elizabeth wrote.

All things considered, Elizabeth told reporters that year, she led a "very depressing, confining, rather zoo-like existence." Jail was dull, repetitive, and dehumanizing rather than brutal or horrifying. "Whatever the discomforts of jail," she later said at a hearing in Dixon's courtroom, "being here lacks the horror, anxiety, and grief that I felt throughout the spring and summer of 1987, knowing that I was subjecting Hilary to sexual abuse by sending her on the unsupervised weekend visitations. I now have the peace of mind that comes from knowing that I am finally protecting my daughter. I feel it every hour of every day. . . . When Judge Dixon expanded the visitation to the two weeks, there were no alternatives to noncompliance with the court's order."

After Dixon's September hearing, Elizabeth made her preparations for a long stay in jail. In March 1988 she closed her medical office, broke her lease, terminated her office staff, and stored away her patient records. Her relationship with Michel did not change. She called her fiancé every day on a prison telephone. He visited about twice a week, and the couple exchanged letters. Michel also became one of Elizabeth's chief legal strategists in those first few months.

Since Sachs's pleas for special, expedited court treatment for Elizabeth had failed (appellate courts evidently felt she had more than her fair share of hearings before Dixon), the lawyer began to look for a new strategy in early 1988. He eventually found one in the time-honored writ of *habeas corpus,* which can lead to the release of persons who have been unlawfully imprisoned or detained. A *habeas corpus* petition forces the "jailer" (here the D.C. government) to go before a judge and give a legal justification for the imprisonment; if no adequate justification exists, the prisoner goes free.

As of February 1988, the busy D.C. Court of Appeals still had not even scheduled oral argument on the appeal Elizabeth had filed six months before, the day before she went to jail. So that month, Sachs filed a *habeas corpus* petition with the U.S. District Court for the District of Columbia, the trial-level federal court in Washington, D.C. He asked the court to order Elizabeth freed. Under federal law, federal district courts have the power to grant *habeas* petitions for persons they feel to have been wrongfully detained by states or the District of Columbia.

In the District Court, Sachs presented a new and imaginative argument, one that would be his theme for a year. Although it seemed paradoxical to many listeners, it packed a legal logic that was surprisingly compelling. To make the argument, Sachs examined the basis for civil contempt and for the summary, shortened procedures trial judges use in handing down contempt citations. No indictment, no jury trial, no formal sentencing. The only recognized justification for all that, indeed the only possible justification, he said, was the possibility of coercing the contemnor. But if in a particular case that coercion is not going to take place, the jailing is left without purpose—or has the purpose solely of punishing the prisoner. And the Constitution doesn't permit courts to punish people without a trial. So if shorn of its coercive rationale, the prison term is unconstitutional. "If Elizabeth Morgan is to be punished," Sachs was in the habit of saying, "let's do it the old-fashioned way, with a trial and a jury of her peers and a presumption of innocence."

To make this argument succeed, Sachs had to prove that jail time would never force Elizabeth to relent and permit Eric his visit with Hilary. The best evidence of that was Elizabeth's state of mind and her actions. The longer she remained in jail, the more intransigent she became, and the clearer it became that she had shut the door on her life as a surgeon and begun a new life as a prisoner, the more likely it was that she would have to be released. In that lies the paradox. Precisely those prisoners who are most contemptuous of the court—those who make it clear beyond the shadow of doubt that they will never relent—are those who must be freed.

Although there was no precedent either way in the courts of the District of Columbia, the argument had been accepted by several courts in other parts of the country. The due-process clause of the Constitution protects citizens against arbitrary imprisonment, courts had explained, and it was arbitrary to keep someone in jail to comply with an order when the facts showed that the person would never comply. To force Elizabeth's release, Sachs argued, the District Court need not decide anything about whether Eric abused Hilary, only that "the depth of her conviction is such that she will not relent." Elizabeth's unshakable commitment to her cause made her an ideal client for Sachs's contention. "As the record makes plain, there is no likelihood at all that Dr. Morgan will comply with the extended visitation order," he told the District Court.

In 1987 and early 1988, Sachs's argument had seemed unpersuasive since Elizabeth had hardly been in jail long enough for her will to be tested. A court would not order her release before the coercive power of the jail cell had first had the opportunity to do its work. Sachs thought that six months might be enough time for the argument to be persuasive.

But he and Elizabeth first ran into a procedural snag. On April 11, 1988, a U.S. district judge denied Sachs's *habeas corpus* petition on the grounds that Elizabeth had not fully "exhausted her remedies" in the D.C. court system, and, under a principle of law called "comity," the federal court was not going to consider intervening in a local District of Columbia case until it was satisfied that the local D.C. courts had first had their chance to hear the issues. That meant Sachs had to wait for the D.C. Court of Appeals to decide his appeal of Dixon's visitation order the previous August.

If that appeal did not succeed, Sachs realized that his next step had to be to walk right back to the D.C. Superior Court and file a *habeas* petition there. By then, Elizabeth would have been in jail longer, and Sachs's arguments would presumably be stronger.

While Elizabeth stayed in jail, ever more confident, ever more determined, the situation continued to unfold in other courts. Sharon's custody litigation, back before Judge Jane Delbridge in the Fairfax juvenile court yet again, continued with another abuse hearing in November 1987. Dr. James McMurrer, Heather's therapist, testified that Heather had described sexual abuse to him that September; but he cautioned that her allegations "are new to me, she never having said this to me two years ago." (The period two years ago would have been the fall of 1985, when Eric still had visitation with Heather and when the abuse was allegedly occurring. The September 1987 session took place almost two years after visitation stopped.)

McMurrer concluded that Eric appeared to be "a caring concerned father who wants visitation with his daughter soon." Sharon was "a concerned caring mother," the psychiatrist said, and Heather was doing well, except for her seriously impaired relationship with her father. To reestablish that relationship, the seven-year-old needed psychotherapy. In her January 1988 ruling, Judge Delbridge ordered therapy for Heather—as well as supervised visits for Eric, progressing to daytime unsupervised visits by June 1988 and, later, weekend visitation. Valerie Szabo, Sharon's lawyer, appealed to the Court of Appeals of Virginia, and that court stayed the visitation orders of Delbridge and of Judge Bach of the Virginia Circuit Court, preventing them from taking effect until the appeal was completed. Eric did not see Heather during 1988.

Also moving forward was the federal court case in Alexandria that had resulted in the jury verdict in February 1987 rejecting the claims of both Elizabeth and Eric. Almost a year after the trial, the Fourth Circuit in Richmond was getting ready to hear James Sharp's appeal on behalf of Elizabeth. Eric had gotten into a dispute with Thomas Albro, his lawyer in the Alexandria case, over what Eric thought was an exorbitant bill Albro had sent him. (Eric eventually paid the bill.) Learning of the fee dispute, Bob Machen, Eric's lawyer friend who had warned him about Elizabeth in 1983, volunteered to represent Eric before the Fourth Circuit. The argument was scheduled for January 6, 1988.

Machen had represented Eric in Sharon's case in 1987, so he knew something about the abuse charges. But he was soon overwhelmed by serious legal problems of his own unrelated to the Morgan case. In 1987, Machen was tried and convicted on federal charges of obstruction of justice in connection with a tax matter he was handling for a client. He, too, was caught up in the "Rocket Docket" of the Eastern District of Virginia, where justice is meted out swiftly, and he faced sentencing on January 8, 1988, just four months after a grand jury had indicted him.

The problem for Machen was that on January 6, he had to go down to Richmond to argue Eric's case. In their appeal papers, Elizabeth's lawyers had raised serious questions about Judge Williams's handling of the trial. The evidence that Williams had excluded about Heather "was obviously relevant," they said in their brief, "to rebut [the Foretiches'] contention that Hilary's physical injuries were accidental or self-inflicted." And the judge should have permitted Elizabeth to testify about Hilary's descriptions of abuse, on the grounds that these qualified under evidence law as "excited utterances," admissible as exceptions to the usual rule against hearsay evidence.

Eric, Doris, and Vincent knew about Machen's personal problems. Over and over, they asked him if he was sure he could do his best for them, and he reassured them that he would have no problem. The Foretiches may have been right in being concerned. For several nights before the hearing, Machen, preoccupied with his sentencing, had slept only an hour or so. At the Morgan hearing, the three appellate judges, who included retired Supreme Court Justice Lewis Powell, Jr., interrupted him over and over again. That is not necessarily a bad sign for an advocate, but, according to three people who were there, the judges' questions, which began as innocuous requests for clarification, gradually became testier. "There was some confusion in his presentation," an observer recalls. (Machen has explained that since he had helped Eric in Sharon's case, he gave little credence to the allegations about abuse of Heather. He was surprised that the appeals court granted those allegations any weight, since they had never been upheld by a court.)

Mark Katz, a lawyer in James Sharp's firm, was effective on Elizabeth's behalf, and Eric and Vincent, who had driven to Richmond for the argument, left the courtroom convinced they had lost. They could see the verdict of the year before slipping away. Machen's performance was "that of a man who was under extreme mental stress," the Foretiches told the judges later that month in a letter requesting a new hearing. (Albro had agreed to handle the appeal by then.) Appellate courts rarely if ever agree to start all over just because an attorney was distracted by personal problems, and the Fourth Circuit did not bother even to reply.

Another oral argument soon followed, in a different court with a different cast of characters. In March 1988, the D.C. Court of Appeals finally scheduled its hearing on the appeal Sachs had filed for Elizabeth when she went to jail the previous August. That argument would be April 25. After eight months in jail, Elizabeth was finally getting her first chance since the fall of 1986 to challenge Dixon's findings head-on. (The attack on the jailing through *habeas corpus* had just been turned aside in U.S. District Court.) At the April 25 argument, Sachs brought up the necessity defense again, telling a three-judge panel of the court that the evidence showed that what Elizabeth did "was reasonably believed to be necessary in order to avoid the court-ordered destruction of her child." The appeals judges did not let Elizabeth out of jail to attend the hearing.

Eric not only attended, he argued his own case. Still concerned about his mounting legal fees—John Lenahan would have charged him $15,000 to $30,000 to handle the appeal—Eric took the unusual and risky tack of doing it himself. (Lenahan came back into the case later after he and Eric reached an agreement about his fees.) Eric wrote a thirty-seven page brief in support of Dixon's handling of the case, and he told the judges in a calm, almost subdued manner, "I think that the real victim in the case is not here, and that's my daughter. We don't know where she is. . . . The other victim in this case, I believe, has been myself." For the first time, Eric accepted Linda Holman's suggestion that a multidisciplinary team should be named to evaluate Hilary; in the past, he said, he had feared (as he had been told by Dr. Benedek) that too much evaluation was itself harmful to his daughter.

In effect, Eric was telling the court that Dixon was right in putting Elizabeth in jail and keeping her there. With his efforts to find Hilary still stalling, that was his only tether to his daughter. (Police efforts, although still halfhearted, picked up a bit in early 1988. In February the department assigned Detective Tom Harmon, a top-notch investigator who had found hundreds of abducted children around the nation and the world, to the case.)

Eric felt uncomfortable saying publicly that he wanted his ex-wife to stay in jail. He thought that sounded vindictive. "I do not wish to continue to devote limited resources to keep Elizabeth Morgan in jail," he wrote in a letter to the editor of Washington's *Legal Times* in July 1988. "I will continue to marshal those resources to locate and salvage the life of my little girl."

Linda Holman had no satisfactory course at the April 25 argument. She had disagreed with Judge Dixon's handling of the visitations, contending that he had rushed Hilary into them. She was also compelled to admit that Dixon's orders were "not based upon speculation or conjecture" and that there was enough evidence on Eric's side that an appellate court could and would sustain them. She was angry at Elizabeth for hiding Hilary, fearing that the separation from her mother would be the final blow to Hilary's shaky emotional health. She could only conclude:

> This Court has before it the weighty task of deciding the course of the life of an innocent, young child . . . it is Hilary's legal position that the lower court's rulings should be affirmed.
>
> Whatever this Court's rulings, we must again join Dr. Morgan in a request: a multi-disciplinary team evaluation is still crucial to this case, to provide this Court and the lower court with guidance in making decisions that will affect this child's life forever.

At oral argument, Holman told the court that whether or not the allegations were true, she was concerned for Hilary's well-being, because the little girl had been "thrust in the middle of too much conflict." She referred to the possibility that it was the Morgans who had caused Hilary to be unhappy at home.

As both appeals courts, the D.C. Court of Appeals and the federal Fourth Circuit, were considering whether they should listen to Elizabeth and overturn the results of the 1987 trials, Elizabeth got some backing from an unexpected source. That spring, Alice Monroe, a speech pathologist who knew Elizabeth slightly from Fairfax Hospital, organized a grass-roots group called "Friends of Elizabeth Morgan" (FOEM) to garner support for the jailed surgeon. All through 1988, FOEM gained strength, drawing feminists to its ranks. The group picketed in front of the Superior Court Building every Wednesday at noon and held a series of teach-ins to publicize Elizabeth's case. At a June symposium in Washington, the speakers

included Elizabeth's psychiatrist Carol Kleinman and Hilary's therapist Mary Froning, who shared details of some of her eighty-seven
therapy sessions. (Froning also founded her own activist organization, the Coalition Against the Sexual Abuse of Young Children,
listing her home address as the group's headquarters.) Soon Molly
Yard, president of the National Organization for Women (NOW),
heard about FOEM and threw her organization's support behind
Elizabeth.

By now, *Morgan* v. *Foretich* was more than a simple custody case;
at least in the Washington area, it had become a political issue
dividing people along the fault lines of gender. Women tended to
sympathize with Elizabeth, finding her a role model for self-sacrifice;
they wondered if they themselves would have responded as nobly
if placed in her position. Men generally took Eric's side, pointing
out that the courts had never accepted Elizabeth's charges and that
Eric had never been charged with a crime, let alone convicted of one.

In Washington, Elizabeth's name was on everyone's lips: a woman
who had always embraced the national limelight was becoming a
minor feminist icon. A front-page article by reporters Elsa Walsh
and Michael York in *The Washington Post* that spring was one of
the few that disputed any of Elizabeth's claims while she was in jail.
Instead, it summarized some of the public's uncertainty: "The stalemate, whose most obvious victim is the child, remains unbroken
because although no court or investigative agency has found enough
evidence to support abuse charges against Foretich, Morgan has
continued to press her allegations. . . . While medical and psychological experts disagreed sharply . . . questions about the credibility
of Foretich and Morgan also have clouded the picture."

That same spring of 1988, Elizabeth got a major boost from the
courts. In James Sharp's appeal of the Alexandria case, the Fourth
Circuit ruled that Judge Williams was wrong in excluding the evidence from Charles Shubin and Dennis Harrison about Heather;
this entitled Elizabeth to a new trial in the Alexandria federal court.

The question before the appeals court was a frequent and an
important one in the law of evidence. It was whether the testimony
about Heather was relevant to some specific issue already part of
the case about Hilary—in which case it should have been admitted—
or whether Elizabeth was just trying to use the evidence to show
that Eric and his parents tended to do evil, depraved things—in
which case Judge Williams was right in keeping it out. Courts do
not admit evidence whose only relevance is that it denigrates someone's character and creates an inference from the person's "prior
bad acts" that he is also guilty of the acts that are the subject of the

trial. Evidence of these "prior bad acts" can be introduced only if it is relevant to some specific point such as the defendant's motive, *modus operandi,* or the like.

In its May 17, 1988, decision the Fourth Circuit found that the evidence about Heather was "essential in that it tended to identify the defendants as the perpetrators of the crime against Hilary. . . . Given the similarity of the injuries [testified to by Shubin] and the fact that only the defendants had access to both girls, the identity of the perpetrators becomes clearer."

The relevance of the evidence about Heather was that, according to Shubin, her genital injuries were similar to Hilary's. If it turned out at a later trial, of course, that Hilary's and Heather's injuries were not similar, this evidence would not necessarily have been convincing, but the appellate court properly left it up to the trial court to weigh the evidence. The circuit also concluded that the trial judge should have permitted Elizabeth to testify about the "excited utterances" that she said Hilary made to her when she returned from the visits.

The decision was Elizabeth's first unalloyed court victory since she was awarded custody of Hilary in 1984. It breathed new life into the civil suit in Virginia, and Elizabeth and her attorneys were delighted. Sachs said Elizabeth would proceed with a retrial in the Alexandria court.

Whatever the Fourth Circuit did for Elizabeth's spirits and her chances in federal court, it did nothing to get her out of the D.C. Jail.

The next appellate decision dimmed Elizabeth's prospects. On August 5, the D.C. Court of Appeals unanimously rejected all of Elizabeth's major grounds of appeal on Dixon's contempt decision a year earlier. Eric, acting as his own lawyer, had bested Sachs and the blue-chip Wilmer, Cutler firm—though, as the winner in the trial court, Eric had admittedly gone into the case with the upper hand. On the key issue of whether Judge Dixon was justified in ruling that Eric had not abused Hilary, the court explicitly followed Linda Holman's suggestion that the rulings were not baseless and that the judge did not abuse his discretion in making them. The court rejected the "necessity defense" to the contempt charge in unusually blunt language. It said the whole notion of civil contempt could become meaningless if someone could defy a court with impunity just because he or she took a different view of the issue than the court. "The defier," the court continued, "acts at his or her own peril in so doing."

Finally, the appellate court went out of its way to take notice of the human tragedy before it, in words that have been quoted so often that they have become almost emblematic of *Morgan* v. *Foretich*:

> A Kikuyu proverb tells us: "When elephants fight, it is the grass that suffers." Here, the grass is a little girl who will be six years old this month. For almost a year, she has been deprived of the company of both father and mother. She is the principal figure in a drama of appalling proportions, no matter what the outcome.

That month, as Elizabeth marked the end of her first year in jail, Sachs's efforts to cast the custody case as a constitutional issue, pitting the heroic individual against the amassed forces of society, were beginning to influence public opinion. "This is civil disobedience in the tradition of Gandhi and Martin Luther King," said Arthur Miller, a Harvard law professor quoted in *The Washington Post*. The tradition of resistance to an unjust authority, Sachs pointed out in an interview at the time, goes back even farther, to the Greek tragedy of Antigone. By the end of 1988, he said, Elizabeth would break the record for the longest term ever served in the United States by a civil contemnor.

In its August 5 opinion, the D.C. Court of Appeals told Sachs that his argument that the contempt citation had lost its coercive force and was unconstitutional—the same contention that the U.S. District Court in Washington had declined to consider in April— had to be addressed first to Judge Dixon's trial court. In September Sachs did just that, filing a *habeas corpus* petition in the D.C. Superior Court accompanied by affidavits from Elizabeth; from therapists Mary Froning, David Corwin, and Carol Kleinman; and from the Reverend Caroline Pyle, a pastor at Elizabeth's Episcopal church in Washington. *Habeas* petitions are, as a matter of form, addressed to the authority holding the prisoner, and Sachs accordingly called his new case *Morgan* v. *Plaut* (William Plaut was the administrator of the D.C. Jail). Eric was not brought into the case.

At a November 1 hearing, Sachs told Dixon that the authority of the law had already "been vindicated every hour of every day for 14 months," with no effect on Elizabeth's determination. But rather than either grant or deny Sachs's petition to release Elizabeth, Dixon deferred a decision until he could hear from Eric. There would be no separate case of *Morgan* v. *Plaut*; the case was merged back into *Morgan* v. *Foretich*, and the judge set a hearing for December 13.

John Lenahan, for Eric, and Linda Holman were both asked to participate.

That news did not bode well for Elizabeth; the news from the federal court in Alexandria was worse. After the Fourth Circuit sent the case back for a new trial, Eric asked the court to reopen the pretrial discovery process in the case to take a new deposition—that of Hilary, who had just turned six years old and was presumably a more reliable witness as she grew older. "We need to know if she's been brainwashed, damaged, injured, or, indeed, even if she's alive," Eric said. Eric knew well that Hilary had been hidden and that Elizabeth would not bring her back. His tactic was clever—and legitimate. As Eric fully expected, Elizabeth refused to permit the deposition; she feared that if Hilary were returned to the D.C. area, the little girl would be brought back to Dixon's court.

The result was that Judge Williams dismissed Elizabeth's case in late November 1988. When a party to a lawsuit willfully refuses to cooperate with a legitimate request for discovery, a judge may order the case dismissed. Here the U.S. district judge wrote:

> She attempts to justify her obstinance by claiming that Dr. Foretich will abuse Hilary. The defense fails for several reasons. Most importantly, it begs the fundamental question: it essentially claims that Dr. Foretich is not entitled to defend against the charge of abuse because he is guilty of it.

Judge Williams then went further in his efforts to expose what he viewed as Elizabeth's deliberate effort to flout the law. Williams also pointed out that Sharon's case in Virginia had been no more successful than Elizabeth's in the District of Columbia:

> . . . Dr. Morgan has failed to convince any jury that her assumption is correct. The Superior Court, with a special expertise in child custody issues, already determined that Dr. Morgan has not proven her case and granted visitation to Dr. Foretich. Despite that result, Dr. Morgan brought the same claim in federal court, and the federal jury also returned a verdict for Dr. Foretich. Although the Fourth Circuit reversed that judgment because certain evidence was not admitted, some of the most crucial evidence concerned abuse of Hilary's sister, Heather. A Virginia state court found that Dr. Foretich has not abused Heather. If Dr. Morgan seeks another bite at the apple . . . she should at least be required to follow the rules.

For all practical purposes, Elizabeth's effort at an end run around Dixon in the federal court was over.

"This was a booby trap," Elizabeth said at the time. "Judge Dixon's standing order is that Hilary must 'visit' her father indefinitely. Thus, on her arrival for the seemingly innocent Alexandria exam she would have been sent to live with her father, perhaps permanently."

The setback did not daunt Elizabeth's activist supporters, either. The evening of November 30, about fifty people, mostly women, participated in a candlelight vigil on the plaza in front of Superior Court. "I find it very hard to forgive Judge Dixon," said Molly Yard, the president of NOW and the featured speaker. "He is condemning a mother and a child." Their voices ringing in the chill fall air, the demonstrators pledged to be present en masse at Judge Dixon's December 13 hearing. This trial, since it did not deal directly with the allegations about Hilary, would be open to the public.

The issue on December 13 was not custody—all the pending motions from the trial of the summer of 1987 were being held in abeyance while Hilary was gone—but the mental resolve of Elizabeth. Testifying on Elizabeth's behalf, besides Elizabeth herself, were Pyle, Kleinman, and Paul Michel. While his fiancée remained in jail, Michel's career had moved forward: the previous December, President Reagan had nominated him for a judgeship on the U.S. Court of Appeals for the Federal Circuit, a specialized appellate court that sits in Washington, and in February 1988 the U.S. Senate had confirmed the nomination. (In his short remarks at his formal investiture at the courthouse on May 23, 1988, Michel referred briefly to his fiancée, who he said was "necessarily absent.") The defiant prisoner and the Republican appellate judge remained engaged to marry once Elizabeth was free.

As snow flurries swirled that December day, all four of Elizabeth's witnesses testified confidently to one proposition: that, in Sachs's words that morning, Elizabeth would "never, ever, ever relent" in her determination to remain in jail indefinitely if that was needed to protect Hilary from what she viewed as the certainty of renewed and repeated sexual abuse.

Paul Michel had no trouble describing Elizabeth's resolve. But he ran into unexpected difficulties on cross-examination as John Lenahan, back in the case as Eric's lawyer, focused on Michel's involvement in the August 26, 1987, meeting with Linda Holman in Warrenton. "Do you recall a time when you participated in a secret meeting between Dr. Morgan, Hilary and the guardian *ad litem*?" Lenahan framed the question with a sardonic stare. Michel explained that he had set up the meeting but that it was not "secret" since it took place in a public restaurant.

Lenahan, taking advantage of the trial lawyer's once-in-a-lifetime opportunity to cross-examine a sitting judge, tried to pounce for the kill:

Q. The arrangements for that meeting were made in a rather surreptitious manner, were they not, Judge Michel?

A. I don't know anything about the arrangements for that meeting. I was asked to contact Miss Holman and be sure that she came to the location of where Hilary would be and I did that.

Q. It was necessary for you to lead Linda Holman to the location of this meeting in a remote section of Northern Virginia, isn't that correct?

A. Well, I don't know what you mean it was necessary.

Q. Did you not lead her?

A. I was asked to lead Miss Holman to a meeting site and I agreed to do so and I did that.

Q. Judge Michel, let's stop beating around the bush.

A. I'm not beating around the bush, Mr. Lenahan. I resent that kind of insinuation. I'm trying to answer your questions as clearly and as accurately as I can and I am answering them completely honestly and I do not appreciate and think uncalled-for that comment.

Q. Do you know why the meeting was held in Warrenton?

A. Not really.

Q. Did you inquire at the time?

A. No.

The colloquy, meaningless to most of those present who did not know the intricate background of the case, was the first time Michel's conduct in the case had been publicly called into question; it would not be the last.

Elizabeth's testimony on December 13 was much easier for the spectators—who included *New York Times* columnist Anthony Lewis and *Washington Post* columnist Mary McGrory—to comprehend. Elizabeth, while in jail, had read the literature of civil disobedience, which she cited on the witness stand in Dixon's crowded, dimly lit courtroom:

There are times in any country when the law itself is immoral, and it is the obligation of a citizen not to condone that kind of immorality but rather to disobey immoral laws so that they may be changed to correct the problem. Thoreau on civil disobedience . . . laid the basis for the subsequent changes in this country's law when he wrote that if the law makes you an agent of injustice to another, then you must break the law. . . . Although on the books in this country it is illegal to abuse a child, in fact it has been my experience with my child that children are not protected. . . .

Lenahan took more than an hour of cross-examination to reexamine the history of the custody case, which by then had been simmering for more than five years. He patiently walked Elizabeth through all the experts on whose opinions she had relied in concluding that Hilary was an abuse victim—and about the ones who had disagreed with her. Spectators at the public trial learned, most for the first time, about the panoply of doctors who had already had their say: Beal, Noshpitz, Kessler, Kanda, Benedek, Shubin, DeAngelis, Froning.

Linda Holman also conducted a brief cross-examination, raising a point of personal privilege. In her testimony that morning, Elizabeth had brushed off Holman's trips to Great Falls during the 1987 visitations as merely "social" in nature, implying that the guardian was quite uninterested in Hilary's welfare. Holman did not raise her voice or resort to open derision, but her tone had an unaccustomed sting. She felt that she had worked hard as Hilary's advocate and that she had taken Elizabeth's fears very seriously in 1987. Holman's first courtroom confrontation with Elizabeth, sixteen months after she had last seen her young ward, was a frosty one:

Q. On what do you base your testimony that my visits with Hilary at Dr. Foretich's home were social visits to the Foretiches and to Hilary?

A. From your description of them and from the length of them. They were conducted in a social manner. From your description of them, they offered you refreshments, you sat in a living room, you observed Dr. Foretich play with Hilary and then after a period of an hour or so, you left.

Q. Would you dispute that my visits to Hilary during those weekend visitations with Dr. Foretich were in compliance with the Court's orders?

A. They were in compliance with the Court's orders, yes.

Q. Would you dispute that the Court directed that I go to Dr.

Foretich's home to visit with Hilary under those circumstances?

A. It was my understanding of the Court's order that you were given the power not to take Hilary to the visits if you felt that they would be harmful to her and that if she did go on a visit, that you were then obliged to visit her for a brief period during that weekend.

Holman also asked Elizabeth about the proposal of Dr. Putnam from the National Institute of Mental Health (Elizabeth's chosen expert on multiple personality disorders) that Hilary be brought back and thoroughly evaluated in a hospital setting. Holman had endorsed that proposal—but Elizabeth rejected it out of hand, saying Putnam "does not know Hilary." It was obvious that Elizabeth had made a clean break with Holman, the court-appointed guardian of her child.

The next day, Sachs, Lenahan, and Holman summarized their cases for Dixon. Alluding to the upcoming Christmas holiday, Sachs pleaded, "We don't ask for the court to reverse itself [on the abuse issue]. We ask only that the court find, in this season of universal brotherhood, that enough is enough." Lenahan, in his usual sardonic, clipped manner, responded, "Elizabeth still has substantial legal remedies available to her. She will not truly be tested until she has exhausted them."

Holman said that Hilary had been seriously damaged because Elizabeth was in jail—and because Hilary was in hiding. "We do not know who is holding Hilary, except that they are committing a crime," she told the judge. "I do not doubt that Elizabeth believes Hilary is safe, but Elizabeth Morgan is incapable of controlling Hilary's environment. Morgan's characterization of my visits with Dr. Foretich as partly social visits is a complete distortion, and her characterization of my proposals [to have Hilary reevaluated] causes me pause that she may not be fully able to help Hilary."

Two days later, Judge Dixon rendered his decision in a voice just barely audible in the back rows of the small courtroom: Elizabeth would stay in jail. Her coercion "has only just begun," he said, taking ten minutes to read a brief opinion from the bench. True, Elizabeth had not yet relented, but she might later change her mind, especially since, as the judge speculated, she "has recently been hit by the thought that she may have to seriously consider the orders in this case. . . . As each day passes, the waste of Dr. Morgan's academic, personal and professional accomplishments will become more and more apparent to her." Elizabeth might miss her daughter,

Dixon concluded; "as each day passes, Dr. Morgan misses a unique opportunity to be a part of her child's life." Eventually, he conceded, he might conclude that there was "no substantial possibility" that Elizabeth would relent, but he did not know when that would be: "It could be in a month, it could be in a year, it could be more than that," Judge Dixon said. And Dixon had several words to say about the missing Hilary:

> This Court is concerned about the welfare of Hilary, her emotional and physical health. Her present circumstances are unknown. Upon her return to this jurisdiction, she will have to be evaluated. The Court will appoint appropriate experts to assist with placement decisions. . . . As each day passes, there is the possibility the child will be located.

A few minutes after the judge uttered these words, the marshals walked quietly over to Elizabeth, who, just as calmly, walked with them to the van that would take her back to jail.

CHAPTER 13

December 15, 1988, through March 1990

As 1988 came to an end, everyone involved in the Morgan case seemed to be a loser. Elizabeth had suffered defeat after defeat in court, and her prospects of release were growing dimmer in the wake of Dixon's latest decision to keep her in jail. Her cause was drawing sympathetic coverage nationwide, it was true. Two days after Dixon's decision, Anthony Lewis of *The New York Times* wrote that although court orders should not be lightly disobeyed, "it is very hard to understand the way the law had been applied in this case." The same day, Mary McGrory wrote in *The Washington Post* that the case needed "more wisdom than Dixon has so far shown." And Lewis, declaring that "it is a story that will not leave my mind," returned to the subject in another column a week later. This time he urged Eric to drop the case and give up his visitation rights—even though, the columnist acknowledged, he had not investigated the case and did not know where the truth lay.

Still, Elizabeth had been unable to convince most of the judges in her cases, the only audience that truly mattered, of the truth of her claims. Eric was a loser, too: his visitation rights were utterly meaningless as long as his daughter was hidden. And Hilary had been separated from both her parents for a year and a half. The only bright spot for her was that she was living far away from the continuing strife of the custody battle.

In July 1988, the six-year-old and her grandparents had been forced to leave England; William and Antonia had only temporary residence permits and feared they would be discovered if they applied to immigration. Although the D.C. police had done little to find Hilary, Detective Harmon had contacted his counterparts around the world and had notified Interpol, the international law enforcement agency. Police sources say Scotland Yard had been informed that the little girl and her grandparents might be somewhere in England. But the Morgans, again eluding the authorities effortlessly, moved on to Christchurch, New Zealand, where they located a furnished apartment in a pleasant but undistinguished motel on a main road in Merivale, a tree-lined suburb of Christchurch.

New Zealand held several advantages for the Morgans as a place of refuge. Antonia had traveled there years before and was somewhat familiar with the country. She thought the island nation, with its slow pace, was an ideal place to bring up Hilary.

William and Antonia also knew that New Zealand, as an English-speaking nation, shares a good deal of its culture with England and, to a lesser extent, with the United States. Christchurch, a city of 300,000 on the South Island of New Zealand, has been called the most English city outside of England. They hoped to minimize Hilary's culture shock. And there was the distance factor as well. Although the jet, computer, and fax machine mean that almost no spot is truly remote now, the Morgans felt that Judge Dixon was on another planet altogether as they settled into their new home, ten thousand miles away from the District of Columbia.

New Zealand held another crucial advantage: its government had not signed the Hague Convention of 1980, the international agreement requiring that wrongfully abducted children must be returned "forthwith" to their country of origin. This legal twist meant that a trickle of Americans—those who had the money and the inclination to start their lives anew in the Southern Hemisphere—were beginning to find their way to New Zealand in the wake of unfavorable custody decisions.

Since the Hague Convention did not apply to New Zealand, local New Zealand family law governed custody cases if they came to its courts. Experts in comparative law say that New Zealand family courts tend to be among the most "child-centered" in the world, designed to protect children from the acrimony of their parents' disputes. "Courts have recognized that young children need the emotional security that comes from stable surroundings and a recognized and predictable routine," says an authoritative treatise on New Zealand law. "A father or mother has no special right to custody simply by virtue of being the father or mother."

Although the law did not tell the New Zealand courts how to treat allegations of sexual abuse by a parent, a 1988 case in Christchurch, which drew publicity throughout New Zealand, gave some indications of the approach they took. In that case, Jeff Spence, a Christchurch construction worker, was accused by social service workers of abusing his severely handicapped five-year-old daughter. The accusations, which Spence denied and which resulted largely from the child's play with anatomically correct dolls, were backed up by Karen Zelas, Christchurch's best-known psychiatrist. A family court judge decided to keep the family together, believing that the girl's mother would act to prevent any future abuse.

Hilary was not thinking about international legal conventions or about trials in family court. In her tree-shaded neighborhood, she found friends her age, learned to ride a bicycle, and attended services every Sunday at the Episcopal church down the road. Still using the name Ellen Morgan, she was enrolled by her grandparents at Selwyn House, an upper-class private elementary school two blocks from her home. With her life framed by the tight circle of home, school, and church, Hilary gradually adjusted to her new country and developed a lilting "Kiwi" accent.

At first, only the family doctor knew her true identity; but as television docudramas and newspaper features began to make *Morgan* v. *Foretich* the most famous custody battle in the world, it was impossible for William and Antonia to thoroughly conceal the identity of the celebrated six-year-old. School officials and a few others in Christchurch also learned who Hilary was, but they kept her secret.

As the 1988 holiday season approached, Eric's spirits dimmed. "After what I've gone through, I'm going to write a book about this case," he told a reporter. "It's a shame the feminists have focused on this case. They're doing American men a disservice. These are women who have an agenda. They're nothing but disruptive to children and families." Elizabeth, sounding more concerned for Hilary and less self-pitying, spoke to reporters of Hilary's "second incest-free Christmas."

Stephen Sachs did not share Elizabeth's optimism. Sachs, who like most litigators usually exudes confidence, struck a rare note of self-doubt and ennui in a late December interview after Dixon's trial. He would go ahead, of course, with an appeal of Dixon's decision, but he conceded that the process of freeing his client was taking longer than he had anticipated. In January 1989, the D.C. Court of Appeals granted expedited treatment to his appeal, but

even so, Sachs knew his case would not be heard again until sometime in the spring. It might be as late as May.

Elizabeth's feminist supporters were dismayed by her most recent
loss in Dixon's court and disheartened by what they saw as the
judge's gratuitously cruel tone in rejecting her claims. They tentatively began to think about a legislative solution to Elizabeth's incarceration. Sachs, accustomed to pleading his case before judges,
not legislatures, downplayed this possibility as 1988 ended. "I just
don't see how that's possible," he said just before Christmas. Sachs's
sober conclusion seemed appropriate at the time.

But the women—activists in the Friends of Elizabeth Morgan and
in the D.C. chapter of the National Organization for Women—were
determined. Acting independently of Sachs, they first approached
Jim Nathanson, a member of the D.C. City Council. Nathanson
consulted with Professor Douglas Rendleman of the Washington
and Lee Law School. Rendleman is one of the few academic experts
in the arcane area of civil contempt. He is also a supporter of legal
reform in the area.

Nathanson was prepared, with Rendleman's help, to draft local
legislation to put a time limit on incarceration for contempt in the
District. It would be written retroactively so as to free Elizabeth;
in fact, she was the only person to whom it would immediately apply.
But Nathanson was soon advised by the council's attorneys that
under the District's home-rule mandate, Congress had maintained
its authority over anything involving the D.C. justice system. Elizabeth's supporters realized that any bill to free her would have to
be passed by the U.S. Congress, not by the D.C. City Council, and
it seemed extremely unlikely that Congress would intervene in a
pending custody case.

So Sachs persisted in his strategy of raising his constitutional arguments—the ones Dixon had rejected—in the D.C. Court of Appeals and the U.S. Supreme Court. If those courts turned him down,
he planned to return to the same U.S. District Court that had rejected his *habeas corpus* petition in April 1988. This time, though,
Sachs would be able to tell the federal district judge that he had
done all he could under local D.C. law and had failed. The federal
court would then feel free to use *habeas corpus* to spring Elizabeth
from jail—or so he hoped.

Sachs's legal strategy was unimpeachable, but even the media-
savvy litigator did not anticipate what would happen next. In late
1988 and early 1989, *Glamour* and *People* magazines ran articles
sympathetic to Elizabeth, who, they asserted, had chosen jail over

her lucrative medical practice to protect her daughter from rape by her father. Elizabeth was "wan and exhausted" in jail, *People* said, and her plight was "a tragic reminder that for those who defy the law to protect their children from alleged sexual abuse, the cost of love can be high." (The article used the word "alleged," but left little doubt that the writer believed the abuse was real.)

The New York Times, the Boston *Globe,* and others soon followed with similar articles. And "rape" was the term Elizabeth was now routinely using for what she said Hilary had undergone. Eric was given the chance to respond in the articles, but his denials, which tended to focus on himself rather than Hilary, as the victim, often sounded self-serving. He told *People,* for example, that "although I'm not behind bars, I'm the one who has taken the heat." He said Elizabeth's accusations had hurt his family and his dental practice, "a sin she is going to pay for someday." Eric sounded defensive in responding to Elizabeth's carefully calibrated emotional appeals.

In jail, Elizabeth became a celebrity; *Morgan* v. *Foretich* became a national story. And the media coverage had a direct impact on the case. It turned out that one of the readers of the newspaper and magazine accounts was Charles Colson, the onetime Nixon White House aide who had been convicted in the Watergate scandal a dozen years before. Colson, having served some jail time himself, had resurfaced as the founder of Prison Fellowship Ministries, a Christian evangelical group that tries to spread the gospel to those incarcerated around the nation. At first glance, Charles Colson and Elizabeth Morgan seem to have little in common, but the personal interest Colson took in Elizabeth's case set into motion a chain of events that soon developed a critical momentum.

As far back as the summer of 1988, the Washington director of Prison Fellowship Ministries had reported to Colson that Elizabeth seemed to have developed a sort of ministry of her own in prison. The female inmate population in the D.C. Jail, mostly working-class black women, seemed to look up to the well-educated doctor for spiritual inspiration. In March 1989, Colson wrote a column in the group's newsletter, supporting Elizabeth as a true Christian who was selflessly protecting her daughter. "There is, she believes, a law higher than civil law," Colson wrote. "It's the law of love." Colson urged his readers to pray for Elizabeth and to write to the congressmen with responsibility for the District of Columbia. On April 6, Colson met with Elizabeth in prison.

Just three weeks later, on April 26, Frank Wolf, a moderately conservative Republican from northern Virginia, introduced a bill in the U.S. House of Representatives that would limit to eighteen months the time a person could spend in jail on a contempt charge in a child-custody case in the District of Columbia. Wolf, who represents the part of Virginia where Elizabeth grew up, had read Colson's newsletter and had chatted with Colson several times on the telephone. It was the Colson connection, not the feminists' behind-the-scenes work, that had gotten the legislative wheels rolling. But Colson was not the first person with whom Wolf had discussed *Morgan* v. *Foretich*. Wolf was also Eric Foretich's congressman, and in January 1989 he had written to Elaine Mittleman, one of Eric's lawyers, that while he understood her and Eric's concerns about the hiding of Hilary, jurisdiction over the case "was completely in the hands of Judge Dixon of the D.C. Superior Court."

Mittleman was incensed when she heard about Wolf's bill. She asked him for an immediate meeting with her and Eric, and Wolf agreed. At the meeting, Wolf said he wasn't really taking Elizabeth's side; he just wanted to break the logjam in Dixon's court. Eric's frustration redoubled. Elizabeth was winning in Congress and the media what she had been unable to achieve through the courts, he told Mittleman.

Wolf was undaunted. "I developed this legislation to correct what I believe to be a flaw in the system that allows an individual in a child custody case to remain imprisoned under civil contempt for an indefinite period of time," he said at a hearing that spring. "I am not taking sides in the Morgan-Foretich case. I am not prepared to say that Dr. Morgan is correct or that Dr. Foretich is correct. . . . I do not believe that a child who is denied the care of either of her parents is being well served." But despite Wolf's protestations, the bill, which moved rapidly through spring hearings in the House and the U.S. Senate, became popularly known as the "Elizabeth Morgan bill."

The bill, which applied to all persons jailed in the District after January 1, 1987, was drafted to affect only one person—Elizabeth. Four members of Congress from the D.C. area quickly joined as co-sponsors.

Elaine Mittleman, whom Eric had hired at the end of 1988 to help him with his appeals, immediately denounced the bill. A feisty attorney who practices law from her modest home in Falls Church, Virginia, Mittleman complained to everyone who would listen that if Congress was only concerned about bringing Hilary back, Wolf's bill was useless. "Dr. Morgan and her fiancé, Judge Michel, have both testified that they plan to get married and live in the District of Columbia," Mittleman told congressmen. "They have stated they will never bring Hilary back to the jurisdiction of the District. Congress will let Dr. Morgan out of jail, and Hilary will never be returned."

Assessing Eric's situation, Mittleman concluded that John Lenahan and Eric's other lawyers had focused only on winning the custody case, not on winning the battle for public opinion. She took Eric's case to the media, arranging press conferences and photo opportunities, and found mixed success. Under the glare of the cameras, Eric sometimes sounded shrill and sometimes cool and rational. Mittleman still preferred her policy of openness to the years when her client had ignored the press and let Elizabeth shape the public consciousness all by herself.

Mittleman also seized the initiative in other areas. Eric was offended that Paul Michel, a sitting federal judge, had testified before Dixon in December 1988 that he had helped Elizabeth plan her legal strategies. He also suspected that Michel might have known more than he had let on about the plans to hide Hilary in the summer of 1987. "I hold this man responsible for hiding my daughter, as much as I hold anyone responsible," Eric said. Eric, who had been in court when Linda Holman testified about the meeting in Warrenton, did not believe Michel when he said he knew nothing of his fiancée's plans and that he never talked about Hilary with Elizabeth.

Mittleman decided it was time for Eric to fight back. Early in 1989, Mittleman filed a judicial misconduct complaint on behalf of Eric against Michel in the court he sat in, the U.S. Court of Appeals for the Federal Circuit. For a judge to devise legal strategies for a private litigant was improper and unbecoming, Mittleman thought. So the Morgan case spilled over into yet a new forum; like all federal appeals courts, the Federal Circuit has an internal mechanism for processing misconduct complaints in which the other judges on the court review the questioned actions. Mittleman's complaint was filed with then Chief Judge Howard Markey.

In a response to Markey, Michel admitted that on rare occasions he had worked on Elizabeth's legal case even after going on the bench. That was at least a technical violation of the code of judicial conduct. In order to dispose of Eric's complaint without further investigation by his colleagues on the court, Michel formally agreed to stop giving advice to Elizabeth's lawyers. This agreement constituted "appropriate corrective action," Markey found. As he had in December before Dixon, Michel vehemently denied that he knew anything about Hilary's concealment, and the Federal Circuit dismissed all of Eric's other allegations. Despite this and later efforts by Eric's advocates, who remained suspicious of Michel's role in the August 26, 1987, meeting with Linda Holman in Warrenton, it has never been conclusively demonstrated that he participated in hiding Hilary or had prior knowledge of the plan.

Mittleman also tried to push along the official efforts to locate Hilary. She called the Federal Bureau of Investigation repeatedly for assistance in finding the missing child. But after much equivo-cation on the part of Justice Department prosecutors, Mittleman was finally told that the U.S. Attorney's Office in the District of Columbia (the prosecutor's office that would ordinarily enlist the FBI's help in a case arising in Washington) had, some time before, recused, or disqualified, itself from the entire Morgan-Foretich case. Elizabeth's brother Rob was still a lawyer in the office.

That meant the U.S. Attorney would not help find Hilary. "Rob Morgan was very interested in the case. He wanted Elizabeth's allegations investigated," recalls Joseph DiGenova, who was U.S. Attorney until he switched to private practice in the spring of 1988. "Other [prosecutors] in the office were very uncomfortable with that idea."

To avoid any appearance of impropriety, DiGenova accepted his subordinates' recommendation that the entire office stay out of the case. "We wanted to make sure that whatever decisions were made would not be suspected as biased," he recalls. The U.S. Attorney's Office eventually sent the case to the Criminal Division of the Justice Department, an office that coordinates important cases around the nation and rarely gets involved in individual prosecutions. Al-though it could have brought in the FBI, the Criminal Division took no action to locate Hilary.

The U.S. Attorney's recusal also slowed the decision on the police investigation of Elizabeth regarding the allegedly pornographic pic-tures from 1985. That investigation was still hanging fire as late as July 1987, when Detective Williams's testimony about his chat with Hilary at the hospital was rejected by Judge Dixon in the last stages of his custody hearing.

Although Eric repeatedly aired his belief that Rob Morgan had intervened on behalf of his sister to halt the child-pornography in-vestigation, DiGenova and other top-ranking prosecutors say this was not the case, and Rob has denied that he exerted such influence on the office. Rob's interest in Elizabeth's case, however, may have led to the U.S. Attorney's recusal decision, which in turn put the whole matter on the back burner at the Justice Department.

In any case, there were solid legal grounds for not prosecuting Elizabeth. Sometime in 1988, the National Obscenity Enforcement Unit, a part of the Criminal Division, declined to pursue the case on the grounds that it could not be shown that Elizabeth had derived any sexual gratification from the photos or had intended that anyone else would.

Legal or not, the photographs of the naked two-and-a-half-year-old child remain repulsive to anyone who has seen them, and the fact of the repeated picture sessions does not aid Elizabeth's effort to cast herself as an advocate of children's rights. Some media accounts mentioned the photographs but tended to dismiss their significance. A much-reprinted November 1988 article in *Glamour* magazine emphasizes that some of the pictures were taken in April 1985, after the inconclusive Fairfax Social Services determination on the abuse charges. "Her child was being destroyed before her eyes and no one believed her. She had to do something," the writer said. The article, portraying Elizabeth as a desperate woman, downplays the fact that Elizabeth first took nude pictures of Hilary in early February, just weeks after she first suspected abuse and just days after the Social Services inquiry began.

As another part of his spring 1989 offensive, Eric went public with an effort to settle the whole case and bring Hilary back. In a *Washington Post* op-ed article, Eric urged that Elizabeth be released, whereupon he would drop his request for custody. Meanwhile, Hilary would be in foster care while both parents had supervised visitation. The next step would be to have Hilary evaluated by a multidisciplinary team and to have Elizabeth's mental status evaluated by a trained psychiatrist picked by Linda Holman. If Hilary's psychiatrist found it best that Eric give up visitation, he would agree to do so, although that step would be "extremely painful." All this would be on condition that Elizabeth not exploit the situation through a book or a movie.

Elizabeth rejected the proposal out of hand. Unless Eric were willing to acknowledge that he had abused Hilary, she would make no deals with him, and that is one thing he refused to do.

While Eric's renewed efforts were meeting mixed success, Elizabeth's odd coalition of feminists, born-again Christians, and friends and colleagues from her hospital days pulled itself together with amazing speed. Participants at a noon rally in front of the Superior Court Building on May 17, 1989, carried signs reading: THE WRONG DOCTOR IS IN JAIL. Eleanor Smeal, the former president of NOW, addressed a crowd of about fifty people: "We stand here to fight sex discrimination in the courts until women are empowered and have equal rights to justice in our land," she said. Doug Rendleman, the professor from Washington and Lee, ambled through the fringes of the group. Sharon Foretich was to have been a featured speaker that day, but she never showed up. Instead, the organizers read a letter to members of Congress by Sharon's father Cornelius Sullivan, supporting Wolf's bill and declaring that Eric had "raped and abused" Heather.

That was not what a three-judge panel of the Virginia Court of Appeals had decided a few weeks before. Affirming Judge Bach's ruling of nearly two years before, the state appeals court declared on March 28 that the trial judge "was entitled to accept the testimony of those witnesses who concluded that there was no sexual abuse over that of those who concluded that abuse had occurred." Specifically noted as convincing witnesses for Eric were Catherine DeAngelis, the Johns Hopkins pediatrician; James McMurrer, Heather's therapist; and Daniel Gollhardt, the police investigator who had interviewed Heather. This decision, from a court system entirely separate from the D.C. family court and from Judge Williams's federal court, was unanimous.

Judge James Benton, Jr., in a lengthy concurring opinion, described all the key evidence in Heather's case and reached the same conclusion: Judge Bach had a reasonable basis for deciding in Eric's favor. But, this judge said, there was "strong evidence that some touching did occur; however, the evidence did not address the issue whether the touching was accidental, contrived, or innocuous." By "touching," the judge was referring to the possibility that sometime in the far distant past, Heather had touched Eric's penis. But whether or not Heather was sexually abused, the judge said, "the child believes that she was." All the judges agreed that for that reason alone, further therapy was needed.

This was essentially the last court ruling on the validity of Sharon's allegations of abuse. After four years of litigation, the courts of Virginia had found that there was serious doubt that any abuse had occurred, but that there was little doubt that Heather believed it had.

The case went back, for the last time, to juvenile court so that a visitation schedule could be arranged. Psychiatrists and psychologists wrangled incessantly about whether the father-daughter relationship was in permanent disarray or merely temporary disrepair. Finally, a year later, Vincent and Doris, and then Eric, received supervised visitation privileges with Heather in her psychiatrist's office. The visits were mostly unsatisfactory, the Foretiches said. It was obvious that Heather, turning ten years old, thought her father and grandparents were bad people because of something she had been told had occurred when she was five.

As Heather's case began to wind down in the spring of 1989, Elizabeth's case started to pick up speed. On May 23, six days after the demonstration at the courthouse, a House subcommittee held hearings on Wolf's bill to change D.C. contempt law. A standing-room-only crowd braved a driving spring rain to listen to a panel of legal experts, who explained that eighteen months should be enough time to break the wills of those prisoners whose wills could be broken. After that, they said, contempt tended to become punitive, not coercive. Despite everyone's pretense that the bill had nothing to do with Elizabeth, the custody case kept coming up.

"My personal observation is that Morgan is a woman of great character and resolve," said Stan Parris, a conservative congressman from northern Virginia who was a co-sponsor. "She has determined, correctly or not, that the interests of her child will be served by her incarceration. . . . At some point we will say, 'This lady is really serious about this.' "

The only open dissenter was the forlorn Elaine Mittleman, who circled through the crowded hearing room, passing out fact sheets on Eric's view of the case to anyone who would take them. "This bill will not help Hilary," Mittleman said. "The amount of time Dr. Morgan has been incarcerated is the same amount of time Hilary has been abducted." Eric and Mittleman had both asked permission to testify but had been denied by congressional staffers, on the disingenuous grounds that the hearing was not about *Morgan* v. *Foretich* and that no one identified with a party in the case would be allowed to appear. Elizabeth's lawyers did not have to show up at the hearing, though; her cause had come through loud and clear.

That afternoon, at a hastily convened press conference at a down-town Washington hotel, Eric, flanked by his parents and a publicity agent, again declared his innocence of Elizabeth's abuse charges. "I would like to direct attention away from Elizabeth Morgan and toward the plight of Hilary, an innocent child who's not in this room," Eric said, this time emphasizing his daughter rather than his dental practice. "We seem to have forgotten about her." Mittleman said she had just been in touch with Linda Holman and that Holman had told her she opposed the legislation to free Elizabeth. In response to a question about Hilary's whereabouts, Eric said, "I have fears about what Elizabeth has done to my daughter. I've seen the photographs she took, and if I could show them to you, I'd need to say no more." The dozen or so skeptical reporters present remained skeptical, and the session broke up quickly.

Echoes of the congressional hearing rang the next morning, as the D.C. Court of Appeals finally convened the long-awaited appeal of Dixon's December 1988 decision. Sachs presented his case that Elizabeth would never be coerced and that Dixon had no reasonable basis for concluding that she would be: "I wish I could capture for this court the harshness of this verdict," he told the three judges on the panel. When her turn came, Mittleman immediately tried to pull the argument away from the narrow issue on which Sachs was appealing. Within seconds, she found herself in a tug-of-war with an almost incredulous appeals court Judge John Ferren, who tried to return to the subject at hand:

Mittleman: Hilary is the hostage here. She's hostage to her own mother's delusional beliefs that her daughter was sexually abused.

Ferren: Do you agree that the sole question before us is whether the jailing is coercive or punitive?

Mittleman: No. That's playing Elizabeth Morgan's game. She's focusing on herself, not on Hilary's interests.

Mittleman pleaded with the judges to take notice of the sudden upsurge of support for Elizabeth on Capitol Hill: "The events of the last 24 hours have radically changed the situation before this court," she said. Because of the pending bill to set Elizabeth free, Mittleman insisted, it was necessary to send the case back to Dixon with instructions to locate Hilary. Perhaps a special prosecutor should be appointed to look for the girl, Mittleman said. At one point, a frustrated Sachs took the unusual step of rising from his chair to interrupt her argument. He tried to remind the judges that the issue was the reasonableness of Dixon's decision, not Hilary's welfare or the workings of Congress.

Turning to the question at hand, Mittleman told the judges that "Elizabeth's needs are being met in jail; it's a secure environment for her." Perhaps, Mittleman suggested, Elizabeth would truly be coerced to disclose Hilary's whereabouts only if she were transferred to Alderson, a federal women's prison in West Virginia, away from the media spotlight. A collective gasp was heard in the courtroom, which was packed with journalists and Elizabeth's supporters.

Many people at the hearing thought Mittleman's high-risk strategy of leaving behind the narrow question of the appeal and focusing on the missing child was a failure. Two days later, on May 26, the court produced some support for that view, issuing an order that sent the case back to Judge Dixon for additional conclusions. The appeals court told Dixon to take evidence on whether Elizabeth's continued incarceration from December through June "is likely to cause her to comply with the trial court's outstanding order to produce her daughter," and then to send the case back up for a decision on Elizabeth's appeal. To most observers, it sounded as if the appeals judges didn't think Dixon had yet provided them with enough evidence to sustain his conclusion. Mittleman thought otherwise. "It is the first time of which I am aware when it is possible to discuss Hilary, rather than just Dr. Morgan. It is an opportunity which cannot be missed," she told Eric.

Dixon convened his court again on June 8, six months after the December *habeas corpus* hearing. Elizabeth had been in jail for almost twenty-two months. Her resolve hadn't changed. Neither had her lawyers' arguments. One new witness was Charles Colson, who described Elizabeth's "composure and commitment to Christ" when he had visited her in jail. Paul Michel took the stand again to describe his conversations with his fiancée: "We talk," he said, "as if Hilary is not coming back, since Elizabeth predicts that Hilary will never be fully protected by the courts." Finally, Elizabeth testified again on her own behalf. In measured, singsong tones, she told her story yet another time. The very first thing she said was that she had gone to jail to prevent Hilary from having unsupervised visits with her "incest father." At counsel table, Eric recoiled in his chair, and Doris and Vincent, sitting in the audience, let out an angry and shocked "Ooooooh."

After Elizabeth completed her testimony the next day, she was followed to the stand by her brother Rob Morgan. Rob had been subpoenaed by John Lenahan, Eric's attorney, and both he and Elizabeth's lawyers had objected vigorously to his appearing in the case. (Rob hired a former high-level Justice Department prosecutor as his lawyer to make the arguments.) After all, the ostensible reason for the hearing was to test Elizabeth's will to stay in jail, and Rob could add little to that. But Dixon, asserting that as a family court judge he had "continuing full jurisdiction" over Hilary's welfare, overruled the objections.

In court, it immediately became clear why Rob Morgan did not want to testify. Lenahan, back in charge of Eric's case, had accepted

Mittleman's view that it was time to focus attention on Hilary. He thought Rob might know where Hilary was. On twenty-six separate occasions, Lenahan asked Rob about his parents' whereabouts and the whereabouts of his niece, and on twenty-six occasions, Rob refused to reply, even after Dixon threatened him with a contempt citation of his own. "I respectfully decline to answer any question that might lead to the discovery of my niece," Rob responded, quietly but firmly.

Eric had been stymied again by the strong-willed Morgans, but Rob Morgan's career as a prosecutor was over. An assistant U.S. attorney is sworn to uphold the law. He is not supposed to defy a court order. The following Monday, after a meeting with his supervisors at the U.S. Attorney's Office, Rob cleaned out his desk and was placed on administrative leave. He said at the time that he had already resigned in early May, giving sixty days' notice, before he even appeared before Dixon. "I always wanted to go out and work on my own as a lawyer," he said. But one source says Rob was gently urged to leave by U.S. Attorney Jay Stephens, who didn't want to keep a lawyer so strongly identified with a woman accused of flouting the law.

The June 9 hearing ended with Linda Holman's summation. Although Hilary's guardian expressed no view on Elizabeth's incarceration, she warned Dixon that Hilary was in hiding with "desperate people, people who are only concerned with keeping her secreted away." Elizabeth's bland assurances that Hilary was happy and healthy, Holman said, were unsatisfactory to her and "should be unsatisfactory to the court." From Holman's perspective, the "possible physical, emotional, and mental dangers to which Hilary may be subjected" were "frightening." Holman renewed her suggestion that Dixon appoint a multidisciplinary team to evaluate Hilary once she was brought back.

In the findings he issued and sent up to the appeals court ten days later, Judge Dixon adopted the essence of Holman's views.

> Six months later [after the December hearing] this court is even more concerned about the welfare of Hilary. Her emotional and physical health remain unknown. The fitness of her current providers to be custodians is undetermined. [T]his court will not place the child with either parent until she has been initially evaluated by a neutral team of appointed experts, a multi-disciplinary team.

In these findings, Dixon proposed a new way out of the dilemma: Elizabeth had never stated explicitly, he said, that she would not turn Hilary over to the social services division of the court, or to the D.C. Department of Human Services, both of which provide care to abused or neglected children. "The alternative method to purge her contempt," he said, "has not been addressed." If the only issue were whether Elizabeth would give Hilary to Eric, Dixon conceded that he would consider her will unshakable and order her immediate release. For reasons of personal pride alone, he said, she would never permit a visit with Eric. But as the months in jail dragged on, Elizabeth might agree to a neutral social service evaluation of Hilary. Sachs called Dixon's decision just "a new tactic to keep her in jail." As for the issue of Rob Morgan's contempt, the judge said he was holding that in abeyance.

While Dixon was scrambling to justify his right to keep Elizabeth in jail, Senator Orrin Hatch, the conservative Republican senator from Utah, gave her a huge boost. In mid-June, Hatch introduced a Senate bill that, like Wolf's House measure, would limit the time served for contempt in D.C. custody cases. By now, the eighteen-month cap had been reduced to one year. "It's no use kidding," Hatch told a reporter. "My bill is motivated by the Elizabeth Morgan case." Hatch "has always been a supporter of the underdog," his press secretary Paul Smith said, although in a press release Hatch, like Frank Wolf, said he "was not taking sides in this particular case." Rather than being designed to help Elizabeth, Hatch said, the bill "will go a long way in protecting the child from being the real loser in these cases."

Independently, H. Ross Perot, the Texas billionaire who had read about Elizabeth's plight in magazine accounts, started calling influential senators he knew, asking them to support Hatch's legislation. One of them, Senator John Heinz (R-Pa.) was senior Republican on the Senate District of Columbia subcommittee. When Heinz held hearings on the bill, Hatch was the first witness, and the committee approved the bill unanimously. Beyond Mittleman, there was little organized opposition. What opposition there was came from the American Civil Liberties Union, where the Washington chapter expressed serious concern about limiting the power of the courts. "Civil contempt is often used to protect the rights of minorities. Anything that limits judges' power to compel obedience can hurt civil liberties," said Arthur Spitzer, legal director of the chapter.

But dissenters were rare. Elizabeth's supporters—the feminists and the fundamentalists—kept up their massive letter-writing campaigns, deluging senators and congressmen with information about the Morgan-Foretich case. The grass-roots lobbying effort put the "Elizabeth Morgan bill" on a fast track, and on June 28, Frank

Wolf's bill passed the House of Representatives by a vote of 376 to
34. One of the "no" votes came from Representative Herbert Bateman, the congressman from the Tidewater area of Virginia who was
a longtime friend of the Foretich family. "I would be more than
willing to testify as a character witness for you in any legal proceeding
if it would be helpful in establishing your innocence," Bateman had
written years before to Doris and Vincent.

While Congress lingered in its August recess, Elizabeth, still in
jail, remained outwardly pessimistic about her chances of release.
"I'm not going to delude myself. When it happens, it happens," she
said. "My first time in jail I learned what every inmate learns: If
you plan on leaving soon, you'll go crazy."

A few weeks later, the D.C. Court of Appeals delivered its fourth
and final decision in the Morgan case, one that left Elizabeth tan-
talizingly close to freedom. On August 21, the three-judge panel of
the court, dividing 2–1, reversed Judge Dixon's June finding that
Elizabeth could still be coerced by the jail cell. The majority found
a lack of support in the record for Dixon's notion that Elizabeth's
will was not quite as strong as she wished to believe. The majority
opinion was written by Judge John Ferren, the judge who had been
so skeptical of Mittleman at oral argument. Ferren said he tended
to believe Elizabeth when she said that she was just as unalterably
opposed to turning Hilary over to social services as she was to giving
her to Eric for a visit. He wrote:

> We do have a voluminous record that clearly reflects a consistent,
> convincing stand by Morgan that she will not budge. We are therefore
> convinced that Morgan's incarceration no longer can be said, after
> twenty-three months, to have a coercive effect. . . . In ordering Mor-
> gan's release, we do not condone her conduct and do not express any
> view on where the child's best interest lies—with Morgan, Foretich,
> both, or neither.

For the majority on the panel, the only possible conclusion was
that Elizabeth was being punished, not coerced, and that she had
to be released. It was the first time in the case that the appeals court
had seen fit to reverse Dixon. Even so, the opinion, written by
Judge Ferren, went out of its way to commend the trial judge, noting
that he had shown "remarkable fortitude in the face of long and
gruelling proceedings." It was one day short of two years after that
Saturday afternoon in 1987 when Elizabeth had called Eric to tell

him Hilary would not be attending the eleventh scheduled overnight visit. It was also Hilary's seventh birthday.

Elizabeth would have been out of jail that day, August 21, 1989, were it not for one of those curious legal twists that seemed to pervade the case: At the same time that the 2–1 opinion was issued, the court "vacated" it, i.e., declared it null and void. In doing so, the court announced that before the opinion was issued, a majority of the nine active judges on the court had voted to have the whole appeal reheard *en banc* (by the full court). Rehearings *en banc* are rare in the D.C. Court of Appeals. Rehearings granted simultaneously with the issuance of the opinion of a three-judge panel are rarer still. Once the opinion was vacated, it had no legal effect, and Elizabeth stayed in jail. The court clerk quickly scheduled the rehearing *en banc* to take place on September 20.

The divisions on the District's highest local court, and among its citizenry as a whole, were well illustrated by the dissent from the court panel's 2–1 opinion. Written by Judge Julia Cooper Mack, a black woman who was taking issue with the two white male judges who wrote the majority ruling, the decision urged deference to Dixon's findings that Elizabeth might somehow be coerced by continued imprisonment. But in a passage quite unnecessary to her conclusion, Mack betrayed a personal distaste for one of the parties that is rare in a judicial opinion:

Dr. Morgan has justifiably or unjustifiably wrapped herself in the mantle of motherhood . . . it is Dr. Morgan who has, from the beginning, fought to unseal the record before us to publicly air lurid details of evidence she has submitted which are relevant to, but not determinative of, her right to curtail visitation, and which might run the risk of irrevocably harming her daughter. She has made her daughter a fugitive from the law. A reasonable factfinder could draw the inference that she is willing to risk harm to her daughter to vindicate in a public forum her claim that the man with whom she once shared a mutual obsession has abused his daughter and that the judicial system (which she has exhaustively used) has failed to protect the daughter.

Judge Mack took semi-retired senior status on the court a month later, and this was her last dissent as a full member of the court.

Some court observers, reading passages like this, thought racial politics as well as sexual politics had entered the case. They were struck by the spectacle of a black appeals court judge showing such obvious disdain for Elizabeth, who they guessed was perceived by

Mack as a privileged white woman who had thumbed her nose at the orders of a black trial judge.

Elizabeth's friends on the Hill were determined to make the vagaries of the appeals court irrelevant. The steady advance of the Morgan bill was hardly deflected by the August recess. On September 7, the Senate approved its version of the bill, and all that remained was the appointment of a conference committee to work out minor differences between the two houses. With final passage seeming just days away, the D.C. Court of Appeals convened its *en banc* hearing. The racial animosity was again obvious. Judge Theodore Newman, Jr., an outspoken black judge who had been a prime mover behind the decision to rehear the case, vented his feelings: "Suppose this is Mississippi, and a white mother is required by a court to give a child over to a black father. Is a court order to be at the whim of popular prejudice?"

But the full appellate court never rendered a decision. On September 22, two days later, both houses of Congress gave final approval to the Morgan bill. Immediately, the bill was whisked to the White House, and plans were made to fly it to President George Bush at his vacation home in Maine. The president signed it into law on Saturday afternoon, September 23, in Boston, where he had a luncheon speaking engagement. "It was a matter of compassion" for Elizabeth, said Marlin Fitzwater, a presidential spokesman. Asked whether the president had studied the evidence in the custody case, Fitzwater replied that Bush took no position on the merits of the case. After a last-minute flurry of legal motions at the D.C. Superior Court—Mittleman made a final effort to strike down the new law as unconstitutional—Elizabeth was freed at 8:44 P.M. on Monday, September 25. She had spent almost twenty-five months in jail.

At her first press conference as a free woman in more than two years, Elizabeth, carrying a dozen yellow roses, announced that she would keep Hilary in hiding. She had spoken to Hilary, she said, but refused to say by what means she had done so. Then she, Michel, and her brother Rob drove off in a steady rain to Sachs's Washington law office three miles away. "I don't know that anything is over," Elizabeth told reporters there. "I obviously could be jailed again and am well aware of that. Also, my daughter is not protected. Although I love her and miss her terribly, it is more important that she be safe than that she be with me."

The media storm swirled with renewed force in the days after Elizabeth's release. Elizabeth appeared on the "Today Show," while

Eric went on CNN's "Crossfire." Both warring spouses were interviewed, from separate locations, on ABC's "Good Morning America" and "Nightline." Elizabeth refused to provide any physical evidence of Hilary's well-being, such as letters or videotapes. She told a *New York Times* reporter that the press had not asked for such evidence of well-being when Hilary was being forced to visit with her father. "The press now for their own appetite wants to see her and know about her, but it's too late," Elizabeth said.

At a packed September 27 press conference at his Great Falls home, Eric passed out a typed statement agreeing to supervised visitation with Hilary but refusing to "totally and completely repudiate" his rights as a father. "There is no reason why I should do so, and that would not be in the best interest of Hilary," he added. In a handwritten notation on the bottom, Eric wrote: "I am signing this statement although I am innocent of all Dr. Morgan's allegations." Eric announced that he was calling off Mittleman's efforts to cast doubt on the validity of the legislation. "I hope attention will now be focused on the return of Hilary," he said. "I hope to return to professional life, and I hope this is the last time I have to address all these issues publicly. I would like to restore some dignity to my daughter's life."

Eric, accompanied by Doris, Vincent, Mittleman, and a professional public relations woman, announced the formation of a "Help Hilary Home" fund to solicit private donations to hire investigators. "Apparently Dr. Morgan has no intention of letting this thing abate," he said. "It's time we get over this episode and begin to focus on love, kindness, and family, doing what normal people do. I would have hoped the American public had as much concern for the well-being of Hilary as for Elizabeth Morgan." Again, Eric said, a multidisciplinary team should be named to examine Hilary when she is brought back, to read all the records, and to decide her fate. "I am willing to take the risk of losing my parental rights, if the panel said so. Conversely, if I were given unsupervised visitation, I would make sure someone else was there every single moment," he added.

To the very end, Eric defended Judge Dixon, whom he called a "courageous man." Dixon's fellow judges on the Superior Court also weighed in with support—after all, at least nine of them had also held hearings or issued rulings in the Morgan case over the years. There was outrage at Congress for intervening in a case that was before the courts. "It seems like an intrusion on the independence of the judiciary," one judge said. "There is a strong perception here that if the case had involved a person less prominent, or of a different race, it wouldn't have happened." Dixon himself maintained his silence. He told Mittleman that as long as Hilary was still missing, he would take no action on the motions concerning custody and visitation that remained pending from the summer of 1987. He told reporters that it would be unfair to the parties for him to say anything about the case publicly as long as it was pending.

On December 2, 1989, Elizabeth married Paul Michel in a small private ceremony at St. Alban's Church on the grounds of the Washington National Cathedral. The couple did not announce their honeymoon destination or their address. Although Elizabeth had little to fear from Dixon and the court system at that point, Michel thought he had reason to be security-conscious. A few months earlier, he had complained about a possible break-in at his judicial chambers. He thought he had seen someone rifling his papers, and he suspected that a private detective hired by Eric or the D.C. police was searching for information about Hilary. (Eric denies any such involvement.) Elizabeth settled into her new apartment in northwest Washington with her second husband. She spoke to women's organizations and children's advocacy groups about her experience and about sexual abuse. Her case dropped off the front pages of the newspapers, as the stalemate continued.

Eric tried to keep his surgery practice going while continuing to look for Hilary. In the fall of 1989 he went to England, with his trip partially paid for by a London tabloid, to pursue a tip that Hilary was in school in that country. But his information was out of date. Hilary had left the year before. While Eric was in London, however, he got a call from a BBC television producer who had done a documentary on the case. After the program had been broadcast, the producer had received a telephone call from a parent at the school Hilary had attended in Plymouth. Eric hired British attorneys to interview the producer and eventually had to get a court order. From the information she provided, as well as other tips he had received, Eric got the first solid lead about Hilary's whereabouts. He hired private detectives in Christchurch, who made a positive identification of the seven-year-old and the elderly couple with whom she was living in the motel. Late on February 23, 1990, the world heard the news that Hilary had been found with her maternal grandparents, in apparently good health.

Eric and his parents flew to New Zealand the next afternoon. Elizabeth soon followed, after the D.C. Court of Appeals agreed to give her back the passport that had been confiscated in 1986.

Both hired lawyers in New Zealand, and the courts there, just as the courts in the United States had done, immediately appointed neutral evaluators to help reach a decision. They were Isabel Mitchell, a Christchurch lawyer, as Hilary's guardian *ad litem,* and Karen Zelas, the psychiatrist who had been involved in the controversial Spence sex-abuse case two years before, as a court-appointed expert. Behind the cloak of secrecy imposed by New Zealand law in custody matters, the experts began, yet again, the laborious process of sorting out fact from fiction and reality from myth.

Elizabeth remained in New Zealand, re-creating the family circle that included her parents and her daughter. Paul Michel, her husband, would visit when he could, she said. Eric returned to an empty house in Great Falls and to a life that seemed barren of fulfillment. His oral-surgery patients had mostly disappeared, and with less than one third the income he had had five years before, he found it hard to pay his lawyers and keep up the fight in New Zealand.

So, seven years after the case began unobtrusively with a dispute over custody of a smiling six-month-old baby, it achieved another kind of obscurity under New Zealand's court seal. Now at stake was the life of a seven-year-old girl who wore a private school uniform, played with Cabbage Patch dolls, went to church every Sunday, and had had her picture and her sad story flashed around the world. Hundreds of people—lawyers, judges, psychiatrists, psychologists, social workers, journalists, lobbyists, politicians—had played their roles on the stage of *Morgan* v. *Foretich* and had moved on. But those at the center of the tragedy—Eric, Doris, and Vincent; Elizabeth, Antonia, and William; and especially Hilary—had seen their lives wrenched irrevocably out of shape. The unresolvable passions of the case had taken their toll.

Epilogue

March 1990 through
November 21, 1990

For a few days in the late winter of 1990, Hilary Foretich was perhaps the best-known seven-year-old in the world. When she went to church with Elizabeth and Antonia on March 18 in New Zealand, the minister whisked the family out a back door to avoid television cameras. Later, a parishioner drove the little girl and her grandmother the two short blocks to their motel to escape reporters.

Back in Washington, D.C., the Morgan case continued to stir strong feelings throughout the legal arena. But the action stalled in Judge Dixon's courtroom where the original custody case, *Morgan* v. *Foretich,* remained inactive. Dixon avoided further action until he could determine exactly what the New Zealand Family Court was going to do. (*Morgan* v. *Foretich* did reconvene in late February, when Stephen Sachs applied to Dixon for the release of Elizabeth's passport. But even then, the trial judge sent the request to the appeals court, which returned the passport to Elizabeth.)

Other judges remained busy with Morgan-related matters. During the previous fall and winter, Elaine Mittleman had filed several new lawsuits on Eric's behalf. These included libel suits against *Glamour* magazine and CBS over their coverage of the controversy. A second massive case cited Elizabeth, Antonia, William, Rob Morgan, Mary Froning, Dennis Harrison, Paul Michel, and others for allegedly causing Eric emotional distress by participating in Hilary's concealment. Most of the defendants moved to have the suits dismissed, meeting with mixed results.

In April 1990, just after Hilary was discovered in New Zealand,

Mittleman tried an even more audacious tack—and almost succeeded. She attempted in federal court to prevent the Lifetime cable network from airing *Hilary in Hiding,* a British documentary. Mittleman argued that the film might do "irreparable harm" to Hilary; the lawyer cited a possible invasion of the girl's privacy in scenes showing her playing with anatomical dolls as a four-year-old. Under the First Amendment, though, United States courts almost never grant "prior restraints" against the media, and the show had already been aired once before, on March 6. Still, Mittleman got a federal trial judge to issue a restraining order halting the show temporarily. It took an extraordinary nighttime session of a federal appeals court to reverse that decision.

The rest of Mittleman's lawsuits ground on; portions of the suits were dismissed, other portions allowed to continue. It seemed unlikely that any of the suits would bring out new information any time soon about the abuse charges.

The British documentary had one important indirect result. In that show, Elizabeth was filmed in front of the diner in Warrenton, Virginia, where she and Hilary met Linda Holman on August 26, 1987. Re-creating a key moment in the case, she said on camera that "my father and my fiancé Paul and Hilary and her babysitter all rendezvoused here and my father and her babysitter took Hilary on her next step in the process of hiding her." Bob Kelly, Eric's cousin, who had been present during some of Hilary's 1987 visits at Great Falls, was watching that March evening in his living room in Gaithersburg, Maryland. Kelly had become something of an amateur expert on the case, taking Eric's side. To him, Elizabeth's statement revealed that Paul Michel had a larger role in the hiding of Hilary than Michel had acknowledged.

On April 9, 1990, Kelly, a government scientist by profession, filed a new judicial-misconduct complaint against Michel. Kelly contended that Michel, not yet a judge when Hilary disappeared, was an eyewitness to the girl's "actual abduction" and a co-conspirator with Elizabeth in Hilary's concealment.

On May 4, Judge Howard Markey, chief judge of the appeals court on which Michel sits, dismissed Kelly's complaint as frivolous. The contention that Michel participated in hiding Hilary or knew about Elizabeth's plan, Markey said, relied on an unsupported assumption that Michel "knew what was in Dr. Morgan's mind" that August day.

Michel himself weighed in with a vitriolic six-page letter to Markey, denouncing Kelly as an "unscrupulous" person who was engaged, along with Eric and Mittleman, in a campaign of harassment.

He noted that following the dismissal of Mittleman's 1989 complaint, his judicial chambers were burglarized. He hinted darkly, "One wonders what will follow dismissal of this year's complaint." Moreover, Michel said, "[T]here is reason to doubt Mr. Kelly's good faith. . . . Given the inapplicability of the libel laws to ethics complaints, no matter how false, defamatory, baseless or ill-motivated, one wonders if there is any limit to the vulnerability of a federal judge." In order, he said, to set the record straight, Michel placed his letter on the public record.

Eric, Mittleman, and Kelly all denied acting in concert against Michel and said they knew nothing about the burglary. Linda Holman, the one neutral person who was at Warrenton on August 26, 1987, was not talking. Kelly composed his own letter to Markey: he complained that Michel's allegations had damaged his professional reputation by challenging his truthfulness. He appealed Markey's dismissal to the full Court of Appeals for the Federal Circuit.

While her husband was defending himself against the misconduct charges, Elizabeth was settling down, applying to become a permanent resident of New Zealand. After enrolling as a student in a Christchurch university, she made plans to resume her surgical practice.

Paul Michel, still a sitting federal judge in Washington, could visit his wife only two or three times a year. So, by the fall of 1990, the regular members of the Morgan household included Antonia, Elizabeth, and Hilary. (Sometime during the summer, William had returned to Fairfax County, Virginia, apparently for good.)

In a May 18, 1990, affidavit, Eric told the court in Christchurch that although he ideally would have wanted Hilary returned to the Washington area, he was no longer going to contest custody if Hilary stayed in New Zealand. He wrote:

> For so long as Hilary is living in New Zealand, I wish to spare her from the conflict of litigation that she has been caught up in for so long. . . . I will not try and remove Hilary from the jurisdiction of New Zealand, I will not in any way try and have access to her in New Zealand, and I will not try and remove her from the custody of the people with whom she is living in New Zealand. . . . My only hope is that I can in some way show Hilary that I still love her as my daughter and that I and my parents still want to help her and be part of her life.

Eric explained to reporters that he could not possibly continue to battle Elizabeth, who had uprooted herself and was beginning her life anew in a faraway land. "I am an American," he said, "and I don't live in New Zealand." Eric believed that locating Hilary and telling her he loved her was achievement enough. While in Christchurch, he had had one, quite unsatisfactory, visit with his daughter. He had come away convinced that the reality in Hilary's mind, as long as she stayed with Elizabeth, was that he and his parents were sexual abusers. And there was nothing Eric could do about it.

The New Zealand court rendered its decision, in its own case of *Morgan* v. *Foretich,* on November 21, 1990, in Christchurch. Family Court Judge P. D. Mahony ruled that Elizabeth would retain custody of Hilary. The girl, Mahony maintained, was happy at Selwyn House, her school on a tree-shaded lane. There she was "in every respect a normal child," with plenty of friends. She had her loving mother and grandmother with her, and Eric had agreed to accept that as the status quo. If Hilary was to remain in New Zealand, there was really no alternative to keeping her with Elizabeth.

Mahony placed several conditions on his custody order: Hilary had to remain in Christchurch at Selwyn House School. The court would keep her passport, and she could not be taken out of the nation without court permission. Elizabeth agreed to stop discussing anything about the case in public, at least in New Zealand, and she was ordered to inform Eric of any change of address or significant illness of Hilary's. She was also to send Eric, every six months, a picture of his daughter and her school report cards. (Elizabeth agreed to take all these steps.) Hilary, the judge decided, was not psychologically ready for a visit from her father or her paternal grandparents. Nor could she receive their cards, letters, or phone calls. Dr. Karen Zelas, the court-appointed psychiatrist, and Isabel Mitchell, Hilary's New Zealand lawyer, would decide when these steps would be appropriate.

In words reminiscent of the fond hopes of Judge Bruce Mencher in the D.C. Superior Court in 1984, Mahony said he saw evidence that tempers were finally cooling down:

> It is just possible that the fortuitous involvement of this Court may provide a turning point in this case, rather than a further stage in an ongoing dispute. The restraint of both parties in relation to the media and the major concessions made by Dr. Foretich are steps in the right direction. For the first time both parties are focusing their attention on the child.

The New Zealand court did not hear evidence on the underlying charges of sexual abuse—which occurred, if at all, on another continent, as many as six years earlier. It found definitively, however, that for Hilary, Elizabeth's belief that she was abused "is the reality whether or not her belief has any basis in fact." As Dr. Karen Zelas, the court-appointed psychiatrist, told the court, "It is no longer possible to distinguish fact from belief." Basing his views largely on Zelas's, Mahony concluded:

> In my view it is now part of the family ethos that she is an abused child and it would be impossible for her not to identify with the convictions of her mother and maternal grandparents. This issue, which has been kept alive within the family according to Dr. Zelas, has created distortions in the relationship between the child and her caregivers. She has learned to be oversensitive to their reactions and to respond accordingly. Dr. Zelas referred to her as an "overvalued child," who has been given an inordinate and inappropriate level of power within the family.

Elizabeth was told that the "most needed" step was for her "to relax her determination that Dr. Foretich should not have a meaningful role to play in Hilary's life." Yet Eric, who had been found guilty of nothing, was forced to relinquish his role in Hilary's life, perhaps permanently. Two weeks later, on December 4, Eric lost the right to continue his relationship with his other child. Judge Bruce Bach of the Fairfax County Circuit Court suspended Eric's visits with ten-year-old Heather on the recommendation of a court-appointed psychologist. Things just weren't working out, Bach decided. As in the New Zealand court, sexual abuse was not the question. At issue were Heather's feelings and beliefs about her father. Heather continued to believe that somewhere in the dimly remembered past, Eric had abused her.

As 1990 closed, it appeared that Eric Foretich would be spending 1991 without the company of either of his daughters.

Chronology

August 1981	Dr. Elizabeth Morgan and Dr. Eric Foretich meet in recovery room in Fairfax Hospital.
January 25, 1982	Elizabeth and Eric marry in Haiti.
August 21, 1982	Hilary Antonia Foretich born.
March 11, 1983	Elizabeth files for custody and child support.
May 16, 1983	*Pendente lite* (temporary custody) hearing before Judge Carlisle Pratt in the D.C. Superior Court.
June 15, 1983	Judge Pratt gives temporary custody to Elizabeth and visitation rights to Eric.
September 1984	Four-day custody trial before Judge Bruce Mencher in D.C. Superior Court.
November 8, 1984	Judge Mencher gives Elizabeth custody of Hilary; Eric gets vacations and alternate weekend visitation.
January 30, 1985	Virginia Department of Social Services and police begin inquiry into possible sexual abuse by Eric.

March 8, 1985   Elizabeth moves to suspend visitation on the grounds of sexual abuse. Judge Henry Kennedy of the D.C. Superior Court declines to do so.

April 22, 1985   Virginia Social Services investigation closed. Finding on Hilary is "unfounded with reason to suspect."

November 19, 1985 Hearing before D.C. Superior Court Judge Herbert Dixon, Jr., on Elizabeth's motion to suspend Eric's visits, on the basis of the alleged sexual abuse, so that Hilary can be examined at the Chesapeake Institute, and on Eric's motion for a change of custody.

December 27, 1985 Dixon refuses to suspend visitation, permits the examination at Chesapeake, and denies Eric's motion for change of custody.

February 14, 1986 Elizabeth stops sending Hilary on visits with Eric.

February 26, 1986 Virginia Social Services Commissioner William Lukhard reverses department's findings in abuse investigation.

July 17, 1986   After twelve days of hearings, Dixon rules that Elizabeth has not proved her case regarding sexual abuse. He holds her in contempt, and she serves three days in early August before being released by an order of the D.C. Court of Appeals.

August 22, 1986   Linda Holman named as court-appointed guardian for Hilary in the D.C. case.

August 28, 1986   Elizabeth sues Eric and his parents for damages in federal court in Virginia. The Foretiches countersue for defamation.

January 29, 1987 Dixon again holds Elizabeth in contempt, this time for refusing Eric a supervised visit. The D.C. Court of Appeals suspends Elizabeth's jailing for two weeks.

February 17–20, 1987 Federal case goes to trial. The jury returns a verdict against Elizabeth's allegations of abuse and against the Foretiches' allegations of defamation.

February 17–19, 1987 Elizabeth is jailed in D.C. again. She is released after she promises to permit the supervised visits.

February 24, 1987 Visits begin again, first at D.C. Department of Human Services, later at Eric's house.

April 6 through August 21, 1987 Dixon holds seventeen days of hearings on Elizabeth's motions to suspend the visits on the grounds of abuse and on Eric's motion for change of custody.

June 30, 1987 D.C. Court of Appeals upholds Dixon's 1986 order jailing Elizabeth for contempt.

August 19, 1987 Dixon orders a two-week unsupervised visit, August 22–September 6, 1987.

August 28, 1987 Elizabeth appears before Dixon and says she will not permit the visit or reveal Hilary's whereabouts. She is sent to jail.

May 17, 1988 U.S. Court of Appeals for the Fourth Circuit, reviewing federal case in Virginia, orders a new trial on the grounds that the judge should have admitted evidence about Heather Foretich.

August 5, 1988 D.C. Court of Appeals, reviewing Dixon's actions, upholds Elizabeth's jailing.

November 29, 1988   Elizabeth's federal case is dismissed after she refuses to bring Hilary back for an examination.

December 15, 1988   Dixon, after a three-day hearing on Elizabeth's *habeas corpus* petition, refuses to release her from jail.

August 21, 1989   D.C. Court of Appeals, by 2–1 vote, reverses Dixon's findings on whether Elizabeth should be released. Opinion is vacated simultaneously with its issuance, and Elizabeth remains in jail.

September 25, 1989   Elizabeth leaves the D.C. Jail after twenty-five months when Congress passes a bill intended to free her.

February 23, 1990   Hilary is located living with her maternal grandparents in Christchurch, New Zealand.

November 21, 1990   New Zealand Family Court grants custody to Elizabeth in Christchurch.

Index